In this insightful commentary  combines scholarly
perception and pastoral warr ... ...ost
important exegetical issues ... a of
each section so that readers ... sive
understanding of Mark. At t ...)ints
us to the servanthood of Jesus ... lives
shaped by His example of service.

Peter Orr
New Testament Lecturer, Moore Theological College,
Sydney, Australia

In a world often hurt by ego-driven leaders, Redmond's focused
commentary on the Serving Savior is a welcome addition. Packed
with exegetical insights and cultural awareness, Redmond is an
informed narrator helping readers appreciate and mimic Jesus's
selfless and other-focused ministry. I can think of few scholars
more qualified to write on the juncture of Mark's gospel and Christ-
like servant leadership than Eric C. Redmond. Take and drink
deeply from this well of wisdom.

Matthew D. Kim
Professor of Preaching and Pastoral Leadership, Truett Seminary,
Waco, Texas; author, *Reaching with Cultural Intelligence*

Eric Redmond has provided a knowledgeable, succinct, and
clear exposition of the Gospel of Mark. With a pastoral style,
Redmond brings readers face to face with the servant ministry
of Jesus – a ministry characterized not by weakness, but rather
by the rule and power of the kingdom of God. This commentary
is an excellent resource for the church that will strengthen and
encourage pastors and laypeople alike.

Robbie Booth
Lecturer in New Testament, Union Theological College,
Belfast, Northern Ireland

MARK

THE SERVANT MINISTRY OF JESUS

ERIC C. REDMOND

CHRISTIAN
FOCUS

Eric C. Redmond (Ph.D. Capital Seminary and Graduate School) is Professor of Bible at Moody Bible Institute, Executive Director of the Center for Compelling Biblical Preaching at Moody Theological Seminary, and Associate Pastor of Preaching and Teaching at Calvary Memorial Church in Oak Park, IL.

Copyright © 2024 Eric C. Redmond

Paperback ISBN 978-1-5271-1131-8
E-book ISBN 978-1-5271-1210-0

10 9 8 7 6 5 4 3 2 1

Printed in 2024
by
Christian Focus Publications Ltd.,
Geanies House, Fearn, Ross-shire,
IV20 1TW, Scotland, U.K.

www.christianfocus.com

Cover design by MOOSE77

Printed and bound by
Bell & Bain, Glasgow

Contents

Dedication

To Pamela, my Autumn,
who stands as faithful lover and friend
between me and the raging waters of this fallen world
so that I do not walk storm-tossed alone,
but rather with the best of companionship,
and so that I might rejoice in all the Lord has given to me
in life and love, children and home, work and play –
you are a beautiful servant in the vein of Christ.

And to Laura Johnson,
Deacon Lonnie and Mrs Millie Gilliam,
'Uncle Heaf' and Aunt Bernie Wiggins, our roomies
Ronjour and Annie Locke,
Quincy and Rhonda Jones,
Eden Gordon Hill
Aprella Johnson,
Denise 'Big Sis' Southall,
Dylantra 'Dee' Scott,
Janet Buis,
and Andy Brandt,
who have served our five children
in your roles as faithful godparents, mentors,
unkies, aunties, and adult voices of reason –
thank you for your love.

Preface

'For the Son of Man came not to be served,
but to serve, and to give his life a ransom for many.'
– Jesus Christ, The Son of God in Mark 10:45

Great customer service is becoming a thing of the past. Right next to holding a door for a lady and giving your bus seat to the elderly, good service is about to take its seat in the box labeled, 'Things from days gone by.' Today it is common for you to expect to wait indefinitely in a fast-food line and/or gain a harsh retort to a question about your order from the counter worker rather than to get prompt service with a smile. The old adage, 'The customer is always right,' assumed that a company was willing to serve to whatever degree necessary in order to satisfy a disgruntled customer and retain the customer's business.

In his article, 'Whatever Happened to Good Customer Service?' Dick Yarbrough writes:

> Some years ago, I had gone into the store as a total stranger to buy an inexpensive easel. Although it was shown in one of their ads, it was unavailable. I was not a happy camper, asking an unfortunate salesclerk why they would advertise such an item if they didn't intend to offer it for sale. Besides, I was going out of town and had wanted to take the easel with me. Krimsky's partner, Jay Shapiro, overheard the conversation, apologized for the inconvenience and asked me when I was leaving town. I told him early in the morning. He said the easel would be there before I left. After the store closed, Shapiro drove quite some distance to get the easel and had it at the store when I arrived. I suspect he spent more on gas that I spent on that easel. Tragically, Shapiro died a few years later but I never forgot his efforts on my behalf. I have been a loyal Binders customer ever

since. Why the huge discrepancies in customer service these days, I asked Krimsky? Where are the Jay Shapiros? It seems like retail clerks these days have taken a course in how to avoid eye contact, lest they have to (shudder!) say 'Can I help you?' He said a lot of it is communications. 'You have to talk to employees every day about the importance of the customer,' he said. 'It has to always be at the top of their minds.'[1]

The sort of care represented by a conscientious worker's, 'Can I help you?' reflects much of what we see Jesus doing in Mark, such as in Mark 10:35-36: 'And James and John, the sons of Zebedee, came up to him and said to him, "Teacher, we want you to do for us whatever we ask of you." And he said to them, "What do you want me to do for you?"' Jesus' response to an open-ended request by James and John shows that He seemed prepared to have no limit to His scope of service. 'Whatever' only meets a threshold because part of James and John's request is outside of the scope of Jesus' prerogative (10:40). Jesus gladly served James and John, and as we will see later, He also gladly served as a ransom for many.

Immediately following the episode of the request by the sons of Zebedee, Jesus again gains a request for service (10:46-52). He provides a similar 'Can I help you?' reply to the blind beggar, asking him the same question He asked His two disciples:

> And they came to Jericho. And as he was leaving Jericho with his disciples and a great crowd, Bartimaeus, a blind beggar, the son of Timaeus, was sitting by the roadside. And when he heard that it was Jesus of Nazareth, he began to cry out and say, 'Jesus, Son of David, have mercy on me!' And many rebuked him, telling him to be silent. But he cried out all the more, 'Son of David, have mercy on me!' And Jesus stopped and said, 'Call him.' And they called the blind man, saying to him, 'Take heart. Get up; he is calling you.' And throwing off his cloak, he sprang

---

1. Dick Yarbrough, 'Whatever Happened to Good Customer Service?' Dalton Daily Citizen, March 4, 2017, https://www.dailycitizen.news/opinion/columns/dick-yarbrough-whatever-happened-to-good-customer-service/article_4a60384c-9513-5b52-959b-98273a8608ba.html. The 'Whatever' in the title of the article where one expects to read 'What ever' seems to be a play on words using the dismissive postmodern term of exasperation, i.e., 'What ever happened to good customer service? It has been dismissed as being out of sync. "Whatever" is what happened to customer service.'

up and came to Jesus. And Jesus said to him, *'What do you want me to do for you?'* And the blind man said to him, 'Rabbi, let me recover my sight.' And Jesus said to him, 'Go your way; your faith has made you well.' And immediately he recovered his sight and followed him on the way.

Even for one both unable to see and impoverished – one without means to pay for service and no social standing to bargain for attention – Jesus was prepared to do *whatever* again. His service stands out in comparison to the crowds' rebuke of the blind one for asking Jesus for help. In spite of expectations of service in the world – or the lack thereof – the followers of Jesus are called to display the Gospel of the kingdom by *serving* in the model of our Lord.

Approach of this Commentary
Mark presents a fascinating picture of the servant ministry of Jesus. It begins without a birth story of Jesus, moves at breakneck speed with healings, exorcisms, and other miracles occurring 'immediately' in succession, and oddly ends without a post-resurrection account. Between its pages, the work of the Servant is so powerful that we are left to conclude with a Roman Centurion, 'Truly this man was the Son of God' (Mark 15:39)!

As you read this commentary, my hope is for you to enjoy an incredible journey through an account of a Man who demonstrated that *servanthood* and great *service* should not be associated with being weak, a pushover, or a loser. Instead, we should associate *servanthood* and great *service* with the rule and power of the kingdom of God. Along the way, it is my prayer that your ministry as a servant will begin to look much more like the mighty works of the Servant who came to rule.

I intend to explain each section of Mark according to its unifying subject and the complement of that subject, within the structure and theology of the passage. By 'subject,' I am speaking of the most talked about idea in the passage that unifies all of the ideas in the passage. One could refer to it as the 'central idea' of a passage. By 'complement,' I am referring to the commentary or judgment the author makes on the subject.[2] The

---

2. One might speak of the 'predicate' synonymously with the concept of a complement.

complement *predicates* an idea about the subject in a passage; the complement answers, 'What is the subject *doing*?'

As with any work of literature, the reader reads in order to recover the author's meaning of the words in a passage. In discerning a passage's subject and complement, one is discerning the author's meaning. The subject is completed by the complement to form a statement of meaning. One then reads what the author is talking about in a passage (e.g., the subject), and what the author is saying about what he is writing about (e.g., the complement).

The act of discernment comes only by a working of the Lord's grace as the Holy Spirit of God illuminates the passage and enlightens the affections and comprehension of the reader. As the psalmist prayed, 'Open my eyes, that I may behold wondrous things out of your law' (Ps. 119:18). The psalmist can read the words of the law with comprehension. His prayer, however, is for a knowledge of God's truth inherent within the words of a passage that is not readily evident via the conventional tools of language comprehension. Similarly, Paul spends over a decade praying that the Lord would give the Ephesian believers enlightened insight into the hope, riches, and power provided to believers via their mysterious union with Christ (cf. Eph. 1:16-18). Seemingly, the words of what Christ provides for the believers in Ephesians 1:3-14 are readable and understandable. But the depth of the significance of the words comes by a working of the Father, Son, and Spirit – a work for which Paul prays unceasingly from the time of his earliest report of the Ephesians' faith in Christ through to his first imprisonment. I will approach passages in this commentary seeking to explain what Mark intends for us to comprehend by the combination of his words, structure, and theology, and some of the significance thereof to Christian living.

For example, in Mark 3:20-35, I propose that the subject of the passage is *One's recognition of Jesus' works as works from God*. In doing so, I am saying that the words, structure, and theology of the passage show that the central idea that unifies the passage is *One's recognition of Jesus' works as works from God*. That is, Jesus' family attributes His refusal to stop serving the crowd so that He could eat, to Him being out of His mind instead of recognizing that He is doing work in

God's strength. The scribes accuse Jesus of blasphemy because they do not recognize that He is performing exorcisms by the power of God. Jesus then tells two parables to explain that His works can only be from God, and that the judgment for mistaking His work for the working of the demonic is eternal death. The writer then comments on the failure of the scribes to recognize Jesus' works as coming from God as they said, 'He has an unclean spirit.' The failure to recognize Jesus' works as works from God explains why the family makes erroneous accusations related to the works that Jesus did, why Jesus introduces the parable and condemns the scribes, and the writer's comments.

What Mark predicates about *One's recognition of Jesus' works as works from God* is that it *distinguishes that one as a true family member of Jesus from those eternally condemned as blasphemous*. In the passage, there are those who '[do] the will of God' and Jesus identified them as His *spiritual* family (3:35). His biological family came to arrest him from his service as someone who was not thinking rationally. They think He is crazy! They stand in contrast to those who are clinging on His every word and hoping for healing or exorcism from Him – those who recognize the working of God in Jesus. Jesus rebukes the blasphemous who do not recognize divinity in Him while conferring 'mother' and 'brothers' upon those who do recognize the works from God in Him. The two groups – 'true family member' and 'those eternally condemned' – are evident in the passage.[3]

May you enjoy each chapter of Mark as we discern his meaning for our knowledge of the Son of God, the working of the kingdom of God, and our service in the vein of the service of Christ.

ERIC C. REDMOND

---

3. In landing on the subject or central idea, I am attempting to recover what Mark is communicating by his words within the structure, content, and theology of the passage. I recognize that each individual passage is one part of the larger meaning of the whole of Mark 1–16 and will show how the whole and parts work together.

Brief Introduction to Mark's Gospel Account

Authorship

Mark's Gospel does not have any statement about its author. It is unlike John's Gospel in which the author claims to be a witness of the events described in it (John 21:24). It also does not make a reference to a recipient like Theophilus that helps us identify the author of Luke. In terms of the practice of authorial humility, the best we have is an unidentified young man leaving his clothes and streaking away from authorities (Mark 14:51-52)!

Yet, because the process used to identify a canonical work included authorship by an apostle or close companion of an apostle (like Luke), it is likely that the church would have regarded the most well-known 'Mark' as a canonical author. The church would not have received a book whose authorship was suspicious. John Mark was a companion of the Apostle Paul, a friend of the Apostle Peter, and a cousin of Barnabas (Acts 12:12, 25; 13:5, 13; 15:36-39; Col. 4:10; Phil. 24; 2 Tim. 4:11; 1 Pet. 5:13). It is the uniform tradition of the Church Fathers that John Mark was a companion of Paul, Barnabas, and Peter.

Eusebius' *Ecclesiastical History*, a fourth-century work, quoted Papius' *Exegesis of the Lord's Oracles* (c. 140), which refers to the authorship of the Second Gospel.[1] Papius, quoting another source known as 'the Elder,' who most likely was John the Apostle (cf. 2 John 1; 3 John 1), said that Mark wrote the Gospel associated with his name. Seemingly Mark

---

1. *The Ecclesiastical History of Eusebius Pamphilus*, 3:39:15.

developed his work by following the preaching of Peter and his eyewitness testimony.

Audience

The author of this Gospel wrote for a largely non-Jewish audience, most likely Romans. This accounts for Mark's explanation of Jewish customs and terms like 'Talitha cumi,' 'Corban' and the Unleavened Bread and Passover traditions (5:41; 7:3-4; 14:12; 15:42). It explains why Aramaic words and sentences are translated into Greek (cf. 3:17; 5:41; 7:11; 9:43; 10:46; 14:36; 15:22, 34), and the reason why Latin terms are used rather than their Greek equivalents (cf. 5:9; 6:37; 7:4; 12:14, 15; 15:15-16).

Seemingly, Mark's Gospel met a need for a quickly written, simple account of the life of Christ that affirmed His deity. Mark is the shortest Gospel account, omitting the nativity and genealogies, and including only two long discourses. He uses the term 'immediately' ('straightway') several times, which has the effect of moving his account forward swiftly – an account very appropriate for today's image-driven culture. Importantly, his account records a large number of miracles by Christ, and the Passion Narrative is six chapters long (chs. 11–16), reflecting important theological focuses in Mark.

Literary Features

Several other significant literary features characterize Mark's account of the life of Jesus Christ. First, the author identified Jesus as the divine Son of God. Noteworthy for understanding the second Gospel are the declarations of divine Sonship at the beginning and end of the Gospel (1:1; 15:39). At Jesus' baptism and transfiguration the Father recognizes Jesus as His beloved Son (1:11; 9:7). Even the demonic forces recognize the divine Sonship of Christ, declaring 'You are the Son of God' and 'What have you to do with me, Jesus, Son of the Most High God?' (1:24; 3:11; 5:7). In great contrast, the Jewish leadership is condemned for not recognizing Jesus' divine Sonship (12:1-12).

Second, discipleship and the disciples' role in learning from Christ is prominent. Many passages directly address the disciples' call to follow Christ or to serve as He serves (1:16-20; 3:13-15, 34; 4:1-20; 8:14-26, 35; 10:42-45, 52). In this story of Christ's life, the disciples were called to suffer in the same vein as their Lord (8:34; 10:44-45).

Third, faith is emphasized and commended. One sees the expression of faith especially among women, Gentiles, and others outside of Jesus' primary followers (1:40-42; 2:5; 5:34; 7:24-30; 9:24; 10:52; 12:41-44; 14:3-9; 15:39). As a foil to those who believe, Jesus' family members, those of His hometown, and the Jewish leadership lack faith (3:31-35; 6:1-6; 11:27-33).

Fourth, Jesus often demands silence from people concerning His identity (1:25; 1:34; 1:44; 3:12; 5:43; 7:36; 8:26; 8:30; 9:9); seemingly, Jesus is protecting Himself from 'false messianic expectations.'[2]

Fifth, there is a 'journey motif' in which Christ is frequently 'on the way' (e.g., 2:23; 8:3). The journey follows the 'way' of Christ announced from the beginning (1:2, 3). It is particularly evident in the second half of the account, leading up to the six chapters on the Passion (8:27; 9:33-34; 10:17, 32, 52; 11:7-10).

Sixth, Mark places great emphasis on the authority of Christ throughout the Gospel. Jesus rules over the forces of the wind and the sea, demons, disease, and death (4:35–5:43). He is in control of the events leading to His suffering and death (8:31; 9:31; 10:33-34). His authority extends to the untying of a colt for His entry into Jerusalem (11:2-3), the withering of a fig tree (11:20), His ability to refuse to answer and to silence His critics (11:33; 12:34), and identifying the location of the Passover meal (14:12-16). Although the Jewish and Roman leaderships do not submit to His authority, even in His voluntary submission He is in control of the judgment of His detractors (12:9, 40; 14:20)! Everything in the created order submits to His rule when He applies it to His service in the plan of redemption.

Seventh, Mark addresses his readers directly (2:10; 7:19), sometimes through Jesus' words (13:37), and by the use of rhetorical questions addressed to them (e.g., 4:41).[3] Such direct address seems to have the effect of including the reader in the story as an object of Jesus' ministry. Practically speaking, this

---

2. J. R. Edwards, *The Gospel According to Mark*, PNTC, 19. I develop this idea later in this work.

3. Thomas Constable, 'Notes on Mark, 2019 Edition,' https://www.plano biblechapel.org/tcon/notes/ html/nt/mark/mark.htm, accessed January 3, 2020.

is one of the reasons why the Gospel of Mark works as a good starting point for introducing people to the Christian faith.

The Message of the Gospel of Mark

The subject of Mark is *the servant ministry of Jesus*. Every passage in the book relates to this idea; Mark focuses on serving, whether such service is exorcising demons, healing a fever or leprosy, providing food, opening the eyes of the blind, or dying on the cross. Reading each chapter with *the servant ministry of Jesus* in mind will open up the meaning of each passage. In this book, we are learning to serve as Jesus served. Mark will reveal an uncommon service to us. For example, almost as soon as Jesus begins His public ministry, as Mark records it, Jesus serves a man with an unclean spirit in the synagogue (1:21-28). Immediately following this episode, Jesus serves Peter's mother-in-law, and then the whole city of Capernaum (1:39-34).

Moreover, for the writer, the servant ministry of Jesus *reveals Him as the authoritative Son of God to those who have simple faith in Him*. Simple faith is a theme inherent in this Gospel account, as evident in humble desires like, 'If you will, you can make me clean' (1:40), 'if I touch even his garments, I will be made well' (5:28), and 'Son of David, have mercy on me' (10:47, 48). Such faith *grants the believing ones entrance into the kingdom of God, and calls them to like service in the way of God*. The message of Jesus in Mark is a call to enter the kingdom of God (1:15; 9:1, 47; 10:15, 23-25; 12:34); the message is a call to drink His cup and share in His baptism so that others might enter the kingdom of God.

Again, if you were to ask Mark what his Gospel account is about, he would say, '*The servant ministry of Jesus reveals Him as the authoritative Son of God to those who have simple faith in Him, granting them entrance into the kingdom of God, and calling them to like service in the way of God.*' That is, His process of making disciples (who inherently make disciples) is to serve those who place faith in Him. Mark is an invitation to move from being religious to becoming a disciple.

The General Structure of Mark

This is a broad outline of the structure of Mark:

1. The divine Sonship of Jesus Christ, as attested by multiple witnesses, establishes the servant ministry of Jesus with the authority to proclaim the coming kingdom of God (1:1-15). Here Mark introduces the reader to his protagonist, anchoring the presentation of his Gospel in the plan of redemptive history by tying it to the Old Testament announcements of the coming of the Lord.

2. The servant ministry of Jesus in and around Galilee shows His authority as the Son of Man in encounters with disciples, the demonic, and those who reject Him (1:16-8:26). In this section there is great emphasis on Jesus' identity as the Son of Man (1:16-34; 2:3-12, 23-28; 3:11; 4:35-41; 6:45-52; 7:1-23; see also 10:1-12). There are a number of encounters with the demonic and related miracles (1:23-26; 5:2-8, 15, 16; 7:25-29; see also 9:17-25).

3. The servant ministry of Jesus finds triumph in the disciples' growing understanding of the relationship between His example in suffering and authority in the kingdom as He journeys to the cross in spite of rejection (8:27–16:8). In this section there is great emphasis on Jesus' identity as the Son of God (8:38; 9:7; 12:6-8; 13:32; 14:36, 61; 15:39). Such references tie together earlier themes in the story (cf., 1:11; 3:11; 5:7). Also in this section the writer gives attention to the suffering of Christ (8:31, 34-38; 9:30-32; 10:35-45; 14:24-42). It is in this part of Mark that we find cause for the words on the humiliation of Christ in the *Westminster Larger Catechism*:

> *Q. 46. What was the estate of Christ's humiliation?*
>
> *A.* 'The estate of Christ's humiliation was that low condition, wherein He for our sakes, emptying Himself of His glory, took upon Him the form of a *servant*, in His conception and birth, life, death, and after His death, until His resurrection.'

From the outset, Mark structures a story so that the Son of God journeys toward the cross where He might serve the many in redemption.

1

He Came to Serve as God
(Mark 1:1-13)

Before Mark recorded the calling of the disciples, one healing, a confrontation with the demonic, the proclamation of a parable, or any confrontation with the Jewish leadership, he established the most important fact about Jesus' servant ministry: *Jesus is God.* Mark introduces Jesus as the 'Son of God' in his opening verse. Doing so at the outset means that readers gain an insight into Jesus and His works that the people who encountered Him only gained over the course of spending time with Him.

For example, in His first public encounter with an unclean spirit, Jesus commands the unclean spirit to leave the man who cries out in the synagogue. The response of the people to this miracle is, 'What is this? A new teaching with authority! He commands even the unclean spirits, and they obey him' (Mark 1:27). Their response reveals that they are unaware that God has entered the room in the person teaching with greater authority than the scribes. Yet readers are not shocked when the demons identify the unassuming rabbi as 'the Holy One of God,' and they might expect people to have made this connection between the authority of Jesus' teaching and His person. However, they did not.

Again, when the disciples are caught in a storm while crossing the Sea of Galilee, they are stunned at Jesus' ability to calm the wind and sea. In fear of Him, they talk among themselves, asking, 'Who then is this, that even the wind and the sea obey him?' (Mark 4:41). For readers, this question was answered in the opening verse and passage. They think to themselves, 'Of course Jesus rebuked the winds and spoke calming words to the sea, for He is Lord of heaven and earth. He made the winds, so they obey Him; He formed the sea by speaking it into existence, and it is still listening to His voice as the Word of the Creator!' However, in the Gospel even the disciples have yet to ascertain the deity in Jesus.

Mark kindly offers his readers a way to assume the deity of Jesus while reading so that the focus is not on the discovery of His divine identity. Instead, the focus will be on the manner by which the Son of God *serves*. We will watch the characters in the Gospel account discover the identity of the Son of God through His service to them.

In 1:1-15, Mark's meaning is, *The prophetically-fulfilled,* divine witness *to the identity of Jesus Christ affirms His deity as the Son of God from the beginning of His ministry in the Gospel account.* Mark will portray the work of the One who came to serve as the work of God Himself. This picture shapes the way one reads the rest of the Gospel. The Old Testament prophets, John the Baptist, God the Father (and the Holy Spirit), Satan, wild beasts, and angels all enter into this account to give full color to this picture.

The first indication that Mark intends to communicate something *prophetically fulfilled* are the words, 'As it is written in Isaiah the prophet.' These words tie the events that follow to prophecies in the Old Testament. The coming of John the Baptist fulfills what both Malachi and Isaiah have foretold of the person who will 'prepare' 'the way' for the Lord to come to His people. Isaiah is unspecific regarding the nature of the way to the Lord, even though the herald announces a path through mountains and valleys. Mark draws upon the significance of the prepared 'way' to say that, with the dawning of the Messianic era, *repentance* is the *way* for the Lord to come to His own.

Mark also indicates that there is a *divine witness to the identity of Jesus.* He presents the deity of Christ without the need for a birth narrative announcing the coming of the 'Holy One of God' (Matt. 1:18-25) or a prologue that starts in eternity past to show that the Word is deity (John 1:1-18).

Yet he justifies his opening words by mentioning those who could witness to the deity of Jesus' character.

The Former Prophets Affirm that Jesus is God (1:1-3)

Even though this is 'the beginning,' Mark skips over the first thirty years of Jesus' life. While such details would have been known to Mark via his travels with Paul and Peter, they are not significant to the portrayal of the life of Christ that he wishes to display. Yet this is 'the beginning' in many ways.

First, it is the very *opening* of the story Mark intends to tell. 'Beginning' signals, 'Pay attention and do not miss this part if you wish to understand the rest of the story.' In this way, viewing the introduction is akin to watching the opening in a movie so that one sees the significance of all that will follow in the production.

Second, this is the 'beginning of the gospel of Jesus Christ.' The double-entendre here is evident in the placing of the terms. It is unnecessary to say 'the beginning' at the start of an account, for such is obvious. Differently from the book of Genesis and the fourth Gospel authors, who both draw attention to realities and events at the beginning of creation – i.e., 'These things were so at the beginning,' Mark simply says, 'This is the beginning.' The obvious and redundant nature of the opening sentence invites the audience to ask, 'Is he saying something more, here?' Yes, he is saying more.

Coupled with the lack of a post-resurrection appearance of Christ, 'the beginning of the gospel of Jesus Christ' indicates this story will be the first part of the ministry of the gospel, and not the entirety of the Gospel story. The message of the gospel, as painted by the four evangelists and as repeated by Paul in the ancient creedal formula in 1 Corinthians 15:3-4, shines forth in Mark: 'That Christ died for our sins in accordance with the Scriptures, that he was buried, that he was raised on the third day in accordance with the Scriptures.' Mark establishes a basis for the creedal statement as Jesus acts as 'a ransom for many' and repeatedly foreshadows the resurrection with the words, 'after three days he will rise.'[1]

---

1. Mark 9:31; 10:34, 45. See 8:31, 9:9-10, 14:28 and 16:6 for other references in Mark concerning Jesus' rising from the dead.

Mark draws his account in a manner that causes the reader to look and see how the witnesses came to their conclusion. They will give testimony to the fact that the awaited Hebrew Messiah ('Christ'), seen in the person of Jesus, is God the Son. Mark asserts that the 'Christ' (anointed One) is the 'Son of God.'

Both Isaiah and Malachi foretell of One who would come before the Lord to make a way for His arrival. Mark quotes Exodus 23:20, 'Behold I shall send my messenger before you' (literally, your face), Malachi 3:1, 'who will prepare your way' (literally, 'the way before my face' in the Old Testament), and Isaiah 40:3. All four Gospels refer to Isaiah 40:3 in association with the coming of Christ (Matt. 3:3; Luke 3:4; John 1:23). Isaiah says a messenger will arise before the LORD comes, and Mark says that this prophetic writing is about the gospel of Jesus Christ, the divine God who came in the flesh.

The Forerunner Affirms that Jesus Is God (1:4-8)

John the Baptizer appears.[2] His appearance before the launching of the public ministry of Jesus is significant to each of the Gospel accounts. John serves in the wilderness. Literally, the ministry in the wilderness looks *forward* to (1) Jesus' victory over both the earthly and cosmic forces threatening His work of redemption (Mark 1:12-13) and (2) the later ministry in desolated places.[3] The wilderness will not be an obstacle to John or Jesus.

The ministry in the wilderness also looks *backwards* in the history of Israel to her failure in the wilderness *en route* from Egypt to the Promised Land. Where Israel failed to exercise faith in the promises of God, John will call the nation to repentance. Their immersion in water will signify what is taking place in the hearts of those who respond to John proclaiming the need for repentance. They will be purified of their sins in the way that water washes away external stains. The participants in John's baptism and some of the early readers of this narrative were familiar with the practice in

---

2. In the Greek, John is 'the baptizer,' e.g. 'the one baptizing' or 'the one who baptizes': Ἰωάννης ὁ βαπτίζων (John the Baptist).

3. Mark 1:35, 45; 6:31, 32, 35; 8:4.

Second Temple Judaism of the religiously faithful washing their bodies in water to cleanse themselves from impurity.[4]

John comes from the wilderness, thus identifying himself as the 'messenger' of 1:2 and Isaiah 40:3. He baptized as the means to 'prepare the way.' The *way* for the Lord to come to people is by them having hearts free from sin. The preaching of John alerted the people to their need to acknowledge their actions as sin in need of forgiveness before God. The baptizing follows both the response to the message and acts of repentance rather than providing repentance and forgiveness.

Visually, John's identity comes from the Old Testament, associating him with Elijah (2 Kings 1:8). He comes as one clean according to the law (Lev. 11:20-23). The startling look and diet of the Baptizer would indicate that he is a prophet of the Lord.

Vocally, John's identity is diminished before the coming One, for two reasons. First, the coming One is stronger than John, being sovereign over him; John, acting as the servant in the relationship, does not have enough worth in comparison to the coming One to even act as a servant. A task as menial as untying the strap of a sandal is too high a deed for John (or for any of us!) when the foot and sandal belong to Jesus. One can only say this in truth of One who is beyond human, for each human has equal worth.

Second, Jesus' baptism exceeds John's baptism *in kind*. John, taking advantage of the earthly resource before him, calling people to do what was possible for them to do volitionally, and performing what he was able to do physically, offered a baptism of the human realm. It was a necessary and symbolic baptism, but it also was an anticipatory baptism. What the One coming after John will offer is an experience that immerses people in the Spirit of God. This baptism is heavenly rather than earthly, offers to do for the people what they cannot do for themselves, and performs what only Jesus can do from the heavenly realms into the earthly realm. The superior nature of this baptism points to a Baptizer who has power beyond

---

4. Eckhard J. Schnabel, *Mark* (Downers Grove: IVP, 2017), 40. He also notes: 'At Qumran, immersion signified purification from defilement due to sin and initiation into the community as the true or pure Israel.' Thus, John's repentance would have significance as an act of separation from sin and from the sinful world.

John's earthly realm; the baptism itself affirms the Son of God status of the coming One.

The prophets promised this unique blessing of the Spirit as the mark of the age to come.[5] In the Old Testament, it is the Lord Himself who will bring the comfort and joys of the age to come.

The Father Affirms that Jesus Is God (1:9-11)

John baptized Jesus, but not because Jesus needed to repent from personal sin. The identity of Jesus as the Son of God in 1:1 guards against thinking He needed repentance before His baptism. Instead, in Mark's account, Jesus stood in the place of 'the many' in need of a ransom for sin. The baptism in the Jordan River pointed back to Israel's crossing of the Jordon *en route* to the Promised Land. This time, God's true Son will see that Israel has the righteousness to enter the land. Literally, Jesus was immersed in the waters as the others because He comes from out of the waters upon finishing His baptism.

Three things happened in association with Mark's baptism account: first, the sky was ripped open (by God the Father). One can imagine the happiness of God the Father in seeing the Son come to fulfill the long-awaited plan of redemption! The excitement led to this tearing so that the Father could participate in the celebration of righteousness without the hindrance of the sky. The act itself is reminiscent of Psalm 114 and the trembling of the Red Sea, the Jordan River (mentioned in Mark 1:9), and Mount Sinai. In Psalm 114, the climatic upheaval reveals God's presence in the form of a theophany. Yet one sees no theophany here; one only sees the very presence of the divine Son.

Second, the Spirit coming down like a dove alighted on Jesus. The Spirit already has a divine association (Mark 1:8). Certainly the One upon whom the Spirit alighted will have the ability to immerse others in that same Spirit. The baptism of the Spirit is a promise repeated by all four evangelists.[6] Jesus fulfilled this baptism on the Day of Pentecost with the outpouring of the Spirit of God upon believers to dwell in

---

5. Isaiah 32:15; 44:3; Ezekiel 36:26-27; 39:29; Joel 2:28-32.
6. Matthew 3:11; Mark 1:8; Luke 3:16; John 1:33.

them and His church permanently (Acts 2:1-4). That Pentecost was foretold in this baptism by the Baptizer in Mark (and parallel accounts) and is affirmed by the words of Jesus and Peter: 'For John baptized with water, but you will be baptized with the Holy Spirit not many days from now' (Acts 1:5), and 'And I remembered the word of the Lord, how he said, "John baptized with water, but you will be baptized with the Holy Spirit"' (Acts 11:16).

Third, the voice from heaven – the voice of Father – identified Jesus as His Son (with 'you' being emphatic in the sentence and 'with you' again emphasizing the Father's unique pleasure with Jesus). With no one else will the Father share such words of delight – the delight He expressed in the tearing open of the heavens. The picture is that of the Trinity together as in the first 'beginning' in Genesis 1:1-3 with the 'heavens,' 'the Spirit descending,' and the spoken word: 'In the beginning, God created *the heavens* and the earth. The earth was without form and void, and darkness was over the face of the deep. And the *Spirit of God was hovering* over the face of the waters. And *God said*, "Let there be light," and there was light.'

The echo in Mark 1:11 to Genesis 22 is striking. In the LXX[7] the 'beloved son' translates the Hebrew for 'only son' in Genesis 22:2, 12, and 16. It is there, in the great Aqedah passage, that Abraham binds his only son – the one he loves uniquely and differently than he does Ishmael – as he prepares to sacrifice him in obedience to God. The reader of redemptive history, still hoping in the seed of the woman who will come through Abraham to bless all of the families of the earth, hears the Father speak of His beloved Son and both cringes and explodes with delight. This will be the uniquely loved Son – the only Son of God – whom God, as His Father, will bind so as to sacrifice Him for us.

---

7. The abbreviation, 'LXX' refers to the Septuagint – the Greek translation of the Old Testament that was the first translation of the Hebrew Bible (or Old Testament) into another language. It was completed between the third and first centuries before the birth of Christ. See Karen H. Jobes and Moisés Silva, *Invitation to the Septuagint*, 2nd ed. (Grand Rapids: Baker Academic, 2015), 19-31. The Septuagint often is represented as Roman numerals: 'LXX' (L [50] + X [10] + X [10] = 70) (J. William Johnston, 'Septuagint,' *The Lexham Bible Dictionary* [Bellingham, WA: Lexham Press, 2016], n.p.).

The Forces of Evil and Good Affirm that
Jesus Is God (1:12-13)

The Spirit drives Jesus into the wilderness in a similar way that Israel went into the wilderness. The Spirit of God who descended upon Jesus sovereignly sent Him to the place of temptation. This second use of 'immediately' in the opening scenes serves to move the narrative forward with haste while also showing the determined plan of God in the life of Jesus.[8]

During the forty days in the wilderness, Jesus was tempted by Satan. The forty days indicate that Jesus succeeded where Moses, Elijah, and the nation often failed.[9] Mark presents the enemy as a real person who put forth temptations to sin before Jesus. Mark's account of the temptation is succinct in contrast to the Matthean and Lukan versions. His purpose of calling forth the temptation scene as a witness to the identity of Christ does not require the dialogue between the tempter and Christ, or even the three specific temptations. That Satan came to attack Jesus accords with the Genesis prophecy of the evil one's wounding of the coming seed of the woman (Gen. 3:15). That Christ succeeded in resisting the temptations was inherent in the continuation of His ministry. The victory in obedience to the Spirit further pointed to the deity of the One who was tempted.

Wild animals would be a challenge for any earthly person over the course of forty days. That Jesus survived the wilderness with the presence of wild animals connects Him to the Old Testament portrayal of Israel entering the Promised Land in peace with the wild animals via the working of God.[10] Handling the wild animals and Satan indicated divine power.

---

8. The Greek for 'immediately' – εὐθύς (*euthus*) – appears in 1:10. A form of the word also appears in 1:3, being translated as 'straight,' with reference to the geographical path of the coming king.

9. See Exodus 24:18, 1 Kings 19:4-8, and Psalm 95:10. Moses will fail after his forty days on the mountain upon the revelation of the golden calf (Exod. 32). Elijah seems to fail within the forty days of his journey to Horeb (1 Kings 19). Israel fails at Kadesh-Barnea and wanders in the wilderness for forty *years* (Num. 13-14; Ps. 95:10; Acts 7:36; 13:18; Heb. 3:9, 17). Jesus succeeds with obedience and faith in His measure of 'forty' and thereafter, doing what Moses and Elijah – who later appear together in Mark 9:4-5 – and Israel were unable to do.

10. Exodus 23:29; Leviticus 26:22; Deuteronomy 7:22; Psalm 91:13; Isaiah 11:6-9; 65:25.

The service of the angels revealed Jesus to be the Lord of hosts who has angels to do His bidding (Ps. 103:20-21).[11]

Application

The divine witness to the identity of Christ means believers must present the deity of Christ as part of the gospel message. The witness in Mark's opening – the Old Testament prophets, John the Baptizer, the Holy Spirit, God the Father, Satan, wild animals, and angels – show that deity is inherent in the gospel of Jesus Christ. Mark separately joins the witnesses by identifying Jesus Christ as 'the Son of God.' The entirety of one's reading of Mark 1–16 with understanding rests largely on seeing the divine Son of God at work, and that this work of the divine One is *the beginning* of the good news. This truth infers several things.

First, any proclamation of the gospel must include the explanation that *God* in Christ is the center of the Good News. *There is not a question that someone must believe Christ is God in order to profess and confess the gospel.* While discussion on this truth often devolves into questions about understanding of the Lordship of Christ, the fact remains that for Mark, the *God*-Man Jesus proclaimed the gospel of *God.* God is the One who has come to save. This message rings throughout the Old Testament.[12]

Second, only those professing Christ as Lord are saved. Anyone professing a Jesus who is less than full deity is not professing the Jesus of the gospel. If Jesus is not fully God, then one does not need to *repent* from sin in order to believe the good news. The fact that John announced the need for repentance affirms Christ's deity.

Mark thus excludes those of the Watchtower Society, The Church of Jesus Christ of Latter Day Saints, and seemingly God-fearing practitioners of Islam from being saved, despite the practice of moral behavior by these groups. Neither of the two former cults or the latter world religion profess Christ as having full deity. Confession of Christ's divine nature is

---

11. Mark may have had Psalm 91:9-14 in mind regarding the three wilderness figures; the psalm mentions evil (91:10), angels (91:11-12), and wild beasts (91:13).

12. For example, see Exodus 6:6-8; Psalm 69:35; Isaiah 33:22; Jonah 2:9; 3:5; Zephaniah 3:17.

consistent in the history of the church as expressed in our creeds and confessions:

> We believe in ... one Lord Jesus Christ, the only Son of God, begotten from the Father before all ages, God from God, Light from Light, true God from true God, begotten, not made; of the same essence as the Father ....[13]

> *Q.* Who is the Redeemer of God's elect?

> *A.* The only Redeemer of God's elect is the Lord Jesus Christ, who, being the eternal Son of God, became man, and so was, and continues to be, God and man in two distinct natures, and one person, forever.[14]

> *Q.* What does it mean that He 'was conceived by the Holy Spirit and born of the virgin Mary?'

> *A.* That the eternal Son of God, who is and remains true and eternal God ....[15]

Third, as believers, professing the deity of Christ also means embracing the kingdom-rule of God. This is a product of belief in Christ: 'The *kingdom of God* is at hand. *Repent ...*' Repentance should not be thought of as a simple changing of the mind toward sin, as the Greek term *metanoia* would suggest without context. When one sees repentance in the New Testament, it involves a turning away of one's whole disposition – all of one's affections – from sin and worldliness to submission to the true and living God.[16]

Fourth, vital to seeing the greater significance of the gospel, the story of Mark's Gospel, and the plan of God in redemptive history, is having a working knowledge of the Old Testament. Mark writes so that one without knowledge of the Old Testament will understand the story of the gospel. However, Mark also writes in a manner that one familiar with the Old Testament will find greater significance in the things he has written. Having a working knowledge of

---

13. The Nicene Creed (A.D. 325).
14. The Westminster Confession of Faith (1646), question 21.
15. The Heidelberg Catechism (1563), Lord's Day 14, question 35.
16. Acts 14:15; 19:18-19; 1 Thessalonians 1:9.

the Old Testament allows one to see echoes, allusions, and referents to the Old Testament in the terms Mark employs. One sees every promise concerning fulfillment, even those written in typological form like the 'forty' measurements. To the one thinking in Old Testament terms, Jesus is Moses *par excellence*, Elijah *par excellence*, and Israel the Son *par excellence*. He is the Lord who will provide righteousness to Isaiah's valleys and crooked places, and the Messiah who will bring in a new age of the Spirit. It is clear that Mark would encourage one to read the Old Testament regularly, meditatively, prayerfully, and in anticipation of the Lord's faithfulness to us in Christ.

Fifth, temptations are not insurmountable because Jesus, the divine One, was substituted for us. In the wilderness, Christ had victory over Satan. On this, John Calvin notes:

> It ought to be observed, at the same time, that the Son of God voluntarily endured the temptations, which we are now considering, and fought, as it were, in single combat with the devil, that, by His victory, He might obtain a triumph for us. Whenever we are called to encounter Satan, let us remember, that his attacks can, in no other way, be sustained and repelled, than by holding out this shield: for the Son of God undoubtedly allowed Himself to be tempted, that He may be constantly before our minds, when Satan excites within us any contest of temptations. When He was leading a private life at home, we do not read that He was tempted; but when He was about to discharge the office of Redeemer, He then entered the field in the name of His whole church. But if Christ was tempted as the public representative of all believers, let us learn, that the temptations which befall us are not accidental, or regulated by the will of Satan, without God's permission; but that the Spirit of God presides over our contests as an exercise of our faith. This will aid us in cherishing the assured hope, that God, who is the supreme judge and disposer of the combat, will not be unmindful of us, but will fortify us against those distresses, which He sees that we are unable to meet.[17]

---

17. John Calvin, *Commentary on Matthew, Mark, Luke – Volume 1*, Christian Classics Ethereal Library, https://ccel.org/ccel/calvin/calcom31/calcom31.ix.xxxi.html, accessed March 12, 2020.

Finally, the hope of the service of Jesus also includes the promised peace of His kingdom in which the entire creation will live in the harmony of God's rule over humans and beasts. Yet this is just the beginning of the gospel of Jesus Christ, the Son of God and servant of God.

Reflective Questions

1. How does Mark connect Jesus to what the Lord promised under the Old Covenant? In what specific ways does Jesus excel Old Testament persons in the opening verses of Mark 1?

2. Why would it be important to present Christ as God before arguing that He is the Lord's servant? What does it mean for you that God Himself came to serve you?

2

He Came to Make You Love Fishing
(Mark 1:14-45)

'There has to be more to life than this!' This exclamation represents the feeling of many people, regardless of class, race, gender, or nationality. In its various forms, the cry for 'more to life' represents dissatisfied hopes more than common discontentments. It is not so much that one is unsettled with blessings at hand as it is that in the short span of life that we have in this present world, one could experience so much more of the world, gain so much more out of personal relationships and careers, and do so much more to contribute to the good of the world and benefit of those within one's sphere of influence.

Positively, such hopeful thoughts have launched everything from movements to reduce carbon emissions on earth to a competition to place humans on the Red Planet. Some will divest themselves of great inheritances and family statuses to give themselves to social causes to improve the lives of the less fortunate. Others will participate in extreme and risky leisurely activities, living for the thrill of conquering fears. Still others will take a leave of absence from routine life to spend a year soul-searching through a sabbatical, world travel, a return to study for more or different education, or conquering items on one's before-I-turn-forty-(or fifty)-bucket list. Of course, there also are those who drop all to find success in Hollywood, in Nashville, or on Broadway, and to live out their dreams by becoming celebrities.

Negatively, however, to escape what seems to be a mundane, common, lackluster, stifling dead-end or even oppressive routine, some will turn dissatisfied hope into an excuse for indifference toward responsibilities and for foolish decision-making. Unfortunately, we know those who have quit their jobs while chasing dreams of booming entrepreneurship, even though they lacked start-up funding and financial backing. Some became prey to cults and aberrant political, militant, and social movements, living as anarchists or deceived vagabonds, often to the despair of their families. Others turned their dissatisfactions inward so that it resulted in despair, leading to differing degrees, kinds and scopes of harm to themselves and/or others. To be fair to the picture of risk takers, the percentage of those who find success after striking out for Hollywood, Nashville, or Broadway is very low. Many simply are stuck asking, 'Isn't there more for me in this life?'

The question of 'more' doesn't plague unbelievers only; it is a question of every believer at one point in life at least. Each follower of Christ, wrestling with a call to be a fully committed disciple of Christ and for His kingdom, asks the 'more question.' But we ask it in the guise of worth: 'Is it worth it?' That is, 'If I follow Christ, with the kingdom of God as the priority that permeates all of my life choices, will it be worth it?' Or 'What will I gain if I give my all to follow Christ? Will life be more exciting for me than it is now? Will I make the best and most fulfilling use of my life?' Mark 1:14-45 answers the fulfillment question with a resounding, 'Yes!'

The Meaning of Mark 1:14-45

The meaning of Mark 1:14-45 is that *Jesus' calling of the fishermen to become fishers of men becomes an experience that witnesses the power of the kingdom of God in Christ to change lives of the repentant among those most cast down, and the spreading of the fame of Christ's name.* Consistent with the other Gospels, Mark records the imprisonment of John the Baptist in shortened form at the first.[1] Later he will return to the story of John at length, as do Matthew and Luke.[2] Having been affirmed by

---

1. Matthew 4:12; Luke 3:20; John 3:24.
2. Mark 6:14-29; Matthew 14:1-12; Luke 9:7-9.

many witnesses, Jesus proclaimed the 'gospel of *God.*' This was His express prerogative to do as the Son of God. God's gospel is 'the gospel of Jesus Christ' (Mark 1:1).

Bound up in the proclamation of the gospel, God's good news announced three important truths. First, the time in which one era passes and another arrives had come (e.g., the Messianic era). History has awaited God's visitation to His people;[3] God's people have awaited the day He will restore their fortunes, vindicate them, provide justice upon their enemies, and make His home among them.[4] They have looked for a time when the anointed One of God would fulfill all these hopes in the present realm.

Second, the kingdom of God – its king, its rule, and its domain – was near (or 'at hand'). Jesus will reveal this in His authoritative teaching, His rule over the creation, His subjection of the cosmic forces of evil, and His miracles.

Third, repentance and belief are the means to enjoy the kingdom and its king. The kingdom of God is a place for those turning away from sin and its passions to God, placing faith in the good news of the death of Christ for sin on our behalf and His resurrection from the dead to provide life for us.

In recording the initial call of the disciples and the first miracles, Mark reveals what is in store for the 'fishers of men'(Mark 1:17). In this section, and what follows in the entire Gospel account, the author would have his readers ask, *Could being a disciple of Jesus be exciting enough for me to leave my old way of living? Should I leave being in charge of my life to follow Him completely?* Mark also asks each reader to consider *if one's own life as a disciple is claiming men into Jesus' nets in the same way(s) that Jesus was leading His first disciples to do.* Here is how Mark answers these questions:

By Becoming Fishers for People, One Will Leave the Common for the Amazing (1:16-28)

The Sea of Galilee is often called 'the sea' in Mark. As Jesus passed by the sea, He called four men away from their

---

3. Exodus 29:45; 32:34; Leviticus 26:12; Psalm 90:13.

4. Deuteronomy 30:3; Psalms 14:7; 35:19; 53:6; 60:12; 126:4; Isaiah 42:13; Jeremiah 29:14; 33:7; Hosea 1:10-11.

livelihoods: Simon (Peter), Andrew, James, and John. The phrase, 'they were fishermen,' tells us that fishing was their common way of living. This was their trade and routine in life. The blandness of the description gives a tone of the mundane or the usual.

The invitation of Jesus was for them to become persons who now fish for people – men and women – rather than simply for fish. The assignment is universal, without prioritization of Israel, and without limitations with respect to geography or gender. That they must follow Jesus to become fishers of men placed them in a position to learn from Him in His daily doings. The disciples did this, being in tow and on the hip of Jesus as He proclaimed and demonstrated the power of the kingdom of God in the scenes that follow in the remainder of the second Gospel. One set of brothers left their nets from the shore and followed, while the other set came in from the boat, leaving their nets torn for their father and servants to mend.

That the sons of Zebedee left their father shows the priority God must have over family: *One must honor one's parents, love and respect a spouse, raise children to fear the Lord, but not hold the family's perfection or protection as an idol before God.* The entire scene of leaving fishing for fish to fish for people seems cultic, risky, foolish, amoral, and for these sons, almost anti-family. Yet, the readers of the Gospels know that Jesus desires His own to honor the fifth commandment, and that Jesus established an identity of family that prioritizes the will of God.[5]

Capernaum was the place of the home of Peter. Going directly to the synagogue on the Sabbath to teach revealed Jesus' authority as a rabbi among the people – even if previously He had not taught them.[6] As King, He had this authority; in proclaiming the kingdom of God, serving *through* teaching was a significant task.

What the former fishermen immediately witnessed was a distinct difference between the teaching of Jesus and that

---

5. Matthew 10:35-37, 12:50; 15:4, 19:9.

6. Jesus was recognized as a synagogue teacher: 'Jesus, like Paul (Acts 13:15), used the "freedom of the synagogue" – a Jewish custom that permitted recognized visiting teachers to preach (based on the reading from the Law or Prophets) in the synagogue by invitation of its leaders – to bring the Good News to His countrymen' (Walter W. Wessel, *Mark* [Zondervan, 1995], 26).

of the scribes. The scribes did not have innate authority to teach; they depended upon the authority of others. Jesus had authority to claim the ways of God Himself. The responses of amazement to the unstated contents of Jesus' teaching will reoccur in the story, along with responses of amazement to His miracles.[7] The disciples also witnessed 'a new teaching with authority' when Jesus' rebuke of the demonic spirit authenticated His teaching. Twice it says the people were 'astonished' or 'amazed' (Mark 1:22, 27).

One wonders if the man with the unclean spirit regularly attended the synagogue and if his condition was obvious to those around him. Or was this the one day he entered the synagogue and Jesus went to the synagogue immediately on the Sabbath because of the unique presence of this suffering individual? Either way, the encounter became the first lesson in following Jesus, in being a disciple of Jesus. The four fishermen experienced what they could not experience with fishing from shore or from a boat. In doing so, they will learn that following Jesus involves serving people made unclean by demonic spirits.

The singular 'unclean spirit' indicated the presence of only one demonic force inside the man in the synagogue. Yet he spoke with eschatological concern for the entire host of demons in the cosmos. The reference to destruction seems to be to the promise in Genesis 3:15, as there is no other thoroughgoing discussion of the destruction of the demonic in the Old Testament.[8] The reader learns of the demons' awareness of their shortness of time before judgment and their fearfulness of Christ as judge. 'The Holy One of God' proclaims both the deity of Christ and His identity as Messiah, for the title identifies Him with God, 'the Holy One' of the Old Testament,[9] and the 'Holy One' of God who will not see corruption (Ps. 16:10).[10]

---

7. Mark 6:2; 7:37; 9:18; 10:26.

8. There are references to the destruction of Leviathan and to the destruction of the present earth. There also are references to the subjugation of all climatic powers to the Lord. The destruction of the demonic might be implied by such references but is not stated explicitly.

9. Job 6:10; Psalms 71:22; 89:18; Isaiah 40:25; 45:11.

10. The 'your' in Psalm 16:10 refers to God: 'For you will not abandon my soul to Sheol, or let *your* holy one see corruption.'

The silencing of the unclean spirit was so astonishing that those in attendance at the synagogue had to question the nature of the teaching they had received. Apparently, never had they been taught that One has authority to cast out unclean spirits, or that One will come with such authority. So uncommon was the teaching and the exorcism, that the fame of Jesus spread throughout the Galilean regions. The service brought glory to Christ among many.

By Becoming Fishers for Men, One Will See Some of Those Who Are Sick Become Servers (1:29-31).

'Immediately' in verse 29 should be viewed as a time marker (as opposed to a simple conjunction as in 1:21). Upon leaving the synagogue, Jesus and the four disciples invited to fish for people encountered Peter's mother-in-law, who was ill. Traditionally, the site of Peter's home is in very near proximity to the excavations of the synagogue in Capernaum.[11] We know also from Paul that Peter was still married (1 Cor. 9:5). By the time Jesus and the disciples departed from Peter's home, his *relative* was no longer ill, but now *served* Christ and His followers. 'The mother-in-law is presented simply as a model of discipleship, which requires lowly service from all, male and female.'[12]

A second lesson on discipleship for the followers of Jesus pointed toward serving the infirmed with compassion – the compassion Jesus displayed when taking Peter's mother-in-law by the hand and lifting her. *Sickness* in the accounts in the Gospels and Acts portrays the spiritual sickness of shepherd-less sheep (Matt. 9:35-38). Seemingly, service to one's own relatives is not out of bounds of obedience to the gospel.

By Becoming Fishers for People, One Will See Power over the Demonic (1:32-34)

At the close of the Sabbath – 'sundown' – Jesus will repeat *en masse* what He did in serving two individuals at the synagogue and in Peter's home: He will cast out the demonic

---

11. See additional comments by Schnabel, *Mark*, 59, and James R. Edwards, *The Gospel According to Mark* (Eerdmans, 2002), 59.

12. James A. Brooks, *Mark* (Broadman & Holman Publishers, 1991), 52.

and heal the sick. While the writer mentions both (Mark 1:32, 34), the focus will end on the demons.

As a result of the fame of Jesus' service spreading, all of Capernaum heard of Him, His authority and power, and this brought all of the afflicted to Him. Humorously, Mark portrays an 'open "door"' (1:33) for the gospel of God and the kingdom of God. No diseases were off limits to Jesus' power, and many demons were cast out of the oppressed. *In doing so, Jesus also showed the vastness of His compassion to those in need of compassion, hope, deliverance, and healing.* He showed that His power is not limited to one overcome by an unclean spirit; all who are demonized have hope in Jesus.

Jesus silenced the demon here, as is common in this Gospel account.[13] On this, Calvin notes:

> The devil dexterously acknowledges that Christ is *the Holy One of God* in order to insinuate into the minds of men a suspicion that there was some secret understanding between him and Christ. By such a trick he has since endeavoured to make the Gospel suspected, and, in the present day, he is continually making similar attempts. That is the reason why Christ rebukes him. It is, no doubt, possible that this confession was violently extorted from him: but there is no inconsistency between the two suppositions, that he is forced to yield to the power of Christ, and therefore *cries out* that He is *the Holy One of God* – and yet that he cunningly attempts to shroud in his own darkness the glory of Christ. At the same time, we must observe that, while he flatters Christ in this manner, he indirectly withdraws himself from His power, and in this way contradicts himself.[14]

By Becoming Fishers for People, One Can Experience the Power of Prayer to Wield the Word (1:35-39)

Jesus set an important pattern for fishing for men in this scene. With intentionality, He rose before dawn and the beginning of a new day of ministry. He departed from the home of Simon, from the four following and learning from Him, from the place the crowd knew Him to lodge and serve.

---

13. Mark 1:25, 34; 3:11-12.

14. John Calvin, *Commentary on Matthew, Mark, and Luke*, vol. 1, on Mark 1:21-28 and Luke 4:31-36.

He went to a deserted place – the same term for 'wilderness' in the scenes with John the Baptizer. He spent concerted time in prayer with the Father past dawn and long enough for Peter to become aware of His absence and search for Him. *Because of* the needs of the people, and *because of* the demands of preaching and of casting out demons, Jesus went alone to pray. He spent time in prayer (1) ahead of His schedule, (2) when others were sleeping, and (3) in a place where He could not be interrupted.[15] So in following Jesus, the disciples will learn how to deepen in prayer and how to depend on God to supply what is needed for serving others. Jesus, fully human, models the need for praying to God as a priority.

As a result of the practice of prayer, Jesus met the coming demands of serving. He could traverse the Galilean locales and proclaim the kingdom of God. He could go from village to village and town to town serving those possessed by demons. Surely the grace and mercy of the power of God enabled Jesus to accomplish preaching in multiple venues, let alone the encounter with the supernatural forces of darkness revealing conquering authority. The power to preach, with any hope that people respond in repentance and enter the kingdom of God, rested largely on a prayer practice like Jesus'.

By Fishing for People, You Will See the Transformation of the Socially Outcast (1:40-45)

Leprosy could refer to one of several skin diseases. If one had leprosy, he was an outcast of the community (Lev. 13:45-46). Therefore, the leper risked breaking the law and infecting others by approaching Jesus. His posture, however, was one of helplessness and humility, as he implored Jesus and bowed before Him. He left the prerogative to heal in the hands of Jesus, which was an act of simple faith on his part.

Jesus' act of mercy cleansed this man so that he was now holy according to the standards of the Mosaic Law.[16] It required

---

15. The departure to pray apart from others is Jesus' common practice of prayer, although not exclusive to it. See Luke 5:16; 6:12; 9:18, 28; 11:1; 22:41-45.

16. The manuscript evidence seems to point to Jesus being 'filled with anger' rather than moved to pity. Seemingly, as the more difficult reading, it would be the correct reading, as scribes would have softened this term rather than substituting anger for compassion. If so, it is possible that 'Jesus was angry with the entire evil

a priest to authenticate the cleansing (Lev. 14). However, as one formerly outcast from society into a lepers' zone, and as one previously with little hope of cleansing, this cleansed leper ignored the legal authentication and proclaimed the greatness of Christ.

Still in tow, the disciples witnessed the power of serving this outcast. The life changed from leprosy to the service of Christ became the impetus for telling the towns about Jesus. Like the exorcism of the demoniac, the report of the exhibition of the kingdom of God in the cleansing of the leper brought people to the One who later will die on the cross and rise from the dead.

Reflective Questions

1. In your life, how did following Jesus make worthwhile hard decisions you had to make because you are one of His followers?

2. How should Jesus' practice of prayer in this passage reshape your current practice of prayer?

---

order in which suffering has such a prominent part' (Brooks, *Mark*, 55) or 'Jesus was indignant at the misery of the leper' (Edwards, *Mark*, 70). It also is possible that Jesus was angered over the leper's breaking of the law; this would then heighten the depth of compassion in Jesus' action as wrath against sin mingles with mercy for healing. Yet I agree with Bruce Metzger in seeing that 'moved with compassion' has better textual weight. See Bruce Manning Metzger, *A Textual Commentary on the Greek New Testament, Second Edition, a Companion Volume to the United Bible Societies' Greek New Testament*, 4th rev. ed. (United Bible Societies, 1994), 65.

3

He Came to Free You to Serve Without Human Limitations
(Mark 2:1–3:6)

I remember attending a Saturday morning men's prayer breakfast at my home church. I thought the event was informal, which was a strange mistake because I cannot remember many 'informal' gatherings at my home church other than youth-related events. Even at evening Bible study and prayer meetings, many attendees were professionals coming directly from their jobs or from their homes without having changed out of their white-collar clothing.

At this breakfast, I planned to enjoy the fellowship prayer. I was not scheduled to speak or serve in any way. Yet, upon entering the Fellowship Hall and greeting one of the older members of our congregation, I was asked, 'Reverend, where is your tie?' I was wearing a button-down Oxford dress shirt, sport coat, dress slacks, dress shoes (and socks), a black belt, but no necktie. I thought I was dressed enough to eat and pray. The church officer – who was more than fifty years my senior – did not think so.

Startled by the question, I simply stared back inquisitively. 'Your tie, Reverend; where is your tie?' repeated the gentleman. 'I did not know I needed one,' I said in response. 'You always need a tie, Reverend. Always,' he said, with the last 'always' coming with a tone of, 'and you should know this is the only way you should be dressed in order to minister to the people.'

Even though the saint smiled at me gently, I knew I had been schooled and reprimanded.

That incident represented one of many unwritten rules and restrictions under which I had to keep myself in order to serve people. I could add to it prohibitions on what furniture could not be moved or touched, what questions could not be asked, whose authority could not be challenged (even by comparing Scripture to the actions of a said authority!), the places where young adults could (and could not) congregate or even sit in worship, and the silliest one of all: where one could or could not chew gum. More concern was expressed over chewing gum than over the need to be zealous and bold about sharing one's faith and providing discipleship for younger members of the body of Christ.

Human-imposed restrictions to Christian worship and service, no matter how well-meaning, are a hindrance to the powerful working of the gospel and the kingdom of God. In His time on earth, our Lord Jesus directly confronted those whose imposition of human regulations stood in the way of people enjoying Him. It was an important lesson for the disciples to carry forward in the highly religiously controlling culture of their day.

The Meaning of Mark 2

The meaning of Mark 2 is *Jesus' new way of serving people apart from humanly-constructed limitations revealing Him as Lord of the present age and freeing disciples to enjoy Him.* A key to what Mark is doing in this chapter is recognizing that the audiences were seeing a *new* thing (2:12), *new* cloth (2:21), *new* wine and skins (2:22), and a *new* practice of plucking grain on the Sabbath (2:23-24). The friends of the paralytic, the scribes, the Pharisees and the people were limited by the overcrowded house, by their understanding of Jesus, by traditional fasting practices, and by their misunderstanding of the Sabbath law. Mark 2:1–3:6 centers around the Parable of the New Wine in New Skins. In each of these episodes Jesus revealed that He was not placing Himself or His ministry in the vein of the Pharisees and scribes, their traditions and their teachings (2:6, 16, 18, 24; 3:2, 6; see also 7:1-23). Jesus made His power on earth known despite such limitations. His disciples benefited from

Jesus' new ministry without religious constraint. The chapter reveals a four-part macro structure.

Jesus' Ability to Overcome Your Friend's Depravity and Sin Reveals the Power of the Son of Man (2:1-12)

It is of significance to note that Jesus returned 'home' to Capernaum (2:1; cf. 1:21). It is unlikely that Jesus owned a house there. Rather, Peter's home seemed to serve as His place of lodging while in Capernaum.

The narrative intends readers to expect many in Jesus' home town to come to Him for healing. One is not shocked that the report of His return brought many to Him, for He left Capernaum with His fame spreading everywhere, 'the whole city gathered at the door,' and 'everyone' was looking for Him (1:28, 33, 37).

Jesus, however, was not simply providing physical healing. Consistent with the ministry of the kingdom of God, Jesus proclaimed the Word of God to the people. Mark uses a non-technical verb for 'speaking' here – *laleo* – rather than words for *preaching* (*kerysso*) or *teaching* (*didasko*). Yet, modern versions translate it as preaching because the subject of the speaking was the Word of God. Jesus used the people's desire for healing as an opportunity for meeting the real human need of healing bodies broken by the result of living in a created world marred by the Fall. He also used it as an opportunity to offer healing to the souls of those who willingly rebel against their creator and stand in judgment of His wrath.

The absence of more room at the door posed a conflict in the story for the characters. Like those healed previously in Capernaum and the other towns the paralytic had real hope for complete physical healing if only his friends could get him to Jesus. The friends, however, removed the roof to lower their friend rather than being stymied by the crowd.

Two broad acts took place in this scene of healing. First, Jesus *saw* the persistent faith of the paralytic's friends to get into the house to get their friend healed. This led to a pronouncement of the forgiveness of sins upon the paralytic. The pronouncement came despite there being no room because of the many who had come and despite His preaching of the Word. The friends were not limited by the overcrowding of the house, and neither did they simply accept that they and their friend could hear Jesus preaching. Their persistence to get their friend to Jesus was what brought about his salvation. The perseverance did not produce the salvation, but placed their friend where Jesus was free to respond to their faith.

As it was common in that era to assume that a person's disorder stemmed from personal sin (John 9:2-3, 43), Jesus' proclamation of the forgiveness of sin cut the grain against the linear association of depravity with bodily disorder. Jesus also excelled where the Law and any rabbinic, pharisaical, or scribal interpretations of the Law or additions to the Law could not prevail. The tenderness of Jesus over any legal regulations was evident as He spoke endearingly to the paralytic with a word for 'child' (translated in modern texts as 'son').

In the second broad act, Jesus *perceived in His spirit* the scribes questioning in their hearts His authority to pronounce forgiveness of sins. He also perceived their conclusion that He was blaspheming. For the scribes, Jesus was not using a divine passive that would allow Him to mean 'God [and not I] forgives you of your sins.' Instead, they understood that He was claiming the prerogative to forgive sins as God. Mark makes use of irony here with the play on 'blaspheming,' 'God alone,' and 'glorified God' as the scribes accused Jesus of blaspheming even when their questioning of Him was self-condemning.

Jesus then challenged the scribes to examine their hearts' reasoning for questioning His identity and authority. In the end this made all who were watching glorify God in amazement at the *new thing* being done. The comparison is simple: *If I can make someone walk by saying so, certainly you should trust that I can forgive sins by saying so.* On *earth*, Jesus acted as the Son of Man of Daniel 7 – not simply as a man spouting words of forgiveness – even when there was no room in the hearts of some for His healing.

Despite the lack of room in the house and the opposition of the scribes, there were various expressions of faith toward Jesus' power, His ability to heal, His identity as God, and His authority to overcome a man's paralysis and to forgive his sins. Those displays of power were combined with His preaching of the Word. Their responses resulted in Him revealing the Son of Man's power on the earth to forgive sins; and His words challenged the scribes and made all stand in amazement. The faith-responses toward Jesus' power and preaching left Him free to reveal His authority to overcome spiritual paralysis (e.g., human depravity) and sins, and to amaze the people with His authority to change lives, even when there was no room in the hearts of some for His healing.

Jesus' Reception of Those Whom Society Deems Sinful Reveals Him as Physician for the Spiritually Sick (2:13-17)

Matthew's discipleship process begins in this parallel scene rather than where Mark began in Mark 1. Matthew's house became the basis for Jesus to proclaim the gospel to other toll collectors and sinners (Luke 5:29). The calling terms were the same as the calling of the earlier disciples (Mark 1:16-18). Levi is the same person as Matthew, and both Levi and James are described as 'the son of Alpheus,' indicating that they were brothers.[1] 'Levi was probably an employee at a toll station on the Via Maris, a heavily traveled trade route running from Damascus to Caesarea through Capernaum, working for a man who had bought the right to collect tolls.'[2]

Jesus' solution to teaching crowds of people was to call Levi as a disciple. As a Jewish tax collector on behalf of Rome, even Levi's own people hated him. As Edwards notes, 'It may be that contact with Levi was actually more offensive than contact with a leper since a leper's condition was not chosen whereas a tax collector's was.'[3]

But in becoming a follower of Jesus, this hated man then gave Jesus access to all of those like him who also were rejected by society as sinners. Just as the paralytic gains healing, the tax collectors and other kinds of sinners got to enjoy fellowship with Jesus and the twelve! But the scribes, who are the interpreters of the Law, thought that separation from sinners should be Jesus' practice. For them, righteousness required

---

1. Robert H. Stein, *Mark*, Baker Exegetical Commentary on the New Testament, (Ada: Baker Publishing, 2008), 126. See Mark 3:18 with Matthew 10:3; Luke 6:13; Acts 1:13.

2. ibid.

3. Edwards, *Mark*, 83.

separation from sinners – a concept with deep roots in the Old Testament, for Israel was called to be separate from the peoples of the nations and their idolatrous, amoral practices. However, what was missing in the scribes' worldview was the Lord's pursuit of sinful Israel as a jealous lover so that the sinners in Israel might turn to Him.

In the first parable (or parabolic saying) in Mark's Gospel, Jesus reveals that the service call of a physician is for sick people. While wellness checkups are common in the modern world, historically doctors exist for those who are not well. Predating Christ's ministry by at least three hundred years, the line from the Hippocratic Oath says, 'Into whatever homes I go, I will enter them for the benefit of the *sick*.'

By means of the parable, Jesus reveals that His purpose in coming into the present world was to reach those who were sinful – those who recognized that they were spiritually sick. Like a faithful physician, He did not separate Himself from such persons. Those who saw themselves as *righteous* (and in no need of Jesus) missed out on salvation from Jesus, the healing physician.

Jesus' Refraining from Requiring Traditional Practices Reveals Jesus as the Bridegroom (2:18-22)

Besides the prescribed fast associated with the Day of Atonement, first-century Judaism knew of fasts for lamenting national tragedies, crises like war or drought, and self-imposed fasts for various reasons.[4] The Pharisees fasted on Mondays and Thursdays.[5] Therefore, the comparison of Jesus' practice to the practices of John the Baptizer and the Pharisees manifested the significance of the uniqueness of Jesus' ministry. He was baptized by John, but He was not a follower of John's traditional fasting practice. Neither did He follow the practice of the Pharisees, who were considered to be pious. For Jesus to be at odds with one strand of Judaism might not seem so significant. However, to be at odds with the religious leaders and the prophet from the wilderness

---

4. Edwards, *Mark*, 88-89. See Leviticus 16:19-30.

5. Ben Witherington III, *The Gospel of Mark: A Socio-Rhetorical Commentary* (Eerdmans, 2001), 124.

could be perceived as opposition for opposition's sake, arrogance, or error.

To explain the reason Jesus' disciples did not fast as did the disciples of John and the Pharisees, Jesus told a series of three parables. In the first – a parable about wedding guests – at issue was the correct response of the wedding guests to the bridegroom. For some to fast in the presence of the bridegroom at a wedding feast would be out of place. At a feast, the guests simply have a responsibility to eat and celebrate, thereby enjoying the wedding party.

In an interesting twist to the wedding party celebration, Jesus indicated that fasting properly takes place only after the bridegroom is taken away. The imagery goes beyond the traditional departure of the groom and bride from a wedding to pursue the consummation of the marriage. It seems that Jesus, through use of allegory, stepped outside of the parable to identify Himself as the bridegroom and to speak cryptically of His death on the cross, e.g., 'taken away from them.' Guests at an earthly wedding would have no need to fast when the bridegroom departed from the wedding celebration to be with the bride – it would not be for atonement, tragedy, crises, or piety. However, the followers of Jesus, who were the 'guests' at Jesus' eschatological wedding, would fast in mourning over the departure of the bridegroom in His death and further departure from them to the grave.

The presence of the bridegroom among the wedding guests determined the day of their fasting. The lack of practice of fasting among the disciples pointed to the significance of the presence of Jesus among them, or at least pointed to the message Jesus was indicating by refraining from prescribing fasting for the disciples: *His followers are disciples of the bridegroom and they should anticipate Him coming to wed His own.* The hope of Old Testament Israel was that God would do this very thing.[6]

The second parable concerned an unshrunk cloth. In the story, the intent was for someone to patch an old garment with an unshrunk patch of cloth, only to find that this act was not good for repairing the torn garment. Instead, the problem became even greater. The old garment of fasting

---

6. Isaiah 54:5-8; 62:4-5; Hosea 2:16, 19.

by the disciples of John and the Pharisees stood in conflict with the unshrunk patch of cloth of Jesus and His lack of fasting. Jesus informed His hearers that they should not attempt to make His ministry conform to the practices of the Pharisees. The work Jesus did would not easily fit with the work of the Pharisees.

The third parable used for explaining the disciples' lack of fasting considered the practice of storing wine. In order to store new wine, one needed new wineskins rather than old and worn ones. The thought of storing new wine in old wineskins should yield to storing new wine in new wineskins. This decision would prevent the destruction of the wine and the wineskins. Thus, Jesus again indicated the distinction of His ministry – that His practice on fasting (or to refrain from such a practice) would not conform to the old wineskins of the fasting habits of John and the Pharisees. The practice of Jesus rightly fitted in the context of His new teachings. The identity and teaching of Jesus as the bridegroom explained His disciples' refraining from Jewish traditional practices of fasting.

Jesus' Use of David's Precedent Toward the Bread of the Presence Reveals Him as Lord of the Sabbath (2:23-28)

This is the second Sabbath encounter in Mark. Although the first was with the scribes rather than with the Pharisees, Jesus' fame from the first encounter spread so widely that it is likely the Pharisees had heard of the cleansing of the man of the unclean spirit taking place on the Sabbath (1:21-28).

Plucking heads of grain was honorable work, unless done on the Sabbath. The Dead Sea Scrolls reveal extreme rules for preventing violation of the Sabbath.[7] The question of the lawfulness of the practice raised the Torah instructions against working on the Sabbath (Exod. 20:8-11; 34:21; Lev. 23:3) and both the rabbinic and pharisaic interpretation of those instructions.[8]

---

7. Edwards writes, 'The DSS preserve the most rigorous Sabbath regulations in Judaism, forbidding even the carrying of children, giving of help to birthing animals, or the retrieval of an animal fallen into a pit on the Sabbath (CD 10–11)' (Edwards, Mark, 93).

8. 'The scribes enumerated thirty-nine kinds of work that were prohibited, and the third of these was reaping' (Brooks, Mark, 65.)

In response to the implicit accusation of disregard for the Law, Jesus questioned the Pharisees' knowledge of David and His disciples violating the Law by eating the bread of the Presence.[9] These loaves were holy and set apart, not for public consumption.[10] David (the leader) gave them to his men (his followers) and in doing so broke the Law of Moses at a time of need and hunger. Apparently, the ethics of David's actions considered the Law in light of human need; David's actions, which appeared to violate the Law, were compatible with the intent of the Law.

The juxtaposition of the Torah stipulations against the Davidic actions in the prophetic writings of 1 Samuel did not intend to weigh one part of Old Testament Scripture against another. Instead, the intention was that 'the Law ought to be interpreted according to the design of the Legislator.'[11]

Jesus indicated that 'the Sabbath was set up to benefit humankind; human beings were not created in order to observe the Sabbath.'[12] If ever there was a new wine or unshrunk piece of cloth, here it was! For Jesus, Pharisees and most likely all adherents of first-century Judaism were looking wrongly upon the Sabbath regulations, making them work in contrast to the good of the worshiper of God. The disciples, in contrast, were not in violation of the Sabbath rules by their work, for the work did not dishonor the giving of the Sabbath for people to rest while remembering the holiness of God the creator.

Jesus also rebuked the Pharisees and defended the actions of His followers by claiming Lordship over the Sabbath. This was a direct claim to deity, for the Lord is the giver of the Sabbath, and His resting at the end of the creation week served as the model for keeping the Sabbath. The 'so [that]' at

---

9. 1 Samuel 21:1-6 is the historical reference. The incident took place under Ahimelech, the high priest. Abiathar, his son, was high priest later, and might be mentioned because he was well-known as the one son of Ahimelech who escaped the massacre by Doeg the Edomite.

10. According to the Law, twelve loaves were provided on a table in the tabernacle on the Sabbath and were for the priests alone to eat (Exod. 25:30; Lev. 24:5-9).

11. John Calvin, *Commentary on Matthew, Mark, and Luke*, Vol. 2, commentary on Mark 2:24, https://ccel.org/ccel/calvin/calcom32/calcom32.ii.ix.html (last accessed April 25, 2024).

12. Witherington, *The Gospel of Mark*, 131.

the beginning of the clause (also first in the Greek text) shows that drawing a conclusion toward the Lordship of the Son of Man over the Sabbath comes from rightly understanding the ethics revealed in the Davidic episode.

Seemingly, Jesus was saying that if He is a son of David, then He can do as David did. If He is the greater Son of David, He can do greater than what David did. Moreover, if one of the Law's holiest objects in the Tabernacle could serve David and his followers, then one of the Law's holiest days could *serve* Jesus and His disciples. Yet, by revealing a greater truth of the Sabbath law instituted by the Lord, Jesus showed Himself to be that very Lord. In the purpose of Jesus for the Sabbath, true enjoyment of the Sabbath was more important than ritualistic constraints. *Jesus' use of David and his men eating the bread of the Presence as defense for allowing the disciples to pick grain on the Sabbath correctly identified the role of the Sabbath as servant and revealed the Lordship of Christ over the Sabbath.*

Jesus' Confrontation of the Pharisees' Apathy Toward Doing Good on the Sabbath Reveals Him as the Healer Who They Will Conspire to Kill (3:1-6)

Jesus regularly addressed the hypocrisy inherent in the Jewish leaders' law keeping. The scene in the synagogue allowed for dealing with multiple hypocrisies. First, this was the second scene in the synagogue, so the reader is expectant of a miracle confrontation as much as the Pharisees are. Yet the Pharisees were not hopeful of a miracle for doing good, but to be dismissive of Jesus as a rebel. Second, if the synagogue was to be a place for the Jewish people to gather to meet with God, this scene makes it seem like God is not interested in helping a person in need, for those claiming to know and speak for Him were not interested. Third, blatantly ignoring the problem of the man when they would not ignore the need of their own beasts reeked of hypocrisy.

Jesus' confrontation of the Pharisees received silence from them on the ethics of working on the Sabbath. Mark does not have as many chapters leading up to the Jewish leadership's rejection of their Messiah as do Matthew, Luke and John. But the ethical question and miracle will lead to the leadership's commitment to kill Jesus.

The Pharisees hoped to accuse Jesus of breaking the Sabbath by healing the man with the withered hand. In their minds, if Jesus worked on the Sabbath, even to show mercy to one in need, He was breaking the Sabbath. Apparently, the ability to heal by uttering words was work, even though they were working in their heads in their plot to kill Him.

Their silence on the ethics of healing on the Sabbath meant that they did not want to agree that the miracle was doing good. If the Pharisees were concerned about doing good, they would want Jesus to restore the man's hand and they would have changed their understanding of the Sabbath instructions to include intent, mercy, and grace. In contrast, for them to say that it was not right to heal on the Sabbath would mean that the Sabbath is not for doing good in mercy, when in fact that was the very function of the Sabbath – to show mercy to those who needed rest in God. Being trapped by the ethical dilemma posed by the question, the Pharisees remained silent with their evil thoughts and motives.

The Pharisees' hope of catching Jesus breaking the Law brought the man forward and led Jesus to restore his hand. His action was followed by the Pharisees and the Herodians plotting to kill Him. Religiously and politically, the Herodians[13] and the Pharisees had massive differences. Yet they united to accomplish the destruction of the common enemy of their political and religious rules.

The gospel's power confronts the hypocrisy of ignoring the good of helping a person in need to maintain a church's religious practices. The preaching of the gospel will bring forward the needy – those in need of the saving power of Jesus. The gospel, being full of grace, has the power to silence the hard of heart while helping those in need. Such ministry might yet encounter people who hate Jesus and desire to destroy the work of the gospel.

Reflective Questions

1. What is the connection between your faith in Christ and an unbelieving friend's salvation from sin?

---

13. A party supporting the Herodian dynasty's rule financially and politically.

2. What does the Jewish leadership's response to Jesus' healing of the man with the withered hand reveal about their love of God and neighbor? What would have been a better response to both Jesus and the one healed?

4

He Came to Distinguish the Right Responses to Him
(Mark 3:7-35)

Recently I watched a video of a December 7, 1963 live broadcast of the Beatles in concert. As in other concerts of the young rock band, many fans were screaming at them as they played. As the cameras swept over the crowd, you could see fans holding their hands in their faces, staring as if mesmerized, or nearly fainting with excitement. The responses were frenzied, showing great zeal for the four music stars and their works.

Sometimes people measure the responses of worshipers in modern church gatherings to the reactions of fans at entertainment and sports venues. The thinking behind the comparison seems to be that the fanatical passion that humans display toward other humans of stature or star status should be mimicked or outdone when one is responding to revelation of the greatness of Jesus. Yet in the three episodes in Mark 3:7-12, Jesus' words and actions provide a sobering correction to those who think all sincere responses toward Jesus are correct. Instead, there are some well-meaning responses to Jesus that dishonor Him as much as betrayal and blasphemy. There are some responses that He condemns.

Near the sea, on the mountain, and back in His hometown, the various wrongful human and demonic responses to Jesus' divine identity caused Him to make distinctions between

Himself, His workers, and those whom He condemned. Mark presents distinctions between Jesus and the crowds, the unclean spirits, the betrayer, the scribes, and His true family members. He will identify with Himself the disciples whom He called and who do the will of God.

Jesus Provides Distance and Commands Silence Toward Great but Unclean Responses (3:7-12)

The crowd following Jesus were from regions across the entire country – the south, east, and north regions and Judea. People had traveled a great distance to see the One who had healed many, cast out demons, and claimed to be Lord of the Sabbath. His reputation as One who forgave sins and cleansed lepers had spread and attracted throngs to Him.

Despite their intentions of examining the reports about Jesus for themselves, the outcome was that the large number posed a danger for Jesus. While they only intended to gain healing, the great number of infirmed could have crushed Jesus similar to how one might be run over and killed in the mayhem of many fleeing a dangerous scene. Their hopes to touch Jesus were not considerate of who Jesus is, of other diseased persons' need for Jesus, or that their own approach only sought to gain from Him selfishly.

Jesus did not allow the crowd to be near to Him and to receive a miracle from Him. Instructing the disciples to have a boat ready for Him allowed Him to move away from the presence of the crowd's sinful approach. Some in need of healing would have to wait.

Although the crowd might only understand Jesus to be a miracle worker and healer, the unclean spirits were not so limited in their knowledge of Jesus' identity. They recognized His divine identity. Assuming that the demons were present in people and not appearing before Jesus bodiless, there would have been great chaos as those possessed by demons bowed before Jesus and screamed, 'You are the Son of God!' Imagine this scene: diseased people from all over the country were begging, pressing for a touch, and demon-possessed persons were bowing between the forceful crowd and Jesus.

Jesus' silencing of the unclean spirits showed that He would not accept every response to His identity. The words of the unclean spirit state the truth about Jesus: He is the divine, second Person of the triune God. Post-resurrection, the Apostle Paul indicated that such affirmations should only arise from the presence and working of the Holy Spirit in a person and in a church body; the demonic agents, defeated through the atoning work of Christ, were silenced from making such affirmations. And also during His earthly ministry, Jesus silenced them from making such affirmations. He did not need them or desire them.

Some speculate that the silencing of the demons came from Jesus' need to disassociate Himself from them. That is, Jesus did not allow the demons to act as His publicists and marketeers lest those listening to them imagine that He affirmed the demonic activity or that the demons affirmed His work. Although this speculation might be true, the four evangelists are silent about such reasoning. Instead, in this passage, Mark finds Jesus silencing the demons because He rejected wrongful responses to the revelation of His divine identity.

Jesus Calls and Appoints Those He Desires to Be with Him and to Serve Others on His Behalf (3:13-19)

Walter Wessell proposes reading the Greek of 3:13 as 'into the mountain' rather than 'up on the mountain.' This would mean Mark is describing the hill country of Galilee near the lake.[1] Separating the twelve from those near the lake below, Jesus called them to Himself so that they might enjoy Him as the initial part of their unique roles as apostle-disciples.

Mark then made the first of three parenthetical or editorial remarks about the names of those Jesus called (3:14, 16, 17). The twelve received a new designation as 'apostles,' meaning 'sent ones.' They were not being sent exclusively, but uniquely, as they were to walk with Jesus for the full three-year length of His ministry, even as Peter later said: 'All the time that the Lord Jesus went in and out among us, beginning from the baptism of John until the day when he was taken up from us' (Acts 1:21-22). Differently than others, they would be able to draw upon a special and proximate

---

1. Wessel, *Mark*, 42.

relationship with Him, including words given in private ministry to them. They were to be sent as *eyewitnesses* to all He did, including rising from the dead. Their collective name matches their relationship to Him.

They had three roles as apostle-disciples. First, they were with Jesus to learn of Him and directly from Him the truth about His identity, mission, service, and the kingdom of God. Second, they were to preach (or *herald*) on His behalf. If they followed the model of John the Baptizer, they would proclaim the coming of the One mightier than John – the King of Israel for whom the herald called for straight paths (Mark 1:4, 7). If they also followed the example of John and Jesus, they would herald the coming of the kingdom of God so that people might be prepared to meet the king (1:14).

Third, they would have authority to cast out demons. Until now, only Jesus showed the power to command demons to be silent and leave their hosts (1:26-27; 3:11-12). Going forward, the disciples would have this authority. Complementing their proclamation of the coming kingdom of God, they would have demonstrative power of the kingdom they would proclaim.

The second and third editorial remarks come in association with Peter, James, and John, the three disciples who accompanied Jesus on very special occasions, including the healing of Jairus' daughter (5:37), His Transfiguration (9:2), and in Gethsemane (14:33). Of the twelve sent ones, they alone would witness Jesus raise a dead girl to life and would witness the Transfiguration that revealed a glimpse of His heavenly glory and received affirmation from the Father. It seems that the focused time and experiences with Jesus provided the preparation that these three apostles would need for serving Him: one would be sent to the circumcised (Peter), one would become the first martyr (James), and one would be a leader in the churches of Asia Minor and would be exiled for the faith (John).

Simon was named 'Peter' by Jesus, and after this, only once will 'Simon' appear as a name for Peter in Mark's Gospel – and that alongside the name 'Peter' (14:37). James and John, previously identified with their father Zebedee in 1:19-20, are now identified as 'Boanerges,' with the explanation of its meaning as 'Sons of Thunder.' The significance of these names is unclear to modern readers, although 'Simon' and 'Sons of Thunder' might be associated with the roughness and explosiveness of their characters, respectfully.[2] Changing names often anticipated a role in redemptive history related to the new name, like that of 'Abraham' (Gen. 17:5). However, any conclusions about the significance of each individual name are speculative. As part of the whole of the three editorial remarks, the names point to the callings that further distinguished some persons in the passage from those who made incorrect responses to the revelation of Christ's identity as the divine Son.

The remaining names in the list of disciple-apostles agree with the lists in the other Gospels. James 'the son of Alphaeus' and Simon 'the zealot' have additional designations that distinguish them from their namesakes. Mark expanded the name of Judas Iscariot with 'who betrayed him', thus placing him in the pattern of those in the passage condemned for acting consistent with Satan's kingdom (3:26, 29).

Jesus Condemns His Detractors Eternally and Commends Some as His True Family Members (3:20-35)

Jesus' family and the Jewish leadership raised concern about the true source of the power behind His works. His family had perceptions of how Jesus should act if He was *normal* and in His right mind. The Jewish leadership had a perception of how Jesus should act if He was *obeying the Law* and was religiously sensible. Jesus eternally condemned those who found His works to be of Satan and commended those who do God's will as His true family members.

The three scenes each reveal a distinct truth about the response to Jesus' identity, or, in modern terms, about people's responses to the proclamation of Jesus' identity in the preaching of the gospel.

First, some will label the work of the gospel as *crazy* rather than normal. Consider the crowd gathered about Jesus, now at home. The crowd was so large that to minister to them He had to work through mealtimes. This situation provoked His

---

2. Schnabel, *Mark*, 87-88.

kindred to take custody of Him, having assessed Him to have 'lost His senses.' Thus, His kindred judged Jesus as crazy or without sanity. Family members often are the first to see gospel-related work as something abnormal with respect to how a person should live.

While Mary is a faithful Old Testament-type follower of Christ in the Gospels, it was not beyond reason for her family to conscript her to confront Jesus, appealing to her as a loving mother with traditional sensibilities. Although she appeared here as one providing an incorrect response to Jesus' identity and works as the Son of God, the full narratives of the Gospels show that Mary grew in her understanding of the person and mission of Christ, as did Nicodemus, and she will be welcomed into Christ's kingdom rather than condemned.

Jesus' family members did not yet see the significance of the casting out of demons; even in seemingly acting lovingly toward Jesus and His need for food and rest, His family members' actions were wrong, even though they were not as evil as that of the Jewish leadership. They did not recognize His divinity and wanted to shut down His work.

Second, some will label the work of the gospel as *demonic* rather than heavenly. Coming from Jerusalem, the scribes judged Jesus as 'possessed by Beelzebul,' and to be '[casting out] demons by the ruler of demons,' when He performed His miracles, especially exorcism. Thus, the scribes assessed Jesus as demonic. *Beelzebul* means 'master of the house' and refers to 'the arch ruler of a dynasty of demons and evil spirits.'[3]

The scribes were copyists of the Law and thought by doing so that they were experts of the Law and able to stand in judgment over it. With the introduction of the scribes into the narrative, the reader should see that the issue of legal or correct judgment was at stake in the story.

In the parable that Jesus gave in response, the characters teach truth related to the issues at hand. Jesus questioned the absurdity of saying that He was empowered by Satan to drive out Satan. He built His reply by explaining that a kingdom

---

3. .Edwards, *Mark*, 120.

with civil strife will not stand as a kingdom, neither will a house of family members fighting one another survive as a family (i.e., house of Israel). Satan's end would come if he were working against himself within his own kingdom. Thus, for His hearers Jesus created an impossibility: *Jesus must be from outside Satan's kingdom to defeat unclean spirits.* The irony of the accusation of the scribes is evident to the reader of Mark because he introduced Jesus as the Son of God.

Second, Jesus supported His statement by explaining the impossibility of robbing a strong man's house until the strong man is bound; here He created another impossible scenario. In other words, Jesus must come from outside of Satan's 'house' if He was ransacking Satan's realm. This, however, is not a call for us to 'bind the strongman,' or 'to bind Satan.' Jesus was not giving us authority; neither was He instructing us on how to defeat demons. He was confronting a question about the source of His own power. The job of 'binding' the strong man belongs to Jesus alone.

Jesus then stated that blasphemy against the Holy Spirit is the only type of blasphemy that cannot be forgiven: 'But whoever blasphemes against the Holy Spirit *never has forgiveness*, but is guilty of an *eternal* sin.'[4] The double emphasis indicated the certainty of the leadership's rejection of Jesus' offer of salvation as the Son of God. They rejected His Messianic claim and turned the people from immediately receiving the full redemption of the nation of Israel.[5] They will perish for their decisions.

According to Davids, '[Blasphemy against the Holy Spirit] is the willful and conscious rejection of God's activities and its attribution to the devil .... It is the enlightened, willful, high-handed nature of such a sin that makes it unforgivable (not forgiven at death, as the Jews thought, but punished through eternity).'[6] Darrell Bock writes, 'The blasphemy of the Holy Spirit might be regarded as a by-product of rejecting the Son of Man. The difference between blasphemy of the

---

4. Mark 3:29, cf. Matthew 12:31; Luke 12:10.

5. This seems to be the focus of Zechariah 12:7–13:1.

6. P. H. Davids, 'Blasphemy against the Holy Spirit,' *Evangelical Dictionary of Theology*, 2nd ed., Walter A. Elwell, ed. (Baker, 2001), 174.

Son of Man and blaspheming the Spirit is that blasphemy of the Son of Man is an instant rejection, while blasphemy of the Holy Spirit is a permanent decision of rejection .... Once the Spirit's testimony about God's work through Jesus is refused, then nothing can be forgiven, since God's plan has been rejected.'[7]

The blasphemy of the Holy Spirit passage also represents Israel's national rejection of Jesus. As representatives of the nation, the leaders' attribution of their Messiah's works to Satan represented the nation's rejection. *This rejection, however, does not allow for the Church to mistreat the descendants of Abraham, Isaac, and Jacob. It is to their Messiah the Jewish people must answer, and not to the Church.* We should reject anti-Semitic readings of this passage and all passages of Scripture. Jesus was a servant who came to fulfill God's promises to the Jewish patriarchs, and those who are Gentiles are debtors to the Jewish people for sharing in their spiritual blessings (Rom. 15:8, 27; cf. 9:4-5; Eph. 2:11-13).

Third, some will try to stop the work of the gospel *innocently* while others will do the will of God. Jesus, in a final dialogue, conferred familial status upon 'whoever does the will of God.' Jesus was not dishonoring His mother in doing so, for this would violate the Fifth Commandment. The mother and brothers had good intentions, but they were ill-informed. If one works through a day without eating, especially with work as demanding as Jesus' – including confronting evil spirits – the pace will seem unnatural to many. A loving mother should be concerned about her son eating and taking care of himself. Yet, this was not the time to remove Jesus from His service to the needy in the crowd. He had come to serve them and would find an appropriate time to steal away for personal nourishment. If Mark 1:35 reveals a habit of prayer, Jesus already has spent time alone with His Father in a desolate place early in the morning before others could interrupt or seek Him. His mother and brothers may not have been aware of the significance of the spiritual fellowship that took place between the Son and the Father each morning.

---

7. Darrell Bock, *Luke 9:51–24:24:53* (Baker, 1996), 1143.

Rather than making a statement that is dishonoring to His mother, *Jesus is establishing a spiritual family based on obedience to the work of Jesus.* That is, those sitting and listening were accepting the work of Jesus as He explained the kingdom of God and its implications. Those questioning the validity of His work were not part of His family.

Mary and the brothers are part of both families, as the New Testament later shows. Mary was not accusing Jesus of blasphemy, but of having a schedule that showed imbalance between ministry and personal health. The words about the identity of Jesus' 'brother and sister and mother' may have sobered Mary and the brothers such that they never again attempted to interrupt Jesus' ministry of service.[8] The Apostle Paul twice references the brothers of the Lord as members of the early church.[9] Mark does not record Jesus questioning the identity of His spiritual Father, because that was established.

The correct approach to Jesus is to do 'the will of God.' 'The will of God' is shorthand for 'obedience to the Word of God,' and speaks of doing what God desires a person to do. This phrase is not looking for one to discern a vocation, but for those in the crowd around Jesus to do what God desires people to do rather than doing only what they would do based on a natural worldview of life, on following simple personal desires and pleasures, and on desires toward doing evil. Anyone who desires to please the one true God shows himself or herself to be one adopted by God the Father.

Mark 3:7-35 invites readers to consider how we approach the Lord Jesus in prayer and worship. He is and forever remains the Son of God. We cannot make demands of Him, approach Him glibly, accuse Him of wrongdoing, think that all worship of Him is acceptable, or approach Him apart from seeking to do the will of God. As the Son of God, He is looking for people who will do the will of God. On this occasion, He was looking to serve all people more than He ever could have been concerned about stopping to eat.

---

8. John 7 reveals that much later the brothers still do not believe His Messianic claims. However, John 7 does not show them interrupting His ministry to the people.

9. Galatians 1:19; 1 Corinthians 9:5.

Reflective Questions

1. How should Jesus' statement about His family members inform our thinking about who is a child of God?

2. In your experiences, what are some examples of people's limited cultural exposure and perspective leading to them limiting what Jesus might be doing through you and others to serve people with the gospel?

5

He Came So That We Might Grow Through the Word
(Mark 4:1-34)

Three well-known printed optical illusions are the duck versus the rabbit, the vase and the two reversible silhouettes, and one known as 'My Wife and My Mother-in-law.' Depending upon one's prior experiences, brain stimulation, and/or cognitive perspective, one might see a drawing of a duck head and slightly opened beak where another sees the head of a rabbit with its ears shooting back. In a different drawing, another sees a white vase on the page on which others see two perfectly copied silhouettes in opposition to one another. In the third illustration, as much as one may want to see the younger woman dubbed 'Wife,' many only see an older, haggard-looking woman labeled 'Mother-in-Law.' What anyone sees might differ from the next viewer's perception, even though the picture does not change. Some cannot see both pictures of a given illusion even after great concentration.

The response people have to parables in Scripture is akin to that of viewing printed optical illusions. Some, upon hearing (or reading) a parable, respond in a way that does not make enough sense of the words to receive the kingdom of God. Yet others hear in a manner that gives them the ability to know the secret things of the kingdom. While both types hear, only one discerns the truth and significance of what the parable says.

Literary Design

In Mark 4, the author designs his passage 'to confront the disciples with their responsible privilege to understand, in contrast to the consequences of divine hardening.'[1] Similarly, at length, Stein writes:

> In this section Mark seeks to explain for his readers why the message and ministry of Jesus encountered the opposition described in the previous chapters. Why did Jesus experience opposition from the scribes when He healed the paralytic (2:6-8)? Why did they oppose His welcoming toll collectors and sinners into the kingdom of God (2:16) and complain about His disciples not fasting (2:18)? Why did the Pharisees criticize Him for His disciples' actions on the Sabbath (2:23-24) and for His healing on the Sabbath (3:2)? Why did the scribes absurdly explain His exorcisms as due to His being empowered by Satan (3:22)? Why did His own family think that He had lost His mind (3:21)? And why did the Pharisees and Herodians seek to kill Him (3:6)? In this section, Mark explains that 'those outside' the believing community, while hearing the word and seeing the works of the kingdom, cannot understand what is taking place (4:12). God, however, has given to Mark's readers, as He did to the disciples and other followers of Jesus, the understanding and conviction that the kingdom of God had indeed come in the ministry of Jesus and that the works and deeds of Jesus were evidence of this (4:11, 34). Consequently, having been given ears to hear, they should heed (4:3, 9, 23, 24-25) and make sure that they are good soil, bearing fruit for the kingdom (4:8, 20).[2]

Clearly this section has a definable introduction and closing that show the entire passage is about the parabolic teaching of Jesus:

> Again he began to teach beside the sea. And a very large crowd gathered about him, so that he got into a boat and sat in it on the sea, and the whole crowd was beside the sea on the land. And he was teaching them many things in parables, and in his teaching he said to them (4:1-2).

---

1. Elliott E. Johnson, 'Interpretation of the Soils Parable,' unpublished class notes, Dallas Theological Seminary, 1995.

2. Stein, *Mark*, kindle loc. 5063-73.

With many such parables he spoke the word to them, as they were able to hear it. He did not speak to them without a parable, but privately to his own disciples he explained everything (4:33-34).

The parables allow readers to discern section divisions within the chapter: the Parable of the Sower (4:1-9), Interpretation of the Parable of the Sower (4:10-20), the Parable of the Lamp Light (4:21-25), the Parable of a Man Scattering Seed (4:26-29), and the Parable of the Mustard Seed's Growth (4:30-34). Yet all the parables point toward one idea related to the kingdom of God.[3]

Understanding Parables

Before considering the meaning of the parables, it is helpful to understand how parables communicate meaning. *Parable* is a narrative sequence that makes a comparison between common experiences and historical realities to clarify historical theological discussion. Parables are frame stories. That is, they are stories in which one of the characters portrays or exemplifies what is taking place in the story of which he is a part. Or simply, *a parable is a story within a story.* The parable itself is fictional, while the account of Jesus telling the parable is historical.

Jesus used parables as a form of teaching for two purposes. First, He used it to reveal the mysteries of the kingdom to His disciples (4:11). The followers of Jesus gained insight into truths about the kingdom of God that others did not. Second, the parables serve as a means of keeping the secrets of the kingdom from those who, in the decree of God, have hardened themselves against Jesus and the truth about Him (4:12). Jesus teaches so that they might know the content of what He is saying, but never grasp that the contents point to Him as the divine Savior and King. Thus, they will not be forgiven for their sins.

Like the stories in which they are found, narratives communicate meaning indirectly. Indirectly, the Parable of the Prodigal Son invites one living in sin to return to God

---

3. The five above sub-divisions fall under two macro-sections of 4:1-20 and 4:21-24. The first grouping places the Parable of the Sower with its interpretation. The second grouping gathers the three additional parables as complementary ideas rather than disparate thoughts.

the Father to receive mercy. Indirectly, the Parable of the Unmerciful Servant exemplifies the danger of being a person who lacks forgiveness toward another individual.

The Meaning of Mark 4:1-20

The first parable consists of several elements that direct the reader toward the meaning of 4:1-9:

1. There is a sower who sows seeds.

2. There are four types of soil in which the seed falls: path, rocky ground, thorns, and good soil.

3. There are three obstacles: birds that devour, no depth of soil and no root, and thorns that choke.

4. There is one soil that produces fruit, and it produces thirty, sixty, or even one hundred times the crop expected from the amount of seed sown.

5. There is a call to hear – a responsibility.

6. There is a contrast between those who are given to know the secrets of the kingdom and those who do not 'see' and 'hear.' The seeing is the ability to identify Jesus as the Son of God based upon His deeds. The hearing is the ability to identify Jesus as the Son of God based upon the words He used in His claims to be the Messiah and in His other teachings. Again, there is a responsibility on the part of the person *to respond* to the revelation about Christ.

The combination of these elements reveals that a *welcome response to Jesus' Word becomes the basis for growth in a follower's knowledge and fruitfulness.*[4] In the five parable-sections, Jesus will teach the disciples that only one means of responding to the Word of God fosters spiritual growth in the lives of those who are able to hear it.

Growing Through the Word Is Available to All Generally (4:1-2)

Jesus taught from the boat because of the large crowd on the land. He spoke to more people in this way than He could ashore.

---

4. Johnson, 'Interpretation of the Soils Parable.'

Geographically, note that Jesus was still ministering around the Sea of Galilee as He has been doing throughout 1:14–8:26. Mark emphasizes the proximity to the sea and mentions the land, giving a universal concept to Jesus' teaching.

'Many things' indicates that Mark omits much of Jesus' parabolic teaching. This shows selectivity in the working of biblical narrative. All that Jesus taught is not recorded, but the Gospel writers have recorded only that which communicates the meaning the Spirit intended for us to gain from this combination of words, structure, tone, and theology.[5] The Spirit gives us what the Lord intends for us to gain through Mark's account.

All of those present on the shore heard the same parables. It was possible for each listener to accept Jesus' teaching as the very words of God – which they are. However, the episodes to follow reveal that some did not receive the teaching with understanding and thus did not grow spiritually from what was said. The lack of growth was not due to problems with natural cognition.[6] Instead, Jesus showed that such lack of understanding comes from a disposition that is set against knowing God.

Growing Through the Word Comes by an Invitation for Able Hearers to Hear (4:3-9)

In the parable, the sower and the seed remain constant.[7] Only the soils change, and the result of the seed on the soils differs: On the path, birds get the seed; on rocky ground, the

---

5. See also John 21:25. To say that the writers were selective is not the same as questioning the motives behind the inclusion of books in the canon of Scripture. All historical writers are selective, for they cannot possibly write every bit of history on any given topic. Yet whether the whole of their selected writings should be received as Scripture or rejected is a different matter. There is no evidence for political jockeying with respect to the inclusion of the four Gospels and the rejection of other Gospels from canonical consideration, such as The Gospel of Peter, The Gospel of Thomas, and The Gospel of Judas. For more on the trustworthiness of the New Testament canon and the authority of the four Gospel accounts, see Peter J. Williams, *Can We Trust the Gospels?* (Crossway, 2018), and Michael J. Kruger, *Canon Revisited: Establishing the Origin and Authority of the New Testament Books* (Crossway, 2013).

6. I recognize that persons with cognitive impairments lack the natural capacity to comprehend some or all of what people write or speak. However, Mark 4 is not addressing natural cognitive impairments.

7. Mark 4:3, 4, 5, 7, 8.

seed springs quickly and is scorched; among thorns, plants attempting to grow are choked; on good soil a crop blossoms.

The call to give attention to the parable is strong. Jesus begins with both 'Listen!' (ἀκούετε) and 'Behold' (Ἰδού). Jesus' double call to *listen* and *hear* indicates that more is at stake than a common discussion about the routine of sowing.

Jesus makes a distinction both outside of the parable (v. 9) as well as inside (v. 8): '*He* who has ears to hear, let *him* hear.' This distinction is similar to the call of God in salvation – a *general* invitation to all through the proclamation of the gospel versus an *effective summoning* of some through the preaching of the same gospel, e.g.: 'For many are called, but few are chosen' (Matt. 22:14); 'But many who are first will be last, and the last first' (Mark 10:31); 'And behold, some are last who will be first, and some are first who will be last' (Luke 13:30).

All had physical ears and a mental capacity to hear the words of Jesus. The call to '[those] with ears to hear' went beyond the physical ability of persons to a metaphysical ability – a spiritual ability to grasp the significance of the words of the parable. Jesus invited those with that ability to hear in a different way than what was natural.

Growing Through the Word Is a Kingdom Stewardship Distinct from God's Purposes for Those Not Understanding (4:10-12)

'When he was alone' indicates that Jesus and the disciples had withdrawn from the crowds on the shore.[8] There were others besides the twelve present with Jesus in the house. The explanation of the purpose of the parables in private to this group revealed a stewardship of the secrets of the kingdom given to them, while there was a closing of the revelation of God and His forgiveness to outsiders. Some people had the ability to 'see' and 'hear' the words but not comprehend spiritually the truth revealed about God. With the words, 'have been given,' Jesus indicated the gracious choice of God to grant to some the kingdom's secrets, and also that those outside did not understand due to God's sovereign, determined purpose toward them.

---

8. See 4:33-36 in which they are in private and then return to the boat.

The quotation in 4:12 comes from Isaiah 6:9-10 in which the veiling of God's Word concerned the coming Assyrian and Babylonian judgments upon Israel. Jesus drew from the significance of Isaiah's words to the NINTH-CENTURY-B.C. audience to remind His audience of how significant *hearing with an obedient response to God* is for the hearers. Yet Jesus' scope was not limited to the offspring of Abraham, Isaac, and Jacob; it is available to anyone with the ability to 'hear.'

Growing Through the Word Requires an Accepting Attitude toward the Word (4:13-20)

The interpretation of the Parable of the Soils revealed that only an accepting disposition toward the Word of God brings fruitfulness (contrast 'unfruitful' in 4:19 with 'bear fruit' in 4:20). The disciples and others in the private session were seeking understanding. Understanding the truth that this parable teaches had significance for each parable to follow. Each hearer should listen for secrets of the kingdom – that is, for the parable to communicate an aspect of truth about the coming kingdom of God. With understanding, the significance of what has been learned should bring about faithful obedience to what was heard.

Although Jesus explains the role of God in revealing truth to some hearers, He yet questions their ability to understand any parable if this one remains undisclosed to them. The disciples' inability to understand this parable questions their ability to understand any subsequent parable.

Jesus explains the parable of the soils. For this parable, He will show that He intended the various characters and elements to have a meaning. This is not true of all parables, as one cannot identify the pigs and trough of the Parable of the Prodigal Son with any historical element in Jesus' eating with tax-collectors and sinners (Luke 15:1-2). Even in this parable the sower does not have a historical identity, showing that there is not an allegorical aspect to every part of a parable.

The seed in the parable corresponds to the preaching of Jesus in the historical world of Mark and his readers. In particular, the Word heard was the preached Word to the crowd that was listening. That Word was scattered among them and received even as a seed is scattered on the ground and received by the earth. Four responses came from the scattering of this seed; and four responses come from the hearing of the preaching of the message of the kingdom of God.

First, some became victims of a direct attack from Satan to steal what they have heard. One should view the picture of the activity of Satan in concert with the lack of spiritual capacity to comprehend the message of the kingdom of God. What was heard in the proclamation of the Word, the evil one worked actively to remove those words from any contemplation of their significance in the lives of some hearers. The general opportunity to hear with significance and the offer of the kingdom within the general invitation were removed from the focused thinking of the hearer. Thus, the proclamation of the Word did not bear spiritual growth.

Second, some rejoiced in hearing and sought to put what was said into practice. However, at some point the practice met with 'tribulation or persecution on account of the word.' One does not need to read a later Neronian or post-A.D. 70 persecution into the 'tribulation or persecution on account of the word.' The Mark narrative later portrays the disciples as deserting Jesus at the threat of the mob that came with Judas to capture Him.[9] Those without enough 'root' under the tree of endurance will 'fall away' (or better, 'stumble') when they must make a choice between the demands of the Word of the kingdom and the stresses of living in a world that hates those who abide by such demands.

Third, some who experienced the threefold challenge of present responsibilities and concerns, trusted in the false promise of riches and had a desire for things other than the kingdom of God.

The three responses are similar to cutting off sunlight from getting to a plant in the way larger bushes do with smaller plants beneath them. Hearing the Word of God while being concerned about becoming rich or while trusting in riches as one's hope will keep one from having a fruitful response to the Word of God. Equally so, a good concern for things in this life can hinder a fruit-bearing response to the Word as the concern gains too high a value in the life of the hearer.

---

9. Edwards, *Mark*, 136. See 14:43-50.

Many calls for believers to be 'realistic' or 'practical' rather than trusting in the Lord have the tone of cares that choke the Word.

A fourth response was receptive to what the sower proclaimed, and this was the only response that bore fruit. This response involved immediate receptivity to cut off the work of Satan to snatch the Word. Such receptivity also must value the Word of God about present cares and self-preservation.

Growing Through the Word Comes as Part of a Stewardship of Proper Self-examination (4:21-25)

In 4:21-34, Jesus left the Parable of the Soils for three additional parables: A Lamp Under a Basket, Seed Growing, and Mustard Seed. In the first, the teaching about placing a lamp where light will have the greatest display intends for the readers to see lamps as objects for exposing secrets and hidden things about oneself. It is self-directed because the call was for each individual to hear (v. 23) and measure (v. 24). It is a call to measure according to the Word because Jesus exhorted the listener to pay attention to what was heard. The lamp in question concerns the Word of God – the Word of the kingdom. The Word intends to reveal what is hidden within us (i.e., sin) so that such things might be exposed. Sober judgment is necessary, for one must take what is heard and measure oneself against it. The faithful steward finds that adherence to what he has heard allows the Lord to give him greater understanding (and thus, greater growth). The unfaithful steward finds understanding the Word to be increasingly difficult because he has not used the Word of God to measure himself rightly.

The Growth of the Kingdom Occurs Secretly Until the Time of Its Final Purpose (4:26-29)

The last two parables focus on the growth of the coming kingdom of God. Each reveals that the kingdom has a present working aspect, even if the full reality of the kingdom remains to be made manifest. Each is tied to the message of growth by means of the Word of God because such growth is a response to the message of the kingdom of God. The ones who grow in response to the Word of God are those who are receptive to the message of the kingdom and its implications, who measure themselves against such standards soberly, who repent over where they fall short, and who make corrections in order to obey the dictates of the kingdom. If the kingdom is growing secretly, those responding to its message shall find that their faithful stewardship has not been in vain. When the kingdom will manifest itself in fulness, the stewards will have even greater fruitfulness.

Jesus' likening of the kingdom of God to a man scattering seed reveals the secret and sovereign nature of the kingdom's growth until the time of its final harvest gathering. Just as a man scatters seed and then it grows (1) while the man goes about his normal routines, (2) without the man's knowledge of the full scientific details of the method of growth, (3) and due to the normal (scientific) process of the seed growth in the soil, so will be the growth of the kingdom. As the ripening of the plant at the end of its growth allows for the man to harvest it, so too at the fulness of the time of the kingdom it will be revealed. The kingdom grows presently toward its final growth while the earth's inhabitants continue in their daily lives. The details of the mechanics of the growth of the kingdom are part of the knowledge of the King although not fully disclosed to people. The kingdom will grow as it is intended, and a day will come when its growth is final, and it will be time for it to be revealed.

One should not read such 'growth' as a postmillennial position on the kingdom, but as an acknowledgment of the mysterious nature of the present working and future arrival of the kingdom. The working of the kingdom is mysterious to us. Yet the day will arrive when it will be made manifest to the world. Those who have responded to its message with receptivity will share in its blessings.

The Growth of the Kingdom Hides Its Potential Behind an Appearance of Insignificance (4:30-32)
Akin to the previous parable, Jesus' likening of the kingdom of God to the growth of a mustard seed into a large place of shade reveals the seemingly insignificant yet powerful

nature of the kingdom. In comparison to other seeds the smallness of a mustard seed would not give the impression that it could yield a large tree – certainly not one so large that birds could build nests and find shade on it. The beginning of the kingdom of God in the life of the hearers of its message would not give the impression that the kingdom will reveal the rule of her King to the world. Even today Christian believers represent a small part of the world's population, and the gospel message seems to have a very little seat at the table of worldviews. Yet the kingdom, as the work of God, will not disappoint her disciples. The kingdom will be like the large, shade-providing mustard plant toward those who have received her message.

Conclusion 4:33-34

Speaking in parables became the major component of Jesus' teaching to the crowds. Some were able to hear the words of the parable with receptive understanding (e.g., 'as they were able to hear' [v. 33]). Those who were receptive had the benefit of Jesus' explanations to follow the teaching. This explanation assured growth apart from the snatching-work of Satan. It revealed that these disciples had root within themselves, and that they did not yield to the challenges of this world's present cares, concerns, and falsehood posed by desiring and having money.

Mark 4 invites readers to become humble listeners, asking God to use the Word to critique them rather than critiquing the style of the sermon or charisma of the communicator. Such should come to each sermon assuming God must expose them as sinful creatures and then obey what the preached Word of God says (Heb. 4:12-13). This is the only way for God's Spirit to bring about the fruit of Christ in them in great measure. Also, such must pray for the Lord to open the eyes of the lost in His mercy (Eph. 1:15–2:10).

Mark 4 invites us to look past the one exhorting us in the pulpit to the God for whom the person is speaking. We must go to the Word of God in humility, not simply as hunters for hope. We should listen to the hard things and not only to the sweet things. We must view the kingdom and its message with a receptive heart and with the eyes of faith.

Reflective Questions

1. What would make you a more obedient listener to the preached Word of God? What practices do you need to change on Saturday evening, Sunday morning, and Sunday afternoon to benefit the most from each sermon?

2. Of what does your daily experience in God's Word consist? In what ways has the Word of God worked to produce growth in you related to kindness, patience, selflessness, meekness, and endurance?

6

He Came to Rescue Those in Desperate Situations
(Mark 4:35–5:42)

'One thing was certain, nor did he himself doubt it, that he was no longer the same man, that all was changed in him, that it was no longer in his power to prevent the bishop from having talked to him and having touched him' (description of Jean Valjean in Les Misérables).[1]

On reading the story of the terrible Jean Valjean one initially might think that his transformation from a starving, stealing, ex-convict is impossible. But the overwhelming kindness of Bishop Monsieur Charles François Bienvenu Myriel sparks an almost immediate and complete transformation of Valjean from criminal to model citizen and Christian saint. Surely, if this life can be transformed, then the most desperate of persons can be changed into completely new and whole persons.

The four episodes in Mark 4:35–5:42 bring together people with very desperate needs, and casts them alongside of (1) people desperate for the wrong things and (2) those who mock Jesus' power.[2] Consider the similarities between the Gadarene demoniac, the woman with the discharge of blood, and Jairus:

---

1. Victor Hugo, Les Misérables (Ware, Hertfordshire: Wordsworth Editions Limited, 1994), 77.

2. Robert Stein views the three stories of Mark 5 as part of an account of four stories beginning in 4:35 (Stein, Mark, 247).

Gadarene Demoniac	Issue	Hemorrhaging Woman and Jairus
'He lived among the tombs' (v. 3)	Near Death	'My little daughter is at the point of death' (v. 23)
'He wrenched the chains apart, and he broke the shackles in pieces' (v. 4)	Problematic Strength	'A discharge of blood for twelve years' (v. 25)
'And cutting himself with stones' (v. 5)	Relief Unavailable	'Suffered much under many physicians' (v. 26)
'Night and day among the tombs and on the mountains he was always crying out' (v. 5)	Perpetual Suffering	But rather grew worse' (v. 26)
'He replied, "My name is Legion, for we are many"' (v. 9)	Oversized Enemy	'Spent all that she had' (v. 26)

The situations of the three persons address the same issues in both episodes. The three episodes reveal that *Jesus' power to rescue those in desperate situations seeks a response of faith rather than great opposition, in order that His fame might be known.* In keeping with the meaning of the book of Mark, Jesus will serve the demoniac, Jairus and his daughter, and the hemorrhaging woman. They found themselves in desperate life situations: one could not find relief from possession by thousands of demons, another had a daughter at death's door, and another had a continual hemorrhage that made her legally unclean. Each needed Jesus to act for their situations to change. Jesus served each of them, revealing the power of the kingdom of God.

In the opening episode on the sea, the disciples were as desperate as those Jesus will meet on the land. The disciples would perish in the sea if Jesus did not awake and act in some way to mitigate the effects of the storm and the potential doom of the passengers. Jesus served the disciples, displaying His kingdom power in their lives in anticipation of the three encounters to follow. Mark teaches four things concerning Jesus entering desperate lives.

Those Being Taken Down by the Storms of Life Will Find That Jesus Provides Peace (4:35-42)

'On that day' indicates the freshness of the kingdom parables' discussion in the minds of the disciples and to this entire scene. One would expect to observe the characters in focus responding to the words of Jesus with a fruitful response of faith, or an unfruitful response as those who 'hear but [do not] understand.' The readers also should look for a display of the kingdom of God – the subject of the previous two parables (4:26-32).

'Leaving the crowd' brings a focus to the disciples, as does getting into the boat, recalling to the readers the words, 'beside the sea,' and Jesus sitting in the boat alone to teach in 4:1. The presence of people in other boats may have provided some who would hear the Word of God with receptive hearts, or the boats may have been filled with many who misunderstood the identity of Jesus. As it is, the scene concluded with the disciples asking, 'Who then is this, that even the wind and the sea obey him?'

The scene introduces a great windstorm without warning. It is all the more startling since Jesus was the One who said, 'Let us go across to the other side.' The reader knows that Jesus is the Son of God; as God He would have knowledge that a storm was approaching. Yet He sent the disciples into a sea-crossing situation in which the potential for them to perish was very real. The waves were coming into their small vessel so that the boat was filling with water. Without a miracle, the disciples would drown.

The fear and lack of faith of the disciples poses a literary conflict in the trajectory of this episode. In a perfect world, the disciples would laugh at the windstorm and waves drowning the boat. They would have been fully assured that the One who cast out demons and healed paralytics would see them to the other side through the storm or else by stopping the storm. They would have acted as those anticipating the kingdom of God of which Jesus spoke earlier in the day. They would have been of those with a crop of fruit with a thirty to a hundred times increase. But they gave way to fear.

The windstorm and waking bring elements from the story of Jonah into this episode.[3] The disciples acted with the same fear as the polytheistic sailors heading from Joppa.[4] In this scene, parallel to where the captain of the boat wakened the sleeping passenger both to question the meaning of his sleeping through the storm and to call upon his God, the disciples wakened Jesus.[5] However, unlike Jonah, when Jesus awoke, He did not find the disciples casting lots in order to identify the source of the storm, showing faith in a localized deity.[6] Neither does He become the immediate subject of a hearing on His involvement in the evil of the storm.[7] Instead, Jesus awoke to perform the work of deity.

To rebuke forces of nature is a prerogative of the Lord: 'You covered it with the deep as with a garment; the waters stood above the mountains. At your rebuke they fled; at the sound of your thunder they took to flight.'[8] Speaking to the waters also is the prerogative of the creator (Gen. 1:20). The two commands of 'Peace' and 'Be still,' and the two results of the wind ceasing and a calm coming upon the sea, were as miraculous as the calming of the storm when Jonah was thrown into the water.[9] The response of the winds and sea to Jesus is not surprising for the readers, who have been informed regarding His divine Sonship.

The responding question of Jesus should be humorous to the reader. The disciples had experienced a storm in which they found themselves helpless and could have lost their lives at sea. Certainly, there was reason for these men to be afraid, as fear in this situation would be natural and warranted. Yet Jesus asks, 'Why are you so afraid?' and then answers

---

3. See Susan M. Rieske, 'Sea Storms, Divine Rescues, and the Tribulation: The Jonah Motif in the Book of Matthew,' in *Christian Origins and the Establishment of the Early Jesus Movement* (Lieden: Brill, 2018): 351-72. Rieske discusses the Matthean version of this episode (Matt. 8:23-27).

4. See the sailors' fear in Jonah 1:5, 10.

5. Compare with Jonah 1:6.

6. Compare with Jonah 1:7.

7. Compare with Jonah 1:8.

8. Psalm 104:7. The LXX translates the Heb. ga'ărāṯ₂kā – 'rebuke' in Psalm 104:7 – with ἐπιτίμησις (*epitimesis*), the noun related to ἐπιτιμάω (*epitimao*) – the word for 'rebuke' in Mark 4:39.

9. Compare to Jonah 1:15.

with a second question, 'Have you still no faith?' Evidently the disciples by now should have concluded that the power to still the storm and prevent death, or to raise them back to life upon drowning, was present in the person of Jesus. Seemingly, the silencing of unclean spirits (1:25-26; 3:11-12), the rebuking of a fever (1:30-31), the healing of a leper and many diseased persons (1:32-34; 40-45), the making a paralytic walk (2:11-12), the restoring of a withered hand (3:5), and the proclamation of the kingdom of God largely through parables (1:38-39; 2:19-22; 3:24-27; 4:1-34) should have worked together as a signpost to the identity of the figure in the boat with the disciples. The question in effect asks something like, 'Haven't you yet reasoned from the power to overcome leprosy and paralysis that you have nothing of which to worry in a near-death situation on the sea if I am in the boat with you?' The same peace Jesus brought to the sea is what His presence among them offered the disciples.

The fearful response of the disciples again recalls Jonah 1 and the response of the sailors to the calming of the sea.[10] Yet the fear of the sailors on Jonah's rebellious voyage led to faith in the God of heaven who made 'the sea and the dry land' (1:9). The sailors' subsequent sacrifices and vows revealed their belief. But the disciples questioned the very identity of the One who gave orders to the wind and sea and they would not make a conclusion about Him. They still would be evaluating the Lord's servant at the time of the transfiguration (9:5-6).

Those Tormented Will Beg for and Find Relief (5:1-20)

This story is quite unique in the issues it presents for the readers, including the singular demoniac versus the two in a parallel account (Matt. 8:28-34), and the location and name of this region that one should be able to identify by its steep bank. The story shows the interchangeable nature of the terms for demon possession as the writer uses both 'unclean spirit' and 'demon-possession.'

There are three textual options for the name of the region: 'Gerasenes,' 'Gadarenes,' and 'Gergesenes.' There is no final

---

10. The καὶ ἐφοβήθησαν φόβον μέγαν ('and they were filled with great fear') of Mark 4:41 is an echo of Καὶ ἐφοβήθησαν οἱ ἄνδρες φόβῳ μεγάλῳ ('And the men feared with great fear') in Jonah 1:16.

resolution on the location as we are without certainty on the historical reference; both textual and geographical issues are at stake.[11] The parallel accounts in Matthew 8 and Luke 8 reveal the same textual variants as those in Mark 1.[12] In the story of the demoniac, Mark describes him as a man completely under the control of a legion of demons (possibly five or six thousand demons).[13] The immediacy of the encounter seems to have been actual rather than literary, considering both the supernatural possession of the man and the Lukan account of Jesus meeting the man as soon as He stepped ashore (Luke 8:27).

Also in question is the number of demoniacs present: one or two. Matthew's version has Jesus encounter two with unclean spirits (Matt. 8:28). However, Luke agrees with Mark in recording one demon-possessed man (Luke 8:27).[14] The

---

11. 'Gerasa (modern Jerash) was a city of the Decapolis (see 5:20) located thirty-seven miles southeast of the Sea of Galilee. Gadara (modern Um Qeis) was also a city of the Decapolis about five miles southeast of the Sea of Galilee that 'lay on the frontiers of Tiberias' (Josephus, *Life* 9 §42). Ancient coins bearing the name of Gadara often portray a ship, indicating that its territory was seen as bordering the Sea of Galilee (Metzger 1994:19). Although the textual evidence favors 'Gerasenes,' Metzger (1994: 72) gives this only a 'C' rating, indicating considerable doubt as to whether this is the correct reading .... The confusion of the textual evidence is compounded by geographical considerations. Gerasa, favored in Mark and Luke, but barely, requires too long a run (35+ miles) for pigs to the Sea of Galilee. Consequently, some suggest that the 'territory of the Gerasenes' functions as a loose term for the whole of the Decapolis (France 2002: 227) or that the territory of Gerasa extended to the Sea of Galilee .... If, for geographical reasons, we choose Gergesa as the original city designation (Gundry 1993: 256–57), how do we explain its weak textual attestation? Did someone change its relatively unknown name for the name of the better-known Gerasa? Was 'Gerasenes' added by an early copyist unfamiliar with the geographical area, or by an 'ignorant' Mark, to a text that originally had no city designation? Was 'Gerasenes' part of the early form of the tradition, and an ignorant redactor later added the references to the sea and the drowning of the pigs? All such suggestions are highly speculative and not without their own problems. It is probably best to interpret the present form of the story using the designation 'Gerasa' for the city and territory. Apart from the geographical problem, the meaning of the Markan text is clear, but the historical evaluation of the actual site, which is dependent on the original textual designation of Mark, is best held in abeyance due to the textual confusion' (Stein, *Mark*, 250).

12. Brooks, *Mark*, 89.

13. 'A Roman legion consisted of four to six thousand men, but here the word merely refers to a large number ('mob,' GNB)' (Brooks, *Mark*, 90).

14. On this paradox, D. A. Carson writes, 'The best explanation is that Matthew had independent knowledge of the second man. Mention of only one by the other Gospel writers is not problematic. Not only was one sufficient for the purpose at hand, but where one person is more remarkable or prominent, it is not uncommon

record of one man is enough for Mark to achieve his purposes concerning Jesus' work as a servant.

Literally, this demoniac story differs from others in that the demon adjured Jesus rather than vice-versa, there were two directives for the demon to come out (5:8, 13), the demons were sent to a specific location (into the pigs), and the people were not awed positively but had a negative reaction to the healing.

The writer provides the fivefold description of the demoniac in an abb^{1}a^{1}c pattern, referencing (a) activity among the tombs (3a), (b) 'no one' being able to bind the man (3b-4), (b^1) 'no one' being able to subdue the man, (a^1) activity among the tombs and mountains (5a), and (c) the cutting of himself with stones (5b). The writer paints the man as one desperate for help, while unable to relieve himself of the demons or to have outside assistance in gaining normalcy – even for chains strong enough to hold him.

The man was at a short distance from Jesus and ran to meet Him as He came ashore. The demons recognized the identity, deity, and power of God in Jesus. They understood that Jesus had the authority to cast them into eternal destruction.[15] Rightly did Calvin say, 'Now, the devils knew that Christ was the Judge of the world; and therefore we need not wonder that the sight of Him impressed them with dread of immediate torment.'[16] Even so, it seems that the demons were attempting to resist coming out of the man and going to destruction for Jesus commands them to depart multiple times.

The demons implored Jesus for a reprieve from the Most High. They did not wish to be sent away from the country.[17] Instead, thinking that presence in pigs would allow them to stay in the country, they begged to be sent into the animals.

---

for the Gospels to mention only that one (cf. 'I saw John Smith in town today, I hadn't seen him in years' – even though both John and Mary Smith were in fact seen).' D. A. Carson, *Matthew: Chapters 1 Through 12* (Zondervan, 1995), 217.

15. Matthew 8:29; Luke 8:31.

16. John Calvin, *Commentary on a Harmony of the Evangelists Matthew, Mark, and Luke*, vol. 1 (Bellingham, WA: Logos Bible Software, 2010), 432.

17. Rather than see 'territorial spirits' here, it is wise to suggest that the mystery of the geographical nature of the request is unknown to us. There is not much written in Scripture on which to elaborate.

This act of begging is the second of five uses of the verb *parakaleo* for imploring in the episode.[18] Jesus gave consent for the demons to enter the pigs, again demonstrating His power over the spirits as the Son of God. The resulting destruction of almost two thousand pigs does not limit the number of demons to two thousand, for multiple demons could be in one animal. Jesus' power over the demons created a huge economic loss for the herdsmen.

The fleeing of the herdsmen to town did not bring people to worship Jesus. Instead, the townspeople came to observe the loss of the pigs and the subduing of the demoniac. However, seeing what happened did not lead them to see Jesus according to His divinity (4:12).

In great contrast to the healed demoniac, the locals begged for relief from the upheaval of their lives. While the demons begged not to depart from the country, in this third use of the verb for implore, the people of the town sought for Jesus to leave their area. Rather than seeing the significance of one who could now sit peacefully, put on clothes, and have his good sense back, they feared loss of 'pigs' (i.e., their possessions). Yet the healed man will beg to remain with Jesus.

Mark's narrative portrays Jesus crossing the lake only to reach this demoniac on the other side. Having performed this miracle, Jesus got back into the boat to re-cross the lake (5:18, 21). Yet He would not leave the region without a witness to the kingdom of God. He exhorted the healed demoniac to return to those who had known him as demon-possessed, maybe even having developed friendship with him before he was possessed.[19] He did not silence the man as He did upon meeting him.[20]

---

18. Mark 5:10, 12, 17, 18.

19. The timing and nature of the friendships is speculative. What the reader should wrestle with is whether a man fully possessed by thousands of demons and unable to be subdued could have 'friends' in that state. It would seem that the friendships existed before the demon-possession took place and the man is returning home to see those who knew him before his life took a turn for the worse.

20. Edwards notes, 'Curiously, however, Jesus does not swear the man to silence as he has heretofore. It may be supposed that the command to silence is unnecessary in Gentile territory where there is no fear of false messianic expectations. This is not the case, however, for in 7:31–37 Jesus swears a man to silence after a healing in the Decapolis. The reason Jesus sends the man to

Finding relief, the healed man found joy in proclaiming Christ to everyone in the ten cities. He told friends and the peoples of the Decapolis what 'Jesus' did for him. As the command was to tell what 'the Lord' did for him, the obedient actions of the healed man are another means by which the writer affirms the deity of Christ. The sight of the changed demoniac now turned evangelist for Jesus made all who heard him marvel.

Those with Prolonged Pain Will Find Inner Power from Jesus by Faith (5:24b-34)

Mark sandwiches the story of the woman with the discharge of blood between the two episodes of the story of Jairus.[21] The fourfold description of the woman paints her to be as desperate as the demoniac. Her continuous discharge of blood made her unclean according to the law (Lev. 15:25). There was no medical technique that could resolve the discharge. Even if there were, she would have had no means to afford such assistance, having spent her full cache of financial resources. The idea that she was growing worse possibly indicates that her situation would become terminal.

Unlike those in the parable of the soils who heard the Word of God and their hearing was unfruitful, the woman has heard about Jesus' miracles and most likely perceived Him to be the Messiah. She had the simple faith to believe that the power of God in Jesus was not limited by clothing. She pressed her way through the throngs to get near to Jesus' garment and she received instantaneous and complete healing upon touch.

That Jesus perceived power emitting from Himself upon the woman's touch does not question His foresight or omniscience as God. Instead, the power itself and the

---

announce what happened to him may be related to the fact that Jesus has been banished from the region' (Edwards, *Mark*, 160).

21. 'Sandwiching' is a literary technique common to Mark's Gospel in which the writer disrupts one story with what appears to be an unrelated story in an ABA1 pattern. The ending of the inner story gives way to the beginning story in order to rejoin it and complete it. See James Edwards, 'Markan Sandwiches: The Significance of Interpolations in Markan Narratives,' *NovT* 31 (1989) 193-216; and Tom Shepherd, *Markan Sandwich Stories: Narration, Definition, and Function*, Andrews University Seminary Doctoral Dissertation Series 18 (Berrien Springs, MI: Andrews University), 1993.

perception of its discharge both point to abilities that are beyond human. Neither does the question about the identity of the one who touched Him raise a concern about His divine portrait. Jesus raised the question for the sake of bringing the woman forward.[22] If He were not omniscient, He might not be able to discern whether the woman was being truthful and free to receive complete healing.

The woman's fear and trembling before Jesus is reminiscent of the disciples' fear after the calming of the storm (4:41). Differently, however, the woman seemed to understand the identity of her healer whereas the disciples did not. She fell down before Him in humility, with the same posture as the demoniac (5:6).

In great contrast to the woman's faith, the disciples objected to Jesus being concerned about a touch from someone. Their objections, however, did not stop the power of God from working in the life of the one who placed faith in the Lord's power.

Jesus gave the woman a very encouraging fourfold response. She heard the word 'daughter' – a form of the same word that Jairus used – a very endearing term that elevated the woman in the crowd for her actions and also in the response of those who read her story. Jesus affirmed her act of faith as the means that accessed the power to dry up her flow of blood. He pronounced peace upon her, indicated that she has no enmity with God due to her act, and thus had no need to fear. And He reassured her that what she felt as healing in her body she had actually experienced.

Those Concerned About Death Will Find that Jesus Raises the Dead (5:21-24a; 35-43)

Jairus was as desperate as the demoniac and the woman. He begged Jesus to come to his house in the same way the demons, townspeople, and the healed demoniac begged Him (v. 23).[23] Akin to the demon-possessed man and the hemorrhaging woman, in a great act of submission he fell at the feet of Jesus even though he was the ruler of the

---

22. The Greek verb indicates that Jesus kept looking for the person responsible for the emission of power (Edwards, *Mark*, 165).

23. The ESV uses the word 'implored,' but in the Greek it is from the same verb for 'beg' used in the demoniac episode.

synagogue! His daughter would die if Jesus did not come to heal. Jairus hoped for a physical touch by Jesus' hands, maybe not fully understanding Jesus' ability to transcend distance with His power.[24]

En route to the house a great crowd pressed upon Jesus.[25] In such a scenario, it is difficult to see how the synagogue ruler and Jesus would have made it to the house before the daughter died even without the interruption by the woman with the flow of blood. The providential interruption by the bleeding woman may have been the cause of a delay, but not necessarily the complete delay that provided time for the daughter's life to expire.

The report of the death of his 'daughter' immediately followed Jesus' pronouncement of 'daughter' upon the healed woman. If Jairus' daughter were somehow also the 'daughter' of Jesus, there would be hope. Even so, what He could do for the woman, He certainly could do for Jairus' daughter. Jesus is not simply 'the Teacher,' as apparently He was known in Jairus' household. He had shown Himself already to be a healer of no mean strength.

While a report of his daughter's death would have crushed him, and/or caused Jarius to have great anger toward the woman who interrupted Jesus, Jesus will not allow even a hint of such responses. Spurgeon proclaimed,

> It is singular that the case of his little daughter, of twelve years of age, was here placed within the region of hope by our Lord's healing a woman who had been exactly the same time subject to a grievous and incurable malady. A woman who led a living death is healed that Jairus may believe that his dead daughter may be raised to life. Brethren, we never know when God blesses us how much blessing He is incidentally bestowing upon others. It may be that even our conversion had a far-reaching but very distinct connection with the conversion of others. Grace smiles upon its personal subject, but its object reaches beyond the private benefit of the individual. The Lord is strengthening the faith of another of His children, or it may be He is actually working faith in a convinced soul, when He

---

24. Luke 7:6-10; John 4:49-51.

25. The term translated as 'thronged' (συνθλίβω, *sunthlibo*) means to press upon.

is accepting and honouring our faith, and saving us. We speak of killing two birds with one stone; but our Saviour knows how to bless two souls, nay, two thousand souls, with one single touch of His hand.[26]

Mark is intentional in juxtaposing the twelve years of life of the little girl against the twelve years of the illness of the woman. That is information for the reader only, unless the woman shared the length of her suffering in her 'whole truth' story to Jesus, and Jairus also heard her mention the number of years. Nevertheless, when Jesus turned to him and said, 'Do not fear, only believe,' Jairus had every reason to believe based on what he had observed.

Jesus took into the room only those who needed to witness the power of God – possibly due to their later roles in the church.[27] He also put out those who did not have faith, possibly so that they did not discourage Jairus. As David Garland writes, 'Jairus obeys because he leads Jesus to his house, but his faith is again challenged by the grievous chorus of those already assembled to mourn the little girl's death. They do not have the faith of the woman and would undermine the faith of the father.'[28] The laughter of the mourners followed Jesus' words about the girl sleeping; they had heard His words, but did not perceive who He was.

As Jairus requested, Jesus physically touched the little girl, taking her by the hand, and calling her to life with His words. The translation indicates that some of the original readers were not conversant with Aramaic, and that Jesus said words of meaning.[29] The little girl's rising from the dead amazed the disciples and the parents, but Mark seems to construct the story to indicate that both belief (Jairus) and unbelief (the disciples) experience similar amazement to the works of Christ. As seen in the opening episode, only one of the responses – the response of faith – is the right one.

26. Charles Haddon Spurgeon, 'The Touch,' in *Metropolitan Tabernacle Pulpit*, vol. 23, Nov 4, 1877, Sermon No. 1,382.

27. Acts 3:1-8; 8:14-24; 9:32-40; 12:1-5.

28. David E. Garland, *Mark: The NIV Application Commentary* (Zondervan, 1996), 222.

29. Garland, *Mark*, 222-23.

Jesus commanded the silencing of the report of the healing because of the potential to bring harm to Himself and His ministry before accomplishing the atonement on the cross. The command to give the girl food both nourished her, meeting her real need, and proved she was alive. As infirm as she had been, the girl may have been unable to eat previously.

Mark 4:35–5:42 reveals that *simple faith* leads to telling people about the power of God in Christ (5:1-20), simple faith sustains us in the face of death (5:21-24a; 35-43), and simple faith brings inner healing (5:24-34). This section also reveals that *Jesus serves the desperate*, whether such lives are suddenly interrupted on a peaceful journey, troubled and messy, without hope from traditional means, or facing death. By going to the cross and rising from the dead, Jesus can address all desperate situations – situations even as desperate as being crucified unto death.

Reflective Questions

1. Identify two occasions in life when you faced overwhelmingly desperate situations that might have cost you your health, finances, social standing, life, or life of a close family member. What did the Lord do to overcome the situation? How should that inform any future scenarios with overwhelming odds of positive change, success, or survival?

2. Consider Jesus' words to the disciples, the demoniac, the hemorrhaging woman, and Jairus after He acts miraculously in each episode. What do you learn about how we might better respond to people who have faced desperate situations and survived them?

7

He Came So That We Might
Know the Real Jesus
(Mark 6)

Warner Sallman's painting, *Head of Christ*, depicts Jesus as a male of European descent. His 'Christ' has long, flowing brown hair, brown eyes, brown mustache and beard, skin that looks like a slightly tanned European, and a facial structure common to those of Euro-American descent. Copies of the painting have hung in many American Catholic and Protestant churches, including many African American churches – even during the Civil Rights and post-Civil Rights eras. Although this portrait of Jesus in no way resembles Him apart from maleness, it has wielded considerable influence on people's misunderstanding of the identity of Christ.[1]

Both disciples and skeptics hold misunderstandings about Jesus. Disciples of Jesus have in their minds images of Jesus from their childhood readings, how they were taught about Him in church, what they have (and have not) heard preached

---

1. 'Just as the color of Christ influenced broad political and religious problems, it has also figured in the everyday spiritual lives and experiences of Americans. Christ's color has deeply influenced how people relate to God and to others. In very personal ways, many people have close emotional attachments to the Jesus they first beheld in children's Bibles or Sunday School walls or in their bedrooms' ('The Color of Christ: An Interview,' The Newberry, January 16, 2013, https://web. archive.org/web/20131022141546/https://www.newberry.org/color-christ-interview (last accessed April 25, 2024). See also, Edward J. Blum and Paul Harvey, *The Color of Christ: the Son of God and the Saga of Race in America* (Chapel Hill: University of North Carolina Press, 2012).

about Jesus, and their own reasoning based on experiences in their Christian lives. Skeptics may have only what other skeptics have communicated about Jesus, a selective study of theology or religion, or their own experiences and history with those who claim to be followers of Christ.

It would be reasonable to think that an encounter with real, thorough, faithful gospel preaching would be enough to clarify misunderstandings and clear away obstacles to Jesus working powerfully in the life of one rightly informed about His identity. Yet in the encounters in Mark 6, even as people saw the real Jesus at work or gained reports of His working, they did not lose their false ideas about Him. People's interactions with the real Jesus failed to sober them from their misconceptions about Him, due to their own internal noise about Jesus and/or themselves. This was true, regardless of whether Jesus limited or expanded His ministry toward people.

Mark 6 provides four large settings that depict people meeting Jesus on His own terms or hearing of Jesus as He performed miracles among them. The chapter yields four truths about meeting the real Jesus.

Meeting the Real Jesus Reveals a Need for Sobriety about His Authority to Serve (6:1-13)

Jesus left Jairus' home for His hometown, Nazareth.[2] With His disciples still in tow so that they would learn the practices of a servant-disciple, Jesus made a Sabbath entrance into the synagogue to teach. The place He expounded from in the Scriptures is unknown, but the depth of His exposition was beyond anything the listeners expected from the hometown boy.

The questioning by those in the synagogue displayed an understanding of Jesus that saw only His humanity. He was simply 'this [male]' figure who suddenly had wisdom different in quality than that of other teachers. He should not have been able to do the miraculous things He was doing with His hands – hands that seemed commonly human in the years He lived in Nazareth. Moreover, His occupation was that of a carpenter, not of a rabbi or a scribe, following

---

2. Jesus later chose to reside in Capernaum. His previous residence was Nazareth (Mark 2:1; Luke 4:23).

in the footsteps of Joseph (Matt. 13:55). There was not a hint of suggestion that He would do anything other than use His hands to work with wood.

The townspeople also knew Jesus' earthly family well. 'The son of Mary' is used only here in the New Testament, and possibly is the writer's way of indicating the people of Nazareth did not think that Jesus was Joseph's biological son.[3] Mark does not focus on any talk of Jesus having been born of fornication, nor does he make a reference to Him being born of a virgin. The focus is on the commonly known humanity of Jesus.

Readers are aware that Jesus has brothers from an earlier episode in this Gospel (3:31). Here the writer names them: James, Joses, Judas and Simon.[4] The people also mention that Jesus had at least two sisters. The town had assumed that this was an average family of which Jesus was an average person among several offspring.

Their 'offense' toward Jesus seems to have arisen from a comparison of the absolute authority with which Jesus spoke juxtaposed against their conceptions of His identity. The verb for offense, *scandalízō*, is a strong word in the New Testament and is 'exclusively controlled by the thought and speech of the Old Testament and Judaism.'[5] It refers to what causes a fall in faith in an absolute sense. Following the Old Testament, the offense is with God.[6] They have rejected Jesus and will not receive Him as Messiah.

Jesus, in His response, appealed to a common concept and verbal idea.[7] Only in one's hometown – where people are familiar with the humanity of the prophet – does a prophet lack honor. Elsewhere no one measures the prophet according to his family's profession, family of origin, or origin

---

3. R. T. France, *The Gospel of Mark*, New International Greek Testament Commentary, (Grand Rapids: Eerdmans, 2002), 242.

4. The New Testament later identifies James as the brother of Jesus (Gal. 1:19), and 'Judas' (Jude) as the brother of James (Jude 1).

5. Gustav Stählin, 'Σκάνδαλον, Σκανδαλίζω,' ed. Gerhard Kittel, Geoffrey W. Bromiley, and Gerhard Friedrich, *Theological Dictionary of the New Testament* (Eerdmans, 1964–), 344; Henceforth, *TDNT*.

6. ibid.

7. Edwards, *Mark*, 174; France, *Mark*, 243.

of wisdom; others simply receive Him as a mouthpiece of God. The works and wisdom of Jesus should not be causes of rejection, but of reception.

The limitation on miracles in Nazareth was based on the offense of the people. Faith does not make Jesus do more miracles, for Mark presents Jesus as free to make His own schedule of healing (1:35-40; 3:9). Jesus limited Himself to healing a few in response to the offense of the people. Their lack of faith in Him after hearing His teaching and witnessing His works was stunning to Him.

Meeting the Real Jesus Exposes a Lack of Clarity and Conviction Over the Gospel (6:14-29)

King Herod heard of the fanfare surrounding Jesus and His works and the workings of His disciples. He concluded that Jesus' miracle working was the working of John the Baptist raised from the dead with miraculous powers. Herod's reasoning reduced Jesus to a prophetic forerunner rather than concluding that the Messianic Son of God had appeared.

Similarly, some in the general population reasoned that the miraculous workings pointed to Elijah. This reasoning seems to combine the Elijah return tradition with what Old Testament history revealed about the miracle-working ministry of Elijah.[8] Equating Jesus with Elijah again diminished His identity to that of a mere mortal.

Others reasoned that Jesus was a different prophet in the Old Testament tradition. Several prophets were associated with miracles.[9] Yet none of the prophets had the volume of miracles of Jesus. Moreover, the reader has the advantage of having heard the words of the Father at the baptism of Jesus and of seeing the cessation of raging winds and sea by Jesus – items expressly identifying Jesus as the divine Son.[10]

Rather than reasoning towards Jesus' deity, Herod's guilt led him to reason toward the prophet he had beheaded – John the Baptist. Rather than placing faith in the One who will rise from the dead in complete righteousness, Herod had certainty

---

8. See 1 Kings 17-19; 2 Kings 1-2; Malachi 4:5-6; Mark 9:11-13.

9. 1 Kings 20:36; 2 Kings 2:19-22, 24; 3:16-20; 4:1-37, 38-4.

10. See Mark 1:11; 4:39; cf. 1:1.

that John's righteousness had fostered His rising from the dead. Herod held his belief in the absence of any record of miracles performed by John the Baptist. The narrator gives a lengthy explanation for Herod's inability to reason rightly about the identity of Jesus.

Herodias, Herod's wife by adultery, became the impetus for Herod arresting John. John preached the law of righteousness to Herod, being unafraid of his position as king. John was not a respecter of persons when it came to preaching the truth; he was not looking to align himself with the State or wrap himself in Herod's or Caesar's flags.

The straightforwardness of John the Baptist provoked the ire of Herodias. Seemingly, she did not approve of being identified as one of whom the Law of God disapproved. To stop John's heralding of the truth, she wanted John silenced permanently. Yet Herod protected John and prevented Herodias' desire from coming to fruition.

Although Herod feared the prophet enough to keep him safe from his wife, he did not fear John (or the Lord) enough to put away the adulterous relationship. The marriage to Herodias had more power over Herod than the word of the law. John was a holy man whose message of the kingdom challenged Herod morally up to the point where he allowed his Adamic nature to override conviction of sin and unrighteousness.

Herod failed to keep John alive in prison due to his own sexually aroused rashness and pride. When Herod's small convictions about John's righteous and prophetic identity made a collision with his people-pleasing ways, it was John who became the casualty. Herod could not foresee the opportunity afforded to Herodias through his gift to her daughter. Even in feeling remorse over the oaths, Herod did not work to save John. The remorse would be so strong, it would cloud Herod's ability to identify Jesus correctly. Even when the disciples buried John, Herod was unable to see that he did not put to death the One coming as the Messiah of Israel.

Meeting the Real Jesus Tempers Our Temptation to Confuse Our Success with His Shepherding (6:30-44)
The opening line of verses 30-44 returns the reader to the disciples' commissioning in 6:7-13. They now reported to

Jesus their success in casting out demons, anointing the sick and healing. Jesus had given the disciples His authority over unclean spirits. They also were successful in the proclamation of the message of repentance, reporting to Jesus what they had taught the people. They were seeking His approval or affirmation of their work.

Jesus acknowledged the hard work of the disciples, inviting them to rest in a desolate place. The reader should hear an allusion to two earlier departures to a desolate place in Mark – once when Jesus rose early to find a quiet place to pray before a day of full ministry, and once again when the largeness of the crowd influenced a decision to pull away from populated areas (1:35, 45-46). The disciples now had not any time to eat, taking the reader back to the experience with the crowd in 3:20.

By boat, the disciples then traveled to an undisclosed location to find rest. The crowds, however, raced on foot ahead of the disciples to their next location. They came from every town on the route, maybe due to some seeing the crowd and learning of their intent to gain healings and exorcisms from Jesus' disciples. For the disciples to get their needed rest, therefore, they would need to send the crowds away.

However, Jesus saw more than people who could hinder rest; He saw shepherd-less people and began to teach them, indicating that part of their shepherding need was instruction from the Law of God. The idea of Israel as a shepherd-less people hearkened back to Numbers 27:15-18 where Moses petitioned the Lord to appoint a man over the congregation of Israel 'who shall go out before them and come in before them, who shall lead them out and bring them in, that the congregation of the LORD may not be as sheep that have no shepherd.' Micaiah the prophet later drew upon this reference to proclaim to Ahab, 'the king of Israel,' and to King Jehoshaphat of Judah, the fate of Israel's provoking a war with Syria.[11] He foretold the disastrous end of Ahab and the scattering of Israel in

---

11. In 1 Kings 22:1-40, Ahab is not identified by name but is referred to as 'the king of Israel' multiple times.

battle. One also hears a reference to Ezekiel's admonition to the leaders of Israel who had left Israel without any one over them who would care for their needs and guide them safely. In Ezekiel's prophecy the Lord promised to feed His shepherd-less sheep on the mountains of Israel and over all of the country (Ezek. 34:13-14).

The disciples understood that if the people were to eat in the desolated area, they would need to find food. The lateness of the hour was a concern both for the disciples to find time to rest and for the people to find hospitableness if they could not make it back to their homes.

The One full of compassion for shepherdless sheep would not allow the disciples to send away the crowds. Instead, He instructed those successful with casting out demons and healing the sick to provide for them. This would be an amazing feat by the disciples, for they estimated that the amount to purchase food for such a crowd would require six and a half months of income.[12] Jesus invited them, and invites us, to serve shepherdless people.

Jesus sending the disciples to investigate their food supplies further revealed their insufficiency to supply for the crowd's needs by their own power. They had five loaves and two fish among them. But the writer turns away from them to Jesus by His commanding the people to sit arranged in groups on the grass – groups making it easier to feed the multitudes and to count the people (as someone unknown did).[13] The story turns to the actions of Jesus, who will perform several actions that will separate His shepherding from the work of the disciples.

Jesus looked first to heaven, revealing His utter dependence on God the Father to act to feed the people. He added a blessing to God (6:41), a tradition which seems to have influenced the teaching of Paul.[14] In 6:41, one also hears Lukan language of the Lord's Supper in the feeding of the five thousand in the remainder of Jesus' actions: 'Taking the five loaves' (see Luke 22:19a), 'said a blessing'

---

12. A denarius was a day's worth of pay for a laborer.

13. Mark 6:44.

14. See Romans 14:6; 1 Corinthians 10:10-31; 1 Timothy 3:15; 4:5.

(see Luke 22:19b), 'broke the loaves' (see Luke 22:19c), 'gave it to the disciples' (see Luke 22:19c), and 'he divided the two fish among them all' (see Luke 22:17).

As Jesus acted, He fully satisfied the need of the sheep with an abundance of leftovers. Those who were without a shepherd now had One shepherding them. The estimated number of people there may be upwards of ten thousand, as Mark specifies that five thousand men were present.[15] At this point, the disciples were under no illusion that they could shepherd lost sheep to the same degree Jesus did. Jesus demonstrated the divine work of the Good and Great Shepherd.[16] He is the promised Shepherd who prepares tables for His own in the wilderness.

Meeting the Real Jesus Reveals Remaining Fearfulness and Hard-Heartedness toward Him Even as Others Come to Him (6:45-56)

In these final scenes, the disciples' understanding of Jesus' true identity happened as Jesus intentionally separated Himself from them. With sovereign authority, Jesus returned the disciples to the boat and sent them to Bethsaida. He intended for them to go to Bethsaida without Him, and it seems He communicated His intention to rejoin them there. During the time of their travels, Jesus released the crowd to their homes, which would have taken a good amount of time depending upon the size of the crowd and any unrecorded conversations Jesus had in the process of dismissal.

While the disciples were in the boat, Jesus retreated to a place of prayer. Both the disciples' journey in the boat and the isolation in prayer have precedent in Mark (1:35-39; 4:35-42), leaving the reader to speculate on the outcomes: will the disciples fare better on this voyage without Jesus than they did on the previous one? If they meet a storm or other problem at sea without Jesus in the boat, will they exercise more than 'no faith' and survive (4:40)? Will they encounter someone like the demoniac on the other side (5:1-2)? Will Jesus

---

15. Mark uses ἄνδρες (andres – a plural form of the word for 'male') instead of a form of *Anthropos* (man), the generic term that can mean both genders.

16. John 10:11, 14, 16; Hebrews 13:20; 1 Peter 5:4 (cf. Matthew 2:6; 26:31).

be empowered to preach and teach in other towns as He was after His last scene of private prayer (1:39)? Jesus going up on to the mountain to pray comes in the pattern of Moses going up the mountain to meet with the Lord.[17]

Jesus' choice to pray alone after the close of His ministry gives further insight into His uniqueness. Mark 1:35 portrayed Jesus praying alone before embarking upon His ministry routine, seeking power and wisdom for the tasks ahead. Mark 6:46 shows Him praying after a day of full ministry, possibly offering thanks for the strength and discernment provided by the Father through the Spirit throughout the day. However, as the story continues with an additional sea journey and more ministry, the narrative points toward a need for additional power and guidance. The episode in prayer reveals that Jesus sought the Lord's enabling and knowledge so that His identity would be revealed by the activities on the sea and in Gennesaret.

It was nearly dark at the time the disciples' boat was on the lake while Jesus remained ashore.[18] Unlike Jesus, who went to pray before serving further, the disciples attempted to cross the sea without the story referencing them praying. 'Painfully' describes the experience of the disciples pursuing their next task without crying out to the Lord. It appears that they still had no idea that Jesus had the power to help them cross without experiencing pains from the headwinds, even though He stopped the wind on their previous journey.[19]

---

17. Exodus 19:3; 24:15; 34:4; Deuteronomy 34:1.

18. Based on the feeding of the five thousand in the 'late afternoon' (ὥρας πολλῆς γενομένης, v. 35), R. T. France determines that 'when evening came' represents 'a time well into the night.... This is confirmed by the mention of the fourth watch (the last part of the night, before dawn, roughly 3–6 a.m.) in v. 48; indeed, the double mention of 'seeing' (ἰδών, v. 48; ἰδόντες, v. 49) suggests that pre-dawn light already allowed faint visibility. However strong the wind, a rowing boat is not likely to have taken ten hours or more to cross the northern part of the lake of Galilee, as would be required if ὀψίας γενομένης is understood only of the evening' (France, *Mark*, 271).

19. In Mark 4:37, the disciples encounter 'a great windstorm' (Greek λαῖλαψ μεγάλη ἀνέμου – *laílaps* [squall] *megálē* [great] *anemou* [wind]). Mark later says that Jesus 'awoke and rebuked the wind (*anemō*) ... and the wind (*anemos*) ceased' (4:39). Here Mark writes, 'the wind (*anemos*) was against them.' Easily Jesus could have ceased the wind as easily as He ceased the great windstorm, e.g., 'and the wind (*anemos*) ceased' (6:51). But the disciples do not yet see Him as the one completely controlling all winds and storms.

Between 3 a.m. and 6 a.m. – the 'fourth watch' in Roman counting – Jesus made His way to the disciples on the boat. The disciples would be tired, possibly fearful as in a previous experience on the sea recorded in 4:35-41, and certainly not expecting Jesus to approach them by walking on the water. The author indicates that Jesus intended to walk past them unnoticed. This would have left them in the storm facing painful headwinds on their own. Eventually, if they made it to the other side, they would find Jesus there ahead of them and would have had to inquire how He managed to get there before them. Even this would have revealed Jesus' divinity and showed to the disciples their need of Him for them to get across the lake faster and with less difficulty.[20]

The disciples, however, saw Him walking on the sea, but again mistook His identity. Instead of recognizing the One who calmed the storm on the sea, who rebuked a legion of unclean spirits from the Gerasene demoniac, who stopped the twelve-years' hemorrhaging of the woman, who raised a twelve-year-old girl from the dead, who gave them authority over unclean spirits, and who fed upwards of ten thousand people with only five small loaves of bread and two fish, they yielded to superstitious ideas. All of them screamed in fear, having no thought among them about the figure on the waters other than a non-corporeal being appearing.[21] They did not remember that the Lord alone has the power to walk on the waters and in its depths.[22]

At their point of fear, Jesus spoke to bring calm to the situation. Resolving the terror by the power of His words, He simply revealed that He is the One that they saw. His use of *ego eimi*, 'I am' to identify Himself echoes back to Exodus 3:14, connecting Jesus to the One who revealed Himself to the Patriarchs and to Moses, and who led the people of God out of Egypt and through the wilderness to the Promised Land. This presence should have been enough

---

20. Garland recognizes that even the intention to 'pass by' the disciples alludes to the work of the Lord in Exodus 33:22 and 1 Kings 19:11 (Garland, *Mark*, 263-64).

21. Matthew (Matt. 14:26) and John (John 6:19) each record the disciples' experience of fear during this episode on the sea, with Matthew also recording the disciples' conclusion that a ghost had appeared to them.

22. Job 38:16; Psalm 77:19; Isaiah 43:16.

to remove every fear of the disciples. Jesus demonstrated His 'I am' power with the ceasing of the wind the instant He stepped into the boat.

Mark indicates that the disciples responded with simple astonishment rather than with revelatory understanding. At this point, Jesus remained a peace-giving enigma: He had the ability to walk on water and cease winds. The disciples did not understand that the provision of bread for the crowds identified Jesus as the One who had provided manna for Israel in the wilderness – the One holding the power to create and perform miracles within His being. They did not grasp what James Edwards notes: 'Being *with* Jesus (3:14) is not simply a theoretical truth; it has practical and existential consequences, one of which is the safety and peace of disciples. If separation from Jesus brings the disciples into distress, Jesus' presence with them overcomes storms in their lives.'[23]

Their lack of understanding of the provision to the crowds revealed hearts hardened toward the truth of God, which, in this case, is the very identity of Jesus. Previously, Mark wrote that it was Jesus' opponents who suffered from hardness of heart. The 'disobedience, dullness, and obstinacy ... [that] is the predicament of Jesus' opponents' now characterizes the disciples.[24]

The disciples and Jesus land in Gennesaret rather than Bethsaida due to the winds they faced. The people recognized that the miracle worker was among them and immediately brought people to be cured. It seems that Mark paints the disciples and the crowds with the same strokes. Both saw the power of Jesus to perform great works but did not conclude that the works showed Him to have the power of deity. They might be awestruck by Jesus and see the practical importance of His ability to remove sickness by even a touch of His clothing. However, they were far from bowing to Christ as the creator and the sovereign Lord who had defeated Egypt. They were far from seeing their own need to repent before the One who supplies life to all flesh and placing faith in Him for salvation – salvation *from* a fate greater than meeting ghosts

---

23. Edwards, *Mark*, 200.
24. Garland, *Mark*, 265.

or perishing at sea, and salvation *to* a provision greater than receiving physical bread and healing from disease.

Reflective Questions

1. Why is it easy to make the mistake the disciples made about Jesus' identity when we are facing the great storms of life?

2. How would understanding the identity of Jesus portrayed by the second Gospel affect your sharing of your faith regularly, vocally, boldly, and courageously? What can you do differently than you have done previously the next time you are with someone within your sphere of influence who is in need of meeting with Christ?

8

He Came to Free People from Being Tied Up in Human Traditions
(Mark 7)

Mark and Isaiah

In Isaianic studies, Isaiah's Servant Songs are four: 42:1-4; 49:1-6; 50:4-7; 52:13–53:12. Mark cites Isaiah in his Gospel account in 1:2 (Isa. 40:3), 4:12 (Isa. 6:9), 7:6 (Isa. 29:13), 9:48 (Isa. 66:24); and 11:17 (Isa. 56:7); (and 15:28 [Isa. 53:12], depending upon one's reading of the textual evidence).[1]

In his Gospel, Mark seems to be developing both the Isaianic Servant theme and the New Exodus (or Second Exodus) theme.[2] In 1:2-3, Mark begins with the New Exodus with Jesus being the fulfillment of the Old Testament Messiah ('Christ'), who also is God's Son, and who is the Lord for

---

1. Each of the Gospels quotes Isaiah 6:9-10 (Matt. 13:14; Mark 4:12; Luke 8:10; John 12:39), Isaiah 40:3 (Matt 3:3; Mark 1:2; Luke 3:4; John 1:23), and Isaiah 53 (53:4 in Matthew 8:17; 53:12 in Mark 15:28 and Luke 23:37; and 53:1 in John 12:38).

2. Neil Cushman identifies four features of a New Exodus in Isaiah. First, this new exodus event includes a wilderness that separates the people of Israel from the Promised Land; therefore, it needs to be prepared in some way for Yahweh's intervention (40:3-5). Second, following this preparation, God comes and leads His people like a flock (40:9-11). Although some may grow weary along the way, Yahweh strengthens them, assuring them of safe arrival (40:30-31). Third, 'blindness' hinders the exiles from the full realization of these promises, but Yahweh leads them anyway, making the pathway smooth (42:16). Fourth, even though the people of Israel go through fire and water, Yahweh delivers them (43:2, 16). He provides both food and water along the way (48:20, 21; 49:8-12), and He goes before and behind them as in the days of old (52:11-12). Surely His people would go out of Babylon with joy (55:12-13).

whom the messenger (John the Baptist) was preparing a way for the Lord to come and tend His flock like a shepherd (Isa. 40:11). Zion, the (place of the) herald of the 'good news,' is the object of the Lord's coming (Isa. 40:9; cf. Mark 1:1). Mark 4:12 seems to allude to the promise that those 'whose hearts are far from [the Lord]' one day will 'sanctify the Holy One of Jacob' (29:13, 23). Mark 11:17 sees the Lord rescuing His people from exile and bringing them to His house of prayer in Jerusalem, on His holy mountain (Isa. 56:7). Isaiah also will peek through in Mark 7.

In Mark 7:1-23, Jesus took control of a conversation that sought to condemn Him for having disciples who did not wash their hands ritualistically (7:1-3). At issue was the 'traditions' practiced by the Jews ('tradition(s)' are mentioned five times, in verses 3, 4, 5, 8, and 9). Those traditions started out with good intentions from Scripture, then expanded and became layers of rituals to fence the tradition. As the Jewish *Mishnah* says, 'Tradition is a fence for the Torah.'[3] The washing of hands was one such tradition that had taken on a life of its own.

David Garland recognizes that such rituals had three purposes behind their development 'that have affinities with the development of traditions in Christian circles':

1. The tradition of the elders tried to make the basic requirement that Israel be holy to the Lord (Lev. 19:2) something that was attainable in everyday life .... These pious interpreters had a genuine desire to provide precise guidance for laypeople on what one must do to be holy. They did not think they were voiding the commands of God but making them applicable. The tradition was designed to give laypeople a map that charted what was permissible or prescribed, clean or unclean, so that they could live a life of godliness.

2. The tradition of the elders was intended to deter pagan influences that surrounded the nation from making inroads into Judaism (see Lev. 20:1-7) .... Actions such as immersion and washing of hands were tangible,

---

3. *The Mishnah* (London, Oxford, 1974), 452.

positive gestures that displayed who God's elect were who would be vindicated at the end of the age .... The laws created the illusion of an ordered cosmos, with carefully erected boundaries that kept every person and thing in its proper place ....

3. The tradition assumes that God ordered the details, and one must study and erect them to meet God .... The Pharisees affirmed that God created order and that human affairs prosper only when things are ordered. Consequently, they preferred strict rules, orderly programs, and careful debates about the application of texts, lest they lose control. From their perspective Jesus was completely out of control because He disregarded their rules and crossed their boundaries.[4]

The elders were *tied up in tradition.* Jesus took on the tradition of the elders and revealed them as phony religion. He showed three things:

Being Tied Up in Traditions Makes Worthless Worship (7:6-8)

When the Pharisees asked, in effect, 'Why do your disciples not do what everyone else has been doing forever and a day without question?' Jesus appealed to Isaiah 29:13, showing that substituting traditions for real worship of God is a problem of the ages:

And the Lord said:

'Because this people draw near with their mouth
    and honor me with their lips,
    while their hearts are far from me,
and their fear of me is a commandment taught by men,
therefore, behold, I will again
    do wonderful things with this people,
    with wonder upon wonder;
and the wisdom of their wise men shall perish,
    and the discernment of their discerning men shall be
        hidden.'

---

4. Garland, *Mark*, 279-80.

The problem Jesus recognized is that the traditions (i.e., washing hands, etc....) allowed people to praise God vocally without having a heart for Him; the rituals took the place of a genuine faith in God. Also, they raised man-made teachings to the level of 'doctrines [of God].' The commandment they had left was that washing was for the priests (Exod. 30:19; 40:12), not for the people. Peter Bolt notes that they were 'tenaciously and ruthlessly' holding the traditions, for the term for 'hold' indicates 'violent seizure.'[5]

The Pharisees' practices may have been an innocent yet committed following of the practices of the elders they considered to be sacred. They had investigated the history of their faith practices and found bodily washing and the cleaning of cups, pots, vessels, couches and more to be orthodoxy.

What Jesus condemned was not the practice of apostolic traditions, such as baptism and the Lord's Supper, or the use of doctrinal traditions intended to affirm, portray, and review the truth of the Gospel (i.e., the use of the Christian calendar, lectionaries, The Book of Common Prayer, The Apostles Creed, a church covenant, or confessions). He condemned empty rituals and human philosophies that had been elevated to the status of righteous decrees.

Being Tied Up in Traditions Voids the Voice of God (7:9-13)

'Moses' refers to the Law written by Moses. The fifth commandment of the Law commanded honor of one's parents, and in extended form it commanded death for those who cursed a parent.[6] However, the Pharisees had established 'Corban' ('dedicated to God') as a vow to set aside money for the Lord. One did not have to distribute the money; he only had to establish it as Corban. In doing so, if a parent needed financial help, an adult child could say the higher honor would be to hold his money for the Lord, for it was 'Corban.' Jesus revealed that the Pharisees thus allowed the people to refrain from honoring one's parents, which was to nullify the Word of God. They substituted their word – *corban* – for

---

5. Peter G. Bolt, ft. nt. 31, *The Cross from a Distance: Atonement in Mark's Gospel*. NSBT (InterVarsity, 2004), 61.

6. Exodus 20:12; 21:17; Leviticus 20:9; Deuteronomy 27:16; Proverbs 30:17.

God's Word. The practice associated with the Word seemed holy, for it was a vow to God. But the vow was empty since it violated the commandments.

Jesus and Mark indicated similar thoughts about the multiplicity of the human traditions that had been elevated above the Word of God. Mark noted, 'And there are many other traditions they observe' (Mark 7:4). Here, Jesus said, 'And many such things you do.' The Jewish people were filled with all sorts of practices on top of the Law that they considered sanctifying before the Lord. Yet, these many things were voiding what the Lord had spoken in His Law.

Being Tied Up in Traditions Covers Mistaken Morality (7:14-23)

In two changes of scenery (vv. 14, 17), Jesus indicated the true means of defilement. What comes from outside and goes into a person cannot defile (or make one unclean or immoral), for it enters the stomach, not the heart. Instead, what comes out of the heart is what defiles (vv. 21-23). Note that these are things that exterior washing could not possibly cleanse!

It is important to note that Jesus *declared* all food clean, thus showing that the law against certain foods had been fulfilled in Him. Paul picked up on this concept.[7]

Being Tied Up in Tradition Limits Outreach toward Others (7:24-30)

It was not odd for Jesus to try and escape the public eye in Mark, even if only for a short while, as in 1:35, 3:13, 4:10, and 6:31-32. But the withdrawal from public here took on greater significance because Tyre and Sidon was a Gentile region 'with a long history of antagonism to Israel.'[8] Seemingly, Jesus did not want His ministry associated with a Gentile-dominant region before He reached many in Israel, lest the Jewish leadership had fodder to cast dispersion upon His ministry, motives, and love for Israel.

Jesus' fame had already spread to the region of Tyre (3:8). Therefore, news of Jesus' presence in Tyre was an opportunity

---

7. Romans 14:14; 1 Corinthians 10:27; 1 Timothy 4:4-5.

8. Edwards, *Mark*, 217.

for those in need of healing or exorcism to find hope. In a manner untold by Mark, word reached a woman whose small daughter was plagued by a demon. Jesus' encounter with the demonic in Mark permits the reader to anticipate that Jesus will cast out the unclean spirit.[9]

Similar to Jairus' encounter with Jesus, the woman fell down at His feet in humility (Mark 5:22). Again, for the reader, this provides additional anticipation of healing for this little girl even as Jesus raised from the dead the little girl of the last person who approached Him in this manner.

However, one might remember that Tyre was the home of a famous Old Testament female figure: Jezabel, 'who in Elijah's day had nearly subverted the Northern Kingdom with her pagan prophets and practices.'[10] But it is the widow of Zarephath in Sidon whose story shares similarities with this woman whose daughter was ill – both were in great need, desiring healing for a child, and living in Syrophoenicia.[11]

Mark reveals that the woman approached Jesus with two more identifiers that would make anyone in Israel hesitant to serve her and, for the reader, place the hope of exorcism in jeopardy. First, she was a Gentile who would be considered unrighteous. Second, there was the added regional identifier 'Syrophoenician,' which Garland says indicates 'she is a Gentile pagan, which introduces a new wrinkle in the story. She hails from a city that the Old Testament deemed to be a wealthy and godless oppressor of Israel.'[12] Edwards suggests, 'Tyre probably represented the most extreme expression of paganism, both actually and symbolically, that a Jew could expect to encounter.'[13]

In response to the woman's repeated asking for Jesus to cast out the demon, He gave an undiplomatic parabolic saying – one that would be politically incorrect by contemporary

---

9. Previous exorcisms in Mark occur at 1:26; 3:11; 5:8, 13; In addition, Jesus gave the disciples authority over unclean spirits in 6:7.

10. Edwards, *Mark*, 217. See also 1 Kings 16:31-32.

11. Edwards, *Mark*, 217.

12. Garland, *Mark*, 288. Garland references Isaiah 23; Jeremiah 47:4; Ezekiel 26–28; Joel 3:4; Amos 1:9; and Zechariah 9:2 for his conclusions about Tyre in the Old Testament.

13. Edwards, *Mark*, 217.

standards. He commented that it is right to take food intended for children and give it to children rather than take their food and give it to dogs before the children have eaten. As a responsible spiritual parent, Jesus must ensure the nourishment and well-being of His children. To give to dogs while children needed food would be neglectful.

Jesus' use of 'first' placed a priority on serving the children, who represented the people of Israel. Jesus was not speaking of exclusivity in His service, but of primacy. As the Syrophoenician woman was asking for the removal of an unclean spirit, the 'food' of which Jesus spoke was ministry to the children of Israel. Serving Israel with priority had been Jesus' pattern thus far, as was evident in His ministry in synagogues and Jewish regions.[14]

However, in a previous parabolic saying, Mark's portrayal of Jesus left room for those who were 'sick' to receive healing from Him (Mark 2:17). Therefore, His ministry was not exclusive to Israel. Moreover, in His dialogue with the disciples, Jesus indicated that outward concerns, such as being Gentile and Syrophoenician, were not things that defiled people and made them unclean, for they were not 'evil things' or 'evil thoughts' coming from the character of the person.[15] So He could meet the need of the child requested by the Syrophoenician woman, who would have been considered as vile as a dog by Jews. Even as Jesus had no need to follow Jewish washing traditions over keeping the Law, He had no need to follow a Jewish tradition that would have refrained from helping this Gentile woman, when serving a spiritually sick Gentile was in line with the promise to Abraham that people of all nations would be blessed through him (Gen. 12:1-3).

The desperate woman accepted the priority of Jesus' ministry to the Jewish people. Yet, having both a need to rescue her daughter and knowing of the reputation of Jesus to cast out demons, she boldly proposed in reply that it was possible for a faithful parent to simultaneously nourish children properly and feed the dogs that are within the

14. Mark 1:39; 3:1, 7.
15. Mark 7:15, 20-23.

vicinity of the table and seeking crumbs of the children's food. As Calvin appropriately and eloquently commented:

> The woman's reply showed that she was not hurried along by a blind or thoughtless impulse to offer a flat contradiction to what Christ had said. As God preferred the Jews to other nations, she does not dispute with them the honor of adoption, and declares that she has no objection whatever that Christ should *satisfy* them according to the order which God had prescribed. She only asks that some *crumbs* – falling, as it were, accidentally – should come within the reach of *the dogs*. And at no time, certainly, did God shut up His grace among the Jews in such a manner as not to bestow a small taste of them on the Gentiles. No terms could have been employed that would have described more appropriately, or more justly, that dispensation of the grace of God which was at that time in full operation.[16]

It should not be lost on the reader (1) the kindness that Jesus showed to a woman and to a little girl, (2) the reception that Jesus gave to the woman when she challenged His initial reply to her request, and (3) His affirmation of the rightness of the woman's plea. One cannot question Jesus' care for women during His earthly ministry.

Jesus granted the woman what she asked and sent her back to her daughter. Significantly, Mark states that the Syrophoenician woman found her daughter free of the unclean spirit. Jesus removed uncleanliness from this Gentile even as He had from many Jews.

Being Tied Up in Tradition could mean Missing the Transformation of the Troubled (7:31-37)

Jesus returned to the Decapolis region, near to the place of the ministry of the healed Gerasene demoniac (cf. Mark 5:20). Therefore, His fame in the ten cities preceded His presence there. The crowds were aware of Jesus' power to subdue a man who had had an unclean spirit and could not be bound by chains. Now they presented Jesus with the seemingly overwhelming case of a man with both a speech impediment

---

16. John Calvin, *Harmony of the Evangelists*, 268.

and deafness.[17] Having either infirmity would have been challenging; to have both upped the stakes on Jesus' power to overcome human dilemmas and pains. Therefore, the townspeople pleaded with Jesus to lay hands on the man in order to exert His powers of healing.

As when avoiding the tradition of the washings and the standard mistreatment of the Gentiles, Jesus did not conform to a traditional practice of laying hands and healing in front of the crowds. Instead, He took the man apart from the crowd to where they could have no influence, and maybe not even observe the healing. Jesus was not bound by a human standard to heal in front of all.

Moreover, the actions of this healing were unique. Jesus placed His fingers into the ears of the deaf man, portraying the healing to come with a very intimate physical touch. Jesus could have healed by speaking or by the laying on of hands. But here He did not do what was predictable or common.

When Jesus spat, He symbolized the removal of unwanted and undesirable elements from the mouth. One spits out what one wants removed from the mouth. The man's impediment was undesirable, as evidenced by the begging of the friends for healing. It was unwanted, or the man would have stopped his friends from making the appeal. With another very intimate, unique action, Jesus touched the man's tongue. Touching both the ears and tongue indicated to the man an intention toward his hearing and speaking, but the actions were not necessary for his healing. Certainly, the touching would be remembered (e.g., 'How did He heal you?' 'First, He put His fingers in my ears and, after spitting, He touched my tongue with the very same hands').

Jesus then provided three further actions, of which two are unique to this healing. First, He looked up to heaven before performing the miracle. He did the same before providing the miracle of feeding the five thousand.[18] He looked to God the Father – the source of the answered prayer for healing.

17. Although Mark uses the word for 'mute' in 7:37 (ἀλάλους), in 7:32 he uses a word indicating a speech impediment (μογιλάλον). The use of the word is an echo to Isaiah 35:6: τρανὴ δὲ ἔσται γλῶσσα μογιλάλων, 'and the stammerer's tongue will be clear' (LES).

18. See Mark 6:41; also Matthew 14:19; Luke 9:16; John 11:41; 17:1.

Second, He sighed or groaned. Apparently, Jesus was upset over the limits to healing provided by traditional approaches to curing this man (e.g., the people's pleas to lay hands on the man as if this was all Jesus could do).[19] Third, He said, 'Ephphatha,' a word meaning 'be opened.' The translation of this Aramaic word tells the reader that some original recipients of Mark's account could not speak Hebrew or understand Aramaic. More significantly, it was only in the speaking that the man's mouth and ears were opened. It was still the spoken word in combination with the Father's power from heaven that provided healing.

As a result of Jesus' working, three things followed. First, the man gained hearing and speaking. The releasing of the tongue and the correct speaking of the man suggest he had an impediment that prevented clear speaking rather than the complete inability to speak.[20] Figuratively, by providing a healing in an uncommon manner, Jesus broke the chain upon the man's tongue.[21] Also, figuratively, having ears to hear is important to being a follower of Jesus in Mark's Gospel.[22]

Second, the crowd zealously proclaimed the report of the miracle despite Jesus' repeated charges not to tell anyone. Jesus' attempt to silence the report is in keeping with the Messianic Secret theme in Mark. Jesus did not want fame to spread about Him healing in a Gentile land because it could

---

19. Mark does not mention Jesus' disgust with sin's presence in the world, the sin of the deaf and mute man, or the sin of the crowd. Neither does he mention Jesus' personal sorrow over the man's plight. However, the pattern in Mark 7 is that Jesus disagreed with human traditions as paths to pleasing God. Here, Jesus expressed His displeasure with people hoping for Him to lay on hands as the means of healing through a sigh.

20. The ESV, NASB, NET, NIV, NKJV, NLT, and NRSV each say the man spoke 'plainly.' But Luke uses the word ὀρθῶς, a word meaning 'correctly' (Horst Robert Balz and Gerhard Schneider, *Exegetical Dictionary of the New Testament* [Eerdmans, 1990–] 531). See its uses in Luke 7:43, 10:28, and 20:21. 'Clearly' in the CSB is a better translation. The man spoke incorrectly or unclearly prior to the healing.

21. Edwards comments, 'The original Greek is more vivid and concrete, saying that "the chain of his tongue was broken." In the New Testament, the word for "chain" (Gk. *desmos*; NIV, "loosened") most frequently means a chain or fetter that binds a prisoner (Luke 8:29; Acts 16:26; 20:23; 26:29; Phil. 1:7; Col 4:18). The breaking of the fetter by Jesus is a figure of liberation (Luke 13:16)' (Edwards, *Mark*, 226).

22. See Mark 4:3, 9, 12, 15, 18, 20, 23, 24, 33; 7:14; 8:18; and 9:7.

hinder His ministry to Israel. Yet, in the decree of God, the spreading of Jesus' fame in Gentile regions was in keeping with God's intention to bless peoples of all nations and for the entire earth to be blessed under the dominion of an obedient Adam. Refusing to limit Himself to healing through laying on hands and pulling the man aside for healing yielded new, eager witnesses to the power of Christ who proclaimed this good news to all.

Third, the witnesses to the miracle were astounded to an extreme degree. The unconventional ways of Jesus met a deep human need and overcame an incredible set of impairments with such amazement that people concluded, 'He has done all things well.' This is another way that Mark reveals the divinity of Christ in the mouths of the figures in the story. Flawlessly, Jesus provided as only God could provide.

Excursus
Guarding against elevating traditions above the Word of God takes much discernment and humility. Each of us has preferences and levels of comfort with which we do not want others to tamper. We also have well-meaning, embedded ideas about what practices best represent the truths we hold from Scripture, even where such practices are not prescribed in Scripture.

Moreover, in many congregations, the examination of traditional practices divides into two camps: conservatives and progressives. Many factors contribute to whether conservatives will make the case for retaining the practice as following Scripture and a historical doctrinal development or whether progressives will see a practice modified or eliminated as a human tradition. It is with concern for the care and growth of you and your local assembly that I offer the following practical suggestions for examining traditional practices in a local congregation.

If you are hesitant to change a traditional practice, consider a loving approach to change. First, *be open*. Say to your fellow congregants, 'I could consider that.' To say otherwise is to suggest that you already have full knowledge concerning the sacredness of a practice. Listen to those suggesting a change and consider what they have observed in other orthodox assemblies. Be willing to read more about practices outside of your tradition.

Second, *be flexible*. This involves taking a position that says, 'I am willing to try that.' Inflexibility can reveal a lack of humility and consideration of others. Without flexibility, congregations can become rigid in their practices and miss opportunities for the gospel afforded by making key changes to methodology, whether small or great. Removing an icon or flag, incorporating a new piece of modern equipment or technology, changing a longstanding line-item in the church budget, or reconfiguring a church organizational structure or staffing could result in reaching more people with the gospel message and provide wider means for personal discipleship within a local body.

Third, *be gracious*. Ask, 'Does the Bible allow for this change?' Sometimes issues are not a matter of biblical descriptions or historical practices. Instead, some practices simply are a matter of preferences. Asking about the latitude in practice afforded by Scripture is important. Tensions over the forms of the administering of the ordinances can be eased with graciousness toward those wanting a different practice. For example, whether a woman can serve the Lord's Supper or whether the Lord's Supper should be administered weekly are portrayed as matters of Scripture. Yet they are matters of theology, for Scripture does not appoint men, pastors, or elders to serve the Lord's Supper. Neither is there an exhortation on the frequency of holding the Lord's Supper; one must consider historical church practices. *Does the Bible allow for differences in the form of the distribution of the elements?* Gracious answers to this question could help a local body of believers to grow in love toward one another and deepen in their meeting with the presence of Christ during the celebration of the ordinance. Beware of putting your traditions above God and His grace.

Fourth, *be discerning*. In conjunction with your pastor and elders, say, 'Let us examine that.' Commencing into a study of the Scriptures, historical practices, your church's confessional practices, and the practices of gospel-minded congregations near you is a healthy practice. Otherwise you might assume a practice pleases the Lord when it does not.

If you think of yourself as a progressive and are eager for changes in traditions, please also consider a loving approach to changing traditions. First, *be patient*. Give people time to swallow the idea of change. Do not propose your rate of change and openness to be the gospel. Patience is more than a secular virtue. Patience flows from a person who loves others in his/her assembly with the love of Christ.[23] Being zealous over an issue does not make one right.

Second, *be prayerful*. Trust God to make changes when He is ready. Believers before you have been growing in their faith and love for Jesus with this practice in place; so all is not lost if you have to wait months or years for a change. By praying rather than only pushing for change, you are recognizing the warfare that could lead a congregation to division. You want God to put it into the minds and hearts of fellow believers to consider a change. Otherwise, you could simply replace one human tradition with another.

Third, *be pure*. Do not lose your holiness and love while debating with a member of Christ who cannot move off the traditions that you and others think should change. No discussion over a tradition is worth breaking fellowship or dividing the body's mental and emotional unity. The means by which one seeks a change must honor the Lord. Often, forcing a change to happen quickly does not reflect the long-suffering of Christ.

Reflective Questions

1. What non-apostolic traditions characterize your practices in your local congregation's body-life and worship services? What are some possibilities of great things that could happen within the congregation if those who cherish these traditions the most were willing to sacrifice them and yet remain faithful, loving members of the congregation?

2. How might holding to some non-apostolic tradition work to help younger generations of believers

---

23. See 1 Corinthians 13:4.

reconstruct their faith rather than deconstruct their faith? What conversation might you need to have with a younger sister or brother in Christ about a gracious way to view your congregation's non-apostolic traditions?

9

Jesus Came So That We Might
See His Divine Identity
(Mark 8:1–9:1)

It has become commonplace for young couples expecting
a baby to host reveal events to share the identity of their
coming child. Equipped with balls, balloons, piñatas, or
other easy-to-burst containers, the highlight of such events
is the explosion of blue or pink dust or confetti-like materials
into the air to point to the soon birth of a son or a daughter.
Whether done in person or posted as a video online, the sight
of the colorful particles brings cheers from all seeing the news
for the first time.

High school seniors also have become participants in
college-reveal parties, following the long practice of star
athletes to have a special new conference or event to reveal
their undergraduate athletic program of choice over other
contenders. The college student's immediate family will invite
extended family and friends to the home for an affair at which
participants place non-monetary bets on a few viable college
choices for the students. The student's family will disappear
at an appointed time to change into paraphernalia from the
school of choice and they return to receive celebration from
all gathered at the revelation of the college or university.

In Mark 8:1–9:1, Jesus has His own reveal events so that all may
see who He is. While there is no piñata or college flag present, it
is evident that the passage gradually reveals Jesus' true identity

as God the Son – the divine Messiah – as He has been doing in much of Mark's Gospel account.[1] Through five episodes, Jesus will uncover more about His identity for those engaging with Him so that they discover for themselves the truth about Him. The episodes will culminate with the anticipation of seeing Him in glory as the one who delays the tasting of death.

In most modern English translations of Mark's Gospel, the last episode in Mark 8 crosses the boundary to the verse numbered 9:1. That is, even as 3:1-6 is part of a larger idea begun in Mark 2, and 4:35-41 is part of an idea that continues through all of Mark 5, Jesus' statement in 9:1 concludes the major idea of Mark 8. Mark 9:2 begins with an event six days later. The narrator's comments there serve to separate 9:1 from 9:2. In this section, Mark will indicate five things about seeing the divinity of Christ.

Seeing the Divinity of Christ When You're Hungry Requires Disciples to Feed People (8:1-10)

Within proximity of the time of His ministry in Tyre, Sidon, and the Decapolis (7:24-37), Jesus again found an enormous crowd following Him for three days. Stirred by the absence of food to feed them, Jesus invited His disciples to consider how He might serve the hungry crowd that had followed Him. Similar to the events leading to the feeding of the five thousand men, Jesus' action came from a disposition of compassion toward the people.[2] His compassion recognized the physical need of the crowds and the hardship that impacted those coming from a great distance. Both the length of time of their hunger and the distance that some would travel before eating again at home mattered to Jesus.

Once again stymied by the absence of provision in the wilderness,[3] the disciples asked about locating earthly resources sufficient to feed the sizable crowd before them.[4] Yet Jesus asked the disciples the exact question that He had asked them before

---

1. Although this was the focus of Mark 6, it is also the focus of 8:1–9:1, for the disciples did not grasp it in Mark 6. See Chapter 7 in this volume.

2. Mark 8:2. See also Mark 6:34.

3. Mark 8:4. See Mark 6:35.

4. It is a question of the location of the resources, for the disciples ask 'Where?' (Grk. πόθεν), as reflected in the NASB and NET.

He fed the five thousand.[5] One might wonder if any of the disciples had even a momentary recollection of the similarity of the words. But it is certain that Mark intended for his readers to hear the echo of 6:38 and anticipate another miraculous feeding. The greater number of loaves of bread in comparison to the earlier miracle should increase their expectation for Jesus to accomplish the task of feeding with ease.[6]

In a manner like the distribution of food to the five thousand, Jesus had the crowd sit down, gave thanks for the food, broke the bread, and gave it to the disciples to distribute. Similarly, He blessed the fish and had the disciples distribute them to the people. Jesus was both compassionate and God-honoring in His provision for them. He looked to God with thanksgiving for the provision and for Him to bless the food He would serve to the crowd.

The result of the power from God the Father was four-fold. First, the people ate with satisfaction. There was enough for the crowd of about four thousand persons. No one fought for scraps or finished not having enough, for Jesus' provision always was sufficient.[7]

Second, there was an abundance of supply. Akin to the collection of the twelve baskets of fragments in the earlier feeding miracle, the gathering of the leftover fragments showed that the provision of God far-outstripped the need of the people. Jesus gave the same oversupply ministry to this Gentile region that He gave to the largely Jewish region earlier.

Third, Jesus sent the crowd away compassionately, as was His intention before the miracle. They could make their journeys to distant places without concern of fainting on the way due to hunger. Each would remember and report that Jesus satisfied them abundantly before sending them away – that He was a person of compassion, not simply a person of action.

---

5. The wording in the Greek, Πόσους ἔχετε ἄρτους, is the same in 6:38 and 8:35.

6. I am not suggesting that Jesus needed the additional resources; instantly He could make from stones or drop from the sky the bread necessary to feed the crowd (e.g., Luke 4:3; John 6:32).

7. Edwards comments, 'The use of "satisfied" (Gk. *chortazein*) repeats the same word used in the disciples' question of v. 4, "Where in this remote place can anyone get enough bread to feed (Gk. *chortazein*) them …?" In the miracle of the multiplication of the loaves, the answer to the question is supplied: only Jesus can satisfy the people!' (Edwards, *Mark*, 231-32).

Fourth, the disciples and Jesus had the freedom to serve in Dalmanutha. 'Dalmanutha' is a place unknown, mentioned only here in the New Testament and all ancient literature. Matthew, instead, has 'Magadan,' which accounts for the variant reading in Mark. Jesus and the disciples had landed to the northwest of the sea. Their ministry continued in the region of Magdala.

Of further significance in this passage is Jesus' miracle-working, salvific presence within a Gentile-dominant region. On this, Edwards notes,

> From the church fathers onward the church has rightly perceived that in the feeding of the four thousand Jesus brings saving bread to the Gentiles, as He brought it earlier to the Jews in the feeding of the five thousand. The journey to the Gentiles in 7:24–8:9 has evinced that they are neither beyond the reach of salvation nor inured to it. Like the book of Jonah, the three vignettes in Mark 7:24–8:9 reveal that supposed Gentile outsiders are in fact surprisingly receptive to the word of God in Jesus. The journey of Jesus to Tyre, Sidon, and the Decapolis proves that although the Gentiles are ostracized by the Jews, they are not ostracized by God. Jewish invective against the Gentiles does not reflect a divine invective. There is a lesson here for the people of God in every age, that its enemies are neither forsaken by God nor beyond the compassion of Jesus. On the contrary, the Gentiles, like others 'a long distance' away, are the objects of Jesus' compassion.[8]

With similar comments, Garland proposes,

> The context, therefore, suggests that Jesus is now offering a predominantly Gentile crowd the same opportunity to be fed by His teaching and by His miraculous power that He offered to the Jewish crowd. We may think that it is only fair that Gentiles get a share in Christ's benefits, but from Mark's Jewish perspective the inclusion of Gentiles is a token of the end-time reign of God. The miracle signifies that Jesus is not simply 'a redeemer, a messiah like Moses and David'; He is *the* Redeemer, offering redemption to more than just the people of Israel.[9]

---

8. Edwards, *Mark*, 232.
9. Garland, *Mark*, 307.

Jesus fed those following in this largely Gentile region so that they might see His ability to provide salvation. The compassionate act of providing food for the starving pointed to the greater hope of providing salvation for the lost.

Seeing the Divinity of Christ When You're Seeking a Sign Requires Disciples to Preach the Gospel with Grief and Discernment (8:11-14)

This is Mark's third recorded encounter between Jesus and the Pharisees.[10] They already saw Him heal a man with a withered hand. It is likely they returned to confront Him because His fame continued to spread, even into the Gentile regions. It might be that Jesus' serving in the Gentile regions with the same service He gave to the Jews led the Pharisees to this third encounter.

The Jewish religious leaders wanted a sign of proof to verify Jesus' Messianic identity. Although Jesus had not met with, 'If you are the Christ, tell us [plainly],' He had made claims to be able to forgive sins and that He is Lord of the Sabbath. If something came from heaven, fell from heaven, or spoke from heaven, the Pharisees implied that they would believe His claim. Yet they did not believe after the healing of the withered hand, and the reports coming to them about Jesus had not led them to believe. This seeking of a sign intended to draw Jesus into performing a miracle at their demand. They wished for verification of His divinity, not proof of His agreement with the teaching of the Law as in Mark 10:2.

Emotionally, the request disturbed Jesus deeply. Within Himself He made a deep sigh or groan. It came with more intensity than the groaning in 7:34, perhaps reflecting an even greater displeasure with this doubting from the leaders of Israel. The sighing was inner – of the heart, not an external expression; it was over the seeking of a sign from heaven as when He fed four thousand people as if someone had dropped manna from heaven.

What more do these Pharisees want? Fire from heaven? Hailstones? Brimstones? No rain? More rain? God the Father earlier ripped open 'heaven' and expressed His great delight

---

10. See Mark 2:24, 3:6, and 7:5.

with Jesus![11] The readers know that the Pharisees were asking for what had been provided in spades in the narrative. Yet in the next chapter some of the disciples would see another sign from heaven in the Transfiguration.

Jesus refused to offer a sign to the skeptics. That was not His role; that is not the task of believers. The preaching of the gospel is sufficient to produce belief.[12] Yet, like Jesus, the trenchant unbelief of those who have encountered Christ's claims should bring us to grief. The question, 'Why does this generation seek a sign?' indicated that sign-seeking was an affront to Christ. Even those who ask seemingly simple questions of skepticism like, 'If there really is a God, why is there so much suffering in the world?' are acting with the same scoffing of the first-century Israelites.[13]

As is common in Mark's Gospel, the author gives a shorter encounter than that recorded in the parallel accounts. Matthew's account provides a rebuke that discusses the Pharisees' ability to interpret other signs, 'evil and adulterous' as modifiers of 'generation,' and an exception clause related to provision of the sign of Jonah. Mark does not offer these items for they did not fit the purposes of his presentation of the Servant revealing His divine nature. Instead, the generation would not receive a sign. With discernment and a solemn statement of judgment,[14] Jesus left the obstinate leaders to continue ministry on the other side of the lake where greater ministry opportunity awaits. He left the foolishness of the Pharisees.

Seeing the Divinity of Christ as a Disciple Requires One to Beware of the Influence of Skeptics (8:14-21)

The presence of only one loaf of bread among the disciples created a scenario in which a different sort of forgetfulness

---

11. See Mark 1:11-12.

12. Both Jesus (Luke 16:31) and Paul (Rom. 1:16; 1 Cor. 1:24) indicate the power of the Word proclaimed to produce belief.

13. As France notes, the use twice over of the phrase ἡ γενεὰ αὕτη suggests that the unbelief that demands an authenticating sign is not confined to the Pharisees alone (France, *Mark*, 312).

14. The Semitism, 'Truly, I say to you,' gives the clause the force of, 'If a sign shall be given to this generation, may I die!' (Edwards, *Mark*, 236), or 'May God do so-and-so to me, if …' (France, *Mark*, 313).

came to the fore. Jesus warned the disciples against the 'leaven' of the Pharisees and Herodians with the two commands, 'pay attention, beware.'[15] The warning was against pharisaical leavening, which could happen through repeated encounters with the Pharisees akin to that in the previous scene. The warning also provided an alert to the ability of Herod to spread his influence among the disciples.

The episode recounting Herod's beheading of John the Baptist does not bring Herod into direct confrontation with Jesus and the disciples (Mark 6:14-29). However, Mark portrays the Herodian party as antagonists in collusion with the Pharisees.[16]

The disciples were removed from the feeding of the four thousand by only one discussion with the Pharisees. Thus, the warning made sense: the Pharisees' demand for a sign seemingly contributed to the disciples' inability to appropriate the miraculous feeding of four thousand people to their one-loaf reality. Even Jesus' modifying of 'leaven' with 'of the Pharisees' and 'of Herod' was not enough for the disciples to see that physical bread was not Jesus' concern; the most recent miracle should have been on their minds.

Jesus' line of questioning is filled with many echoes to unbelief in Israel's history. Lack of perception looks back to the prophecy of Isaiah and the writing of the Psalmist.[17] The question of understanding hearkens back to the use of a similar construction in Mark 7:18. The hardening of the heart has a long and dark story in redemptive history. Already in Mark the writer associates a hardened heart with the Pharisees and the disciples.[18] But in an earlier century, it was the hardened hearts of Israel that led to the failure at Kadesh Barnea and the forty years of wandering.[19]

---

15. In the clause, καὶ διεστέλλετο αὐτοῖς λέγων ὁρᾶτε, βλέπετε, the Greek verb διεστέλλετο means 'to command.' Jesus commands the disciples both to pay attention (ὁρᾶτε) and beware (βλέπετε). The warning is very strong.

16. Mark 3:6; 12:13.

17. Isaiah 6:9; Psalm 115:5-6.

18. Mark 3:5-6; 6:52.

19. So concludes the writer in Psalm 95:8-11, even though the references to 'Meribah' and 'Massah' speak of incidents in Exodus 17:7, Numbers 20:3, and Deuteronomy 6:16.

Jesus spoke of the blindness and deafness of understanding in the parable of the sower (Mark 4:10-12). The hope of hearing parables is that the listener will be among those who see and hear and not be among those lacking such perception. Yet it seems that the disciples had the same lack of perception that their forebears had when confronted by the Old Testament prophets.[20] *Remembering* the Lord, Passover, Sabbath, full Law, and the covenants was woven into the identity of Israel.[21] To 'remember' went beyond cognition to faithful trust in the Lord. A failure to remember was disastrous for ancient Israel. Therefore, the rhetorical line of questioning should have stirred much alarm in each disciple. Rather than discussing an absence of loaves, they should have had spiritual perception to think of the significance of the two miraculous feedings.

The modern disciple's ability to grasp the significance of who Jesus is and appropriate it to all of life rests, in part, on what one does with the milk and meat of God's Word as the Spirit of Truth opens one's spiritual understanding.[22] Knowing Christ is an act of grace that is not passive on our part. In grace the Lord commands us to think long and hard on His Word – to meditate and become doers of it.[23]

What would it have meant for the disciples to have thought long and hard on Jesus feeding the four thousand from seven loaves and a few fish? By this point in their lives with Jesus, the disciples should have perceived that He was the Messiah – the God of Israel with whom nothing is impossible. This should have changed how they thought of everything and this knowledge should change how modern disciples think of everything in life – work, office politics, promotion, downsizing, upsizing, contentment, marriage, marital conflict, marital goals, children, roles of children, service to children, leisure, play, savings, financial loss, war, recovery from war, natural disasters, contributing to disaster relief, yea, and all other things.

Jesus had fed four thousand people and previously He fed upwards of ten thousand people. Can He not care for

---

20. Jeremiah 5:21; Ezekiel 12:2; Isaiah 42:18-19; 43:8.
21. Exodus 13:3; 20:8; Numbers 15:40; Deuteronomy 5:5; 8:18; Judges 8:31.
22. 1 Corinthians 2:14-16; Ephesians 1:17-19; Hebrews 5:11-14; 1 Peter 2:2.
23. Psalm 1:1-6; James 1:21-25.

one going through great financial loss? Isn't a lack of income as easy for Jesus to address as a lack of bread? Can He not satisfy us if we are wrongly overlooked for a promotion? Does His identity as God determine what drives our conversations with people who are outside of Christ? The leavening of the world raises concerns over such issues to the place where one effectively questions Jesus' divinity. Jesus' warning against leavening is for all His disciples.

In this trip across the sea, the twelve were in a boat without a storm and yet they were concerned. There was no headwind against them and no perceived ghost walking on water, yet they were afraid. Jesus had twice before calmed waves of the sea.[24] Lacking bread should not have concerned them. However, the lack of bread did concern them because twice they had not seen His divinity, in the feedings of the five thousand and the four thousand, even as twice they did not get the significance of Jesus calming the waters. Jesus is greater than Moses who led Israel through the Red Sea and fed them with manna. He is greater than the watery chaos of pre-creation, having the power of God over the seas. When people are hardened against understanding Jesus' divinity, we should think that they have been infected by a skeptic's virus – that a skeptic's yeast has grown in them and spread as in dough, even though Jesus' miraculous power is so evident and historically known.

Seeing the Divinity of Christ Might Mean Multiple Encounters with the Gospel and Departure from Unbelieving Places (8:22-26)

Jesus returned to the place from which He walked on to the sea (Mark 6:45). His fame has so spread that He has gained a reception that sought His power of healing even though Mark does not have incidents of miracles previously taking place in Bethsaida. Seemingly, Jesus' fame as one who healed defective organs preceded Him.

Unusually, Jesus took this blind man out of the village for healing. Taking a person aside is not unusual in this Gospel, as evidenced in the healing of the deaf and mute man in 7:33.

---

24. Mark 4:35-41 and 6:45-52.

But walking outside of a village removed the man from those who possibly could recognize his healing immediately, as in the case of the deaf and mute man.[25]

Readers of the four Gospels are familiar with Jesus spitting on the ground to make mud to anoint the eyes of the man born blind in John 9:6 and spitting before healing the mute and deaf man in Mark 7:33. But spitting directly on the eyes is different and may be distasteful to modern sensibilities. However, France notes, 'The physical contact would be especially important for a blind man,'[26] and, as Edwards says, 'Such gestures, as we noted at 7:33, were not unknown to Hellenistic healers.'[27]

The acts of laying His hands on the blind man and asking him about the healing were full of compassion. Yet, Jesus' first contact with the man did not result in full healing, for while the man could see shapes he could not do so clearly enough to distinguish them as people.[28] For the reader, this could raise questions both about the sufficiency of Jesus' power to heal and reasoning for a multi-stage healing. However, Mark seems to be pointing toward the significance of this blind man remaining unclear in his sight after his first encounter with Jesus. It was only in the second encounter with Jesus' power that the sight he lost was returned so that he saw with full clarity.

To clarify the intent of this episode, Jesus was healing spiritual blindness to show His power as Messiah, as consistent

---

25. In 7:36-37, there are people in proximity to whom the healed man can proclaim the miracle and who can respond with praise to Jesus' power.

26. France, *Mark*, 324.

27. Edwards, Mark, 242. Edwards further states, 'Tacitus records a story of Vespasian (Roman emperor, A.D. 69–79), who was importuned by a person whose sight was failing to "moisten his cheeks and eyes with his spittle." Unlike the account of Vespasian, however, with Jesus there is no calculation, no hesitation, and no use of the infirm individual for ulterior ends' (Edwards, *Mark*, 242, Edwards references Tacitus, *Hist.* 4.81).

28. France's comments about the man are significant here: 'His report is intriguing. Note that περιπατοῦντας agrees with ἀνθρώπους, not with δένδρα: not "I see people who look like walking trees," but "I see people, and I see them walking like trees." The contrast with seeing τηλαυγῶς in verse 25 makes it clear that this is intended as a description of indistinct sight; he sees moving shapes, which because they are walking about ought to be people, but he cannot yet see them clearly enough to identify them – they might as well be trees!' (France, *Mark*, 325.)

with other teaching in the New Testament.[29] Healing lostness is a one-act thing, although it might take two or more encounters with the gospel to see clearly (i.e., savingly). This would be akin to cleaning windows or eyeglasses with glass cleaner twice to make sure they are clean because the dirt film on them was very bad before the first cleaning. After the first cleaning, you stepped back and could see a film was still there because you could not see through the glass as clearly as you should. But with the second cleaning, all became clear.

Further, so that the one who now saw did not become confused – as in the case of the disciples being influenced by the Pharisees' skepticism – Jesus removed him from the realm of the village immediately. Just as contemporary believers cannot escape the world (cf. 1 Cor. 6:9-11), this formerly blind man could not escape everyone who would respond negatively to his claim to have sight via Jesus' spitting and laying on of hands. Nevertheless, contemporary believers should participate in a strong fellowship of believers upon conversion, thus limiting the depth of contact they now have with unbelieving friends. So too this man can live in another village with his new sight away from the village where he was known prior to his conversion.[30]

Seeing the Divinity of Christ Intends to Bring Clarity on His Identity, Mission, and Ideas of Being His Follower (8:27–9:1)

Jesus and the disciples departed for the region of Caesarea Philippi, some twenty-five miles north of the Sea of Galilee. While on the journey, Jesus asked two questions concerning His identity as viewed in the eyes of the general populus and the identity the disciples had concluded by having been with Him for about three years. In general, people had drawn three conclusions about Jesus. First, like Herod, they identified Jesus as John the Baptist. With the Baptizer in prison, it might

---

29. See Romans 2:19, 2 Peter 1:9, and Revelation 3:17.

30. Two additional comments are important. First, the villagers' eagerness for Jesus to heal the man does not mean that they are the best candidates for receiving the man once his eyes are open. Second, one can change primary friendships without sacrificing the relationships one has had with those who do not believe the gospel.

be easy to see how anyone who was not at the baptism might confuse Jesus with John. Yet the Markan account clearly distinguishes them as Jesus comes into the wilderness to be baptized by John.

Elijah's reappearance made sense in the hearts and minds of the people, for he had a strong prophetic role of rebuking the people of Israel and performing miracles. Also, Elijah had been associated with John the Baptist in an earlier scene.[31]

Identifying Jesus as one of the prophets also seems to stem from the role many Old Testament prophets had in calling people to repentance, announcing the kingdom of God, performing miracles, and speaking with authority. Rather than identifying Him with a named prophet within the Old Covenant tradition, Jesus simply fitted the general pattern associated with God's prophetic mouthpieces.

All three descriptions recognized a prophetic role in the ministry of Jesus. Yet all three fell short in associating deity in bodily form with Jesus. 'John the Baptist,' 'Elijah,' and 'one of the prophets' all were shy of concluding that Jesus was the divine Messiah on whom Israel and Judah had set their hopes of deliverance.

Jesus' question to the disciples went to the heart of the people's shortcoming. Had the disciples seen enough to conclude that Jesus was beyond a mere human mouthpiece of the revelation of God? Peter's answer demonstrated that the disciples had reasoned *intellectually* to the correct conclusion, even if emotionally and volitionally they did not yet have full agreement. Peter had the correct conclusion, but this did not keep him from denying Christ or keep the disciples from deserting Him at His hour of greatest need.

Wisely, there was no need for the disciples to engage the people and begin arguments over the identity of Jesus. They would preach to the people of Israel on the Day of Pentecost and following. But at this point in the Gospel, they did not yet need to draw the sort of attention that might invite argument and the possible arrest of Jesus prior to all the events in the path to His mission of the cross.

---

31. Mark 6:14-15.

Mark 8:31-32 is the first of three predictions Jesus gave of His suffering and death at the hands of enemies, and of His resurrection from the dead after three days. The three predictions collectively paint a full picture of those enemies involved in Christ's suffering and death, and of many of the moves involved in causing His suffering and death. Differently from the other two predictions, Mark 8:31 notes broadly the suffering to come but specifically the rejection by the Jewish elders, chief priests, and scribes. The Jewish leaders would not receive Jesus' claim to be the Messianic King and their rejection led to His death.

Jesus did not speak in parables when explaining what shortly awaited Him; He spoke straightforwardly with boldness about what was to happen to Him. He left no doubt that He was going to face much suffering through a wholesale rejection by the Jewish leadership, through crucifixion and death.

Peter understood the plain words of Jesus to some degree. His confession of 'the Christ' demonstrated that he had come to a reasonable conclusion by following Jesus and that he had understood Jesus' talk of rejection, suffering, and being killed. But Peter's conclusions had missed the implications of Jesus' prediction of rising again after three days. Jesus was very specific about the identity of His opponents, that He will be killed, and that there will be three days between His death and resurrection. Considering the frankness with which Jesus had spoken, Peter and the other disciples should have grasped the truth of His resurrection with joy.

The brevity of the Markan account of Peter's confession seems to reflect Mark's intention to minimize shining a light on Peter's successes. Yet a reader of the parallel accounts knows that Peter had received revelation from God the Father regarding the identity of Jesus. Even so, Peter quickly fell to temptation from the evil one to speak against the work of Christ in His suffering and death. 'The things of man' pointed toward desires to avoid suffering and death at the hands of other people. Such avoidance would amount to Jesus not going to the cross. The swift and stern rebuke revealed how evil was the attempt to derail the idea that Jesus would suffer and die on behalf of sinners.

Consistent with the two predictions of His death in the coming chapters, a discourse followed this prediction. In this

teaching, Jesus' explanation of what it means to follow Him
distinguishes those of whom He will be ashamed from those
who will enter the kingdom of God. By calling the crowd and
the disciples together to hear Him, He established the cost of
following Him for anyone and everyone.

'Deny himself,' 'save his life,' and 'gain the whole world,' fill
in what Jesus meant by 'things of men.' Peter was attempting
to save his and Jesus' lives and enjoy life without needing a
suffering Christ. This was not a denial of self; this was an
attempt at the preservation of self. But following Jesus involved
being willing to exchange the desire for self-preservation for
a lifestyle that embraces suffering and death for Christ's sake.

Thus, the saving of life is an attempt at self-preservation,
whereas the losing of life is embracing the life of the cross – a
life that might involve dying on a cross. This requires self-
denial, for it is natural to try to preserve one's own life. But
the attempt at self-preservation will mean loss of eternal life.

In contrast, losing one's life for Christ's sake and the gospel's
will mean the gaining of eternal life. The self-denial required to
follow Jesus and to proclaim the gospel in all the world might
result in actual loss of physical life. But it will be accompanied
by the final realization of eternal life. It is not that eternal life
is earned, but that it is the destiny of one following Christ. The
life of being a disciple of Christ is a life of self-denial.

Jesus reasoned further on the topic of following Him
by asking rhetorical questions to which the answers were
obvious: a man only profits in this life with temporary
material goods if he is willing to preserve his life rather than
follow Christ, and there is nothing one can give to gain back
his soul once it is lost. Therefore, the attempt to preserve one's
life for the sake of gaining more in this present world results
in the loss of one's soul. Self-denial toward the things of the
present world keeps one from compromising one's soul.

Like the words in verse 35, 'for my sake and the gospel's,'
in verse 38 Jesus spoke of shame concerning His person and
words. Immediately, one thinks of Peter's response to Christ's
words about suffering in Jerusalem. Peter did not want to
have the shame of Christ's suffering and death associated
with him because of his choice to follow Jesus. He would find
shame toward himself if the end of following would be death

rather than total victory. (Again, Peter seemed to have missed the significance of the rising after three days!)

Yet the preserving of one's life to avoid the shame associated with Christ embraces the worldview of those in rebellion to God. Like ancient Israel, whose idolatry was an act of adultery against her cosmic husband, the attempt to preserve one's life by denying Christ so that one might gain the things of this life and avoid shame and death is rebellion against God. When Jesus comes with the angels to gather His own as the glorified Son of His Father, He will find shame to be associated with those who have embraced the world. Those seeking to follow Jesus should understand that this One who the disciples are following – that is, the Son of Man – is the very Son of God. Preservation of life is a rejection of the coming glory of the divine Son who is Lord over the host of holy ones.

Jesus' concluding statement about tasting death and the kingdom addressed both Peter's concern about preserving life and the general teaching on life for the follower of Christ. 'Some standing here' addressed the disciples before Him, but not all of them. The idiom, 'taste death,' laid bare what was on Peter's heart and mind when he heard the prediction of Jesus' death. The promised coming of the kingdom revealed that the plan of God and the ministry of Jesus cannot be thwarted by the evil workings of the elders, chief priests, and scribes. 'Power' pointed toward the kingdom and its King being victorious over evil rather than the events in Jerusalem revealing a Messiah whose suffering and death revealed failure.

The statement will find fulfillment in the next episode.

Reflective Questions

1. In your own words, explain what Jesus' two-act healing of the blind man intends to communicate about salvation. What hope does this give you toward those with whom you have shared the gospel on multiple occasions?

2. To what things can you point in your current Christian practice that reflect losing your life for Christ's sake? Where are you most tempted to keep your life for your own sake rather than lose your life for Christ's sake?

10

He Came So That His Greatness Might Be Exalted
(Mark 9:2-48)

Since the time of Jesus' confounding of the Jewish leaders in the Temple, there had been confusion over the identity of Jesus and what He taught about His return. Wrongheaded ideas always tame Jesus into a god bearing the image of man. Such ideas account for some of the puzzling thoughts people have over the return of Christ – thoughts that divorce eschatology from the work of Christ on earth as the substitute for His people.

Mark 9 offers a corrective that reorients our hope: which is, exalt the true greatness of Christ. Mark calls believers to speak of Jesus as presented in this chapter – as greater than human ideals and hopes of greatness. Yet exalting Christ will not answer all our questions about His return, even as Jesus' discourse did not answer all questions for the disciples.

Exalting the Greatness of Christ Prevents Domesticating Him and Divorcing His Return from His Death and Resurrection (9:2-13)

Six days had passed since Jesus proclaimed that some would not experience death until they saw the kingdom of God come with power (9:1). Mark invites the reader to anticipate a display of the kingdom. On this episodic trajectory, the reader should expect Peter, James, and John to experience something unique as they go up the mountain with Jesus. However, Jesus turned into something they had never seen in all their travels with Him, far exceeding any expectations the three (and Mark's audience) would have had about the mountaintop experience.

Immediately upon ascending the mountain, Jesus was transfigured before them. His transformation involved an outward display, not a change in His substance or being. Rather than hiding the full beauty of His glory behind human form, Jesus allowed His glory to shine through His humanity with a brilliance that excelled the bleaching that any launderer could do. The three disciples should have been captivated completely with Jesus and not taken their eyes off Him.

The author mentions the presence of Elijah and Moses without giving details of their glorification or transfiguration, and by merely noting that they appeared with Jesus. He is the one in focus. One would expect the three disciples to have been so enamored with what they saw that they would have failed to do anything else but awed continuously. Yet, with an epic failure, Peter addressed Jesus as 'Rabbi,' suggested Peter's own presence was helpful, and offered to make equivalent tents for Jesus, Moses, and Elijah. In his terror and ignorance, Peter spoke of Jesus in terms that did not fit with the display before his eyes. Jesus had revealed a glory far beyond the assistance of Peter and the Old Testament figures who represented the Law and the Prophets.

Peter's offer to build tents could have been a reference to the 'Tent of Meeting' where Moses met face to face with the Lord (Exod. 33:7-11). If so, then Mark is comparing his transfiguration account with the account of the Lord revealing His glory to Moses in Exodus 33 and 34. In Exodus, the pitching of the tent *preceded* the meetings with the Lord face to face whereas in Mark the revelation of the glory of Christ preceded the call for pitching of the tents. The 'tent' that needed to be pitched had been pitched already with the coming of the Son of God (cf. Mark 1:1).

Observation of Jesus going up the mountain and returning again also brings Moses' experience into the interpretation of the passage. In the Exodus account, Moses went up the mountain to receive the Law and saw the glory of God there.[1] Moses then returned down the mountain to serve the people.[2] Moses again went up to receive the tabernacle design instructions,[3] and he returned forty days later to find the people in disobedience.[4] Moses then went up to see the glory of God;[5] he returned with a need to cover his face with a veil.[6] In the Elijah account, he went up Mount Carmel to confront the prophets of Baal and came down after slaughtering them to look for rain.[7]

The cloud overshadowed those on the mountain and a voice spoke because the One transfigured should have been the focus. The voice identified the transfigured One as the 'beloved Son.' The transfiguration put Jesus in a category by Himself. The terms 'no one' and 'Jesus only' puts Jesus in a category of *exclusivity*. The disciples' domestication of Jesus had been silenced.

Jesus charged them not to tell anyone about His transfiguration. They held what they saw among themselves until He rose from the dead. While this must have been very difficult to do, only John seems to have been affected by it in such a way that he would not desert Jesus when He suffered on the cross.

The passage moves from a discussion about Elijah and Moses to a discussion about Elijah. The disciples asked about the talk of the scribes rather than about what the Scriptures say about the coming suffering of the Son of Man. They still did not grasp what they had seen and heard.

Elijah in this discussion refers to the object of Malachi's prophecy – the one who had appeared with Moses, and who in history past had worked to return the hearts of Israel back to God and of the children back to the fathers in Israel. Peter immediately recognized Elijah – a historical figure who lived in the ninth century B.C. – without any explanation of his identity. To this Elijah the people of the first century A.D.

1. Exodus 19:1-3, 16-20.
2. Exodus 9:14-15, 21-25; 20:21.
3. Exodus 24:1-18.
4. Exodus 32:7, 15-20.
5. Exodus 34:1-7.
6. Exodus 34:29-35.
7. The story is found in 1 Kings 18.

had done nothing of contempt. So Jesus' final use of 'Elijah' referred to John the Baptist, even though Mark only has Malachi 4:5-6 in the background and not a full John the Baptist death narrative. Jesus, however, did not respond to the question about the restoration of all things.

Exalting the Greatness of Christ Offers Understanding for Those Who Doubt His Power and Calls for More Prayer to Defeat the Demonic (9:14-29)

Jesus' resolution of the dispute over the disciples' inability to heal the convulsing son rebuked the lack of faith that the scribes, crowd, father, and disciples had in Jesus' power to heal the boy compassionately and completely. The debate that Jesus encountered upon coming down the mountain concerned the disciples' failure. The crowd rushed to Jesus immediately, perhaps in hope that He would succeed where His disciples failed. The crowd did not necessarily understand Jesus' full identity.

One does not know the content of the argument with the scribes, but it was likely a legal matter related to the failed attempts to heal the boy. It could be that the scribes argued that if Jesus were the Christ His disciples would have been able to heal. Whatever the argument, the crowd quickly ran to Jesus, leaving the debate behind. Jesus invited Himself into the discussion and the father spoke from the crowd to give details on the failure of Jesus' disciples. It is evident that the father looked to Jesus to heal the boy.

Jesus asked the father about the details. In the first series of descriptions, the father related the bodily harm the demon caused the boy: muteness, rigidity, foaming at the mouth, and the grinding of teeth. The description is of a grand-mal seizure, which Matthew identifies as epilepsy.[8]

Jesus witnessed the boy convulse violently, shaking uncontrollably in a seizure following on from when the demon saw Jesus. Mark and Matthew do not divorce the epileptic experience from a concurrent experience of demonic possession. The boy had experienced this for most of his young years, as the father, in replying, described the length of the

---

8. Matthew describes 'seizures' using *selenazomai* – a word that means 'moonstruck,' or epileptic (Matt. 17:15).

suffering as if childhood was long past. Since childhood, the demonic force inside of the boy had tried frequently to drown him or kill him by fire.[9] Mark's forceful terms related to the boy's experience heighten the magnitude of the problem. The length and details of the demonic encounter is reminiscent of the detailed encounter of the Gerasenes' demoniac (5:3-5). But this description bests that previous description with a display of the demon's evil power in the presence of Jesus.

Jesus asked two questions – one to the disciples, and one to the father. The first question – 'What are you arguing about with them?' – invited an answer that would expose lack of faith on the parts of the disciples, crowd, and scribes (by way of their arguing with the disciples). The second question – 'How long has this been happening to him?' – drew out the father's lack of faith that Jesus could overcome the length and depth of this evil.

Jesus challenged the father to trust in God, for to say that all things are possible to one who believes was to claim omnipotence. The father's response recognized the need for the One with strength graciously to grant the faith to trust Him for things of this magnitude. Even a demonic spirit with authority to make a child have seizures and perform acts that would kill him was a problem under God's governance of the universe He had created. For Mark's readers, there should be no doubt that One who had cast out demons, restored withered hands, calmed winds, healed paralytics, stopped hemorrhaging and fed thousands was able to rebuke this unclean spirit and heal the boy completely. Jesus spoke directly of the problems incited by this particular demon and relieved the boy of its influence forever: 'Come out of him and never enter him again.'

The demon's actions surrounding his departure from the boy brought to the fore the worldview issue in question. What all failed to grasp was Jesus' power to raise the dead.[10] Evil did not have the final victory in the life of the boy and his father, revealing a greatness that previously had not seemed possible to the crowd.

---

9. The father uses 'often,' describing a frequent, recurring experience.

10. In 9:26, the boy appears to be dead to many of the onlookers: the words *nekros* (corpse), and *apethanen* (dead) are used. But Jesus lifts him by the hand back to life.

Then the disciples inquired about their own inability to cast out the demon. In private, Jesus spoke about the need for prayer for deliverance from this type of demon.[11] The hope for those with loved ones struck by debilitating, self-harming, life-threatening disorders should not rest in science alone or prayer alone. The identification of this encounter with epilepsy allows us to direct those of faith toward physicians for care for the physical, emotional and mental aspects of this disorder as with any other disorder. But the faithful should be wise: the evil one is behind murder (John 8:44); such attempts to force one's own death reveal demonic influence co-existing with bodily trauma. Much prayer should be made to the Father for the removal of demonic influences surrounding a loved one's need for healing when self-inflicting harm and thoughts of suicide are present.

Exalting the Greatness of Christ Changes Our Ideas of Personal Greatness (9:30-37)

Jesus and the disciples then passed through Galilee. Secrecy was the order of the day because He wished to instruct them privately about His death and resurrection. This would be the second of three occasions when Jesus informed them of the impending events in Jerusalem regarding His death and His rising from the dead.[12] Yet, like modern disciples, they failed to understand the significance of what He was saying.[13] They missed that people, including Israel's leadership, would seek the death of the One who had been transfigured before three of them and had overcome a murderous demon before them all.

Jesus took time on the journey to teach privately about His death and rising. But fear of revealing their lack of understanding prevented the disciples from asking for clarification. The irony of the disciples' argument while journeying is apparent. The One with true greatness revealed His coming death at the hands of people. It must be a voluntary death by One who has power over climatic forces of nature and over the underworld.

---

11. Some translations add fasting to Jesus' response, as reflected in later manuscripts.

12. The first time is in Mark 8:31. Mark will have Jesus return to the foretelling of the events of Passion Week in 10:32-34.

13. In Mark 8:32, Jesus speaks 'plainly,' yet the disciples miss what He means.

It must be a display of unique power if death can be defeated. Yet the disciples, who could not cast out the muting demon and failed to seek clarification of Jesus' words, argued instead about being great. Out of terror Peter spoke of building tents for Jesus, Moses, and Elijah when he saw the transfigured Christ. Now, however, he was among those putting in a bid to be identified as the greatest among them.

The disciples were silent in response to Jesus' inquiry about their conversation. The silence indicated their recognition of wrongdoing before Christ – wrongdoing for which they were ashamed before Him. How could they argue about their greatness when they had recently witnessed true greatness on display, only to hear Him then say that He will be killed by those who have no power over demons and death?

Jesus exposed the disciples' misunderstanding of the relationship between His death and resurrection and the achieving of greatness. Yet He took a humble posture while speaking to the disciples, both by sitting down among them and by taking a child in His arms. Jesus portrayed the very concept of greatness as He spoke to the disciples. To be great (or 'first') – like Jesus – means to serve others because one should seek self-acknowledgment only after all others have had the opportunity to be served (e.g., last). To be first means to be a servant, even as Christ sat with the disciples and instructed them gently, in truth, and embraced the vulnerable child tenderly. Disciples who would yet receive children would have the pleasure of the Son and the Father as they served those less powerful than them.[14]

Exalting the Greatness of Christ Prevents Wrongful Judgments That Could Disrupt Gospel Work or Prevent Eternal Rewards (9:38-50)

Jesus' clarification regarding those for and with Him was intended to prevent the disciples from making wrongful judgments about other people. The disciples wished to

---

14. The issues in the reception of the child are not that they cannot give anything in return (cf. Luke 6:45-35). Neither was the issue one of having the humility of a child (cf. Matt. 18:2-4). Instead, the discussion of greatness was of authority and power, themes that run throughout Mark 9:2-48. The child was frail in power before Jesus and any of the disciples. Greatness uses power to serve the weaker.

stop those casting out demons because they were thinking territorially, imagining that they had privilege in a club with exclusive membership. Only those with them could do the work of the kingdom of God.[15] Jesus indicated that any persons doing such work in His name would not turn quickly to become His enemy. Such persons had encountered the greatness of Christ and would not soon turn to deny Him or walk away from His power. The disciples should not push away such a person. Rewards are at stake for the person who does something as small as giving water to the disciples as they journey.

Similarly, the disciples must avoid causing a child to sin. The one who causes believers of little account (in our eyes) to stumble are warned that they must engage in strong self-judgment. Such self-judgments should give disciples the assurance of eternal life.

Jesus' concern was for the 'little ones,' those 'who are socially invisible and easily ignored .... They are the untutored, the persons on the fringes, the ones whom no one misses when they are absent from worship, the ones who are tolerated but not embraced in fellowship.'[16] In the immediately preceding sections, the disciples encountered a man whose child needed demonic deliverance (9:18), a little child (9:37), and a man outside of the circle of disciples who was casting out demons (9:38). In each case, the disciples showed a wrong reception of those persons. The issue of belief appeared in each episode (i.e., 'believes,' and 'in my Name').[17] The disciples needed more prayer, humility, and an understanding of the unity of believers, but they lacked in each case. 'It becomes an admonition not to discount the faith of another because he or she is not affiliated with an official Christian circle.'[18]

'It would be better' contrasts two fates. It informs the hearer that there is a reality of a danger greater than drowning at sea, or cutting off a hand or foot, or plucking out an eye.

---

15. Those casting out demons are working in the power of the kingdom of God, as Jesus earlier taught (Mark 3:24-26; see also Matthew 12:28 and Luke 11:20).

16. Garland, *Mark*, 375.

17. Mark 9:23-24, 39.

18. Edwards, *Mark*, 292.

A millstone was a large, cylindrically shaped stone used for grounding mill while the power of a donkey or large beast of burden turned the stone. The Romans drowned people in this manner as a form of execution. The concept was greatly terrifying to Jews because of their great fear of the sea and their regard of drowning as a horrible death.[19] For Jesus, it would be better to face this than face Him in judgment if they have caused a 'little one' to 'sin' (see below).

Jesus' prescriptions for the removal of the hand, eye, and foot are *hyperbolic*. That is, to preserve one's soul, one should go to the length of removing acts (hands), places (feet), and sights (eye) that would corrupt the soul and, by corrupting the soul, allow one's life to lead others to 'sin' (which is yet undefined). Hughes comments, 'These gory metaphors tell us that halfway measures just will not do it ... they recommend that we be willing to endure physical pain to conquer our sinful habits.'[20] As Edwards notes, 'If anything, the hyperbole enhances the teaching that God is more important than even those things most indispensable to us.'[21]

'Hell' in Mark 9:43, 45, and 47 is the term *Gehenna*. It translates the Hebrew 'Valley of Hinnom' (*Ge Hinnom*). The term referred to a dump outside of the city wall of Jerusalem in the Hinnom Valley that continually had fires to burn city waste. It had been a place of great slaughter for Judah during a time of divine judgment – the birds and beasts gorged on the dead and joy was absent.[22] It was also a place where maggots ('worms') would eat flesh continually: 'And they shall go out and look on the dead bodies of the men who have rebelled against me. For their worm shall not die, their fire shall not be quenched, and they shall be an abhorrence to all flesh' (Isa. 66:24).

The Gospels also mention *Gehenna* in Matthew 5:22, 29, 30; 10:28; 18:9; 23:15, 33; and Luke 12:5. However, in Mark 9:42-50, Jesus modified and contrasted hell in ways that identify the sense of the term. In 9:43, hell is the 'unquenchable fire' given for causing others to stumble rather than entering life (which,

19. Edwards, *Mark*, 293.
20. R. Kent Hughes, *Mark*, vol. 2 (Wheaton, IL: Crossway, 1989), 40.
21. Edwards, *Mark*, 294.
22. Jeremiah 7:30-34; see also Jeremiah 19:5-6; 32:35.

since they are already living, would be a reference to a future life). In 9:45, hell is held out as judgment for those who cause others to stumble, in contrast to entering life.

Again, in 9:47-48 Jesus speaks of hell as judgment, describing it as a place where 'the worm does not die and the fire is not quenched' (cf. Isa. 66:24). Entering hell stands in contrast to entering the kingdom of God.[23] Jesus taught that hell is a place of unquenchable fire and great death, given in judgment, in contrast to entering life in the kingdom.

Another way to see what Jesus meant by 'hell' is to reason from the context, placing the term *Gehenna* into the meaning of the whole: if the subject of which Jesus spoke is a *threatening danger* (vs. life), and 'hell' is a component of that meaning, then *hell* is a real threat to one who causes another to stumble. Such a threat should force careful self-examination because it is worse than drowning; it is eternal punishment. If it were annihilation or purgatory, it would not exceed a millstone around one's neck or having bodily parts upon entering the grave. Death is not a threat; it is natural. Hell is beyond what is natural. Thus, *Jesus taught that 'hell' is eternal punishment.*

The verb for 'sin' here is *scandalizo*, better translated as 'stumble.' Jesus warned the disciples of behaviors that cause people with basic faith in Christ to have trouble trusting His power. Instead, believers should be 'salt.' One can see the difference in the two usages of 'salt.' In the first usage, the subject of which Jesus was speaking is *threatening danger* (vs. life), and 'everyone will be salted with fire' is a part of that meaning; *then salted with fire* is judgment that all persons will face before God – a testing of the character of the person.

In the second usage, when Jesus warned the disciples to make self-judgment, 'have *salt* within yourselves' is a component for making self-judgment; in this usage, *salt is the capacity for self-criticism that takes the judgment of God seriously.* Without this, one cannot look at oneself to see if one has the marks that indicate one is free from hell-judgment at the hands of God. Therefore disciples, rather than being critical

---

23. In later manuscripts, Mark 9:44 and 46 are added and are identical to 9:48. They are best explained as scribal additions given to strengthen and clarify the concept of hell as fierce judgment.

of those of little account, should strive to live at peace with them as fellow believers.

Reflective Questions

1. When was a time you thought deeply about the fate of unbelievers around you as *hell* – as a place in which *the fire is not quenched and the worm does not die?*

2. What examples do you see in your life of you striving to be first rather than last?

11

He Came to Instruct Us Rightly on Divorce, Wealth and Power
(Mark 10)

Over 689,000 divorces and annulments were granted in the United States in 2021.[1] Despite falling rates of divorce, 689,000 divorces and annulments indicates that almost two-thirds of a million couples were unhappy enough in their marriages to pursue a permanent option for ending it. Yet many divorced persons will try their hands at marriage again.

For the believer, the question of remarriage after divorce can be controversial. Views on the possibility of remarriage after divorce range from remarriage is never allowed to remarriage is allowed regardless of the reason for the dissolution of the previous marriage. However, just as Jesus offered words of correction on the views of divorce and remarriage in His day, His words have a clarifying and correcting force appropriate for contemporary views of the dissolvability and permanency of marriage. Such a teaching comes as one part of Jesus' larger series of corrections on views of family, wealth, and power.

---

1. Statistic from National Center for Health Statistics, Centers for Disease Prevention and Control, https://www.cdc.gov/nchs/fastats/marriage-divorce.htm (last accessed April 25, 2024).

Jesus' Correction of the World and Church's View on Divorce, Remarriage, and the Salvation of Children Reveals the Permanency of Marriage and His Pleasure with Children (10:1-16)

Amid a customary opportunity of teaching large numbers of Jewish people, the Pharisees challenged Jesus in order to trap Him. Their testing of Him sought to measure His teaching against their understanding of what the Mosaic Law taught.[2] If He disagreed with their view, then the Pharisees could say to the Jews that Jesus did not agree with Moses. Thus, they would have reason to provide the Jewish people with doubt toward Jesus' claims to be the promised Messiah.

Rather than responding with His own view, Jesus solicited from the leaders their estimation of the Law of Moses. This allowed Him to discern their angle on the issue, including the points with which they were testing Him. As the Law gave stipulations to follow, Jesus framed the question as a matter of commandment keeping.

The Pharisees spoke of Moses *allowing* a certificate of divorce. They were careful to speak of the certificate Moses mentioned in Deuteronomy 24:1-4. However, they were not careful with their interpretation of the Law, for Moses' stipulations did not speak to the allowability of divorce. Instead, the stipulations accepted divorce as a fact while establishing a prohibition against a remarriage scenario in Israelite society.

Jesus revealed the depravity of the hearts of the ancient Israelites in His reply. 'Your hardness of heart' implied a corporate solidarity between fifteenth-century B.C. Israel and Jesus' first-century audience. The existence of the commandment showed the problem of the Pharisees' spirituality and theology concerning remarriage. Like their forefathers, they needed the Law to prohibit them from violating the mystery of the marital union.

Jesus' appeal to the creation narrative corrected the Pharisees' understanding of the mystery of marriage. Jesus

---

2. It is evident that an *interpretation* of the Mosaic Law is at stake, for the House of Shammai and the House of Hillel had different views on the writ of divorce. See Talmud Yevamot 14a-b.

affirmed God's design for marriage to be a *heterosexual, lifelong, monogamous, sexual, mysterious, inseparable union.*[3] The union is to be heterosexual, as evidenced by Jesus' quotation of Genesis 1:27 and God's making of two separate, biological sexes that reveal gender at birth: 'male and female.'[4]

The quotation from Genesis 2:24 reveals the intention of a lifelong arrangement, as the man leaves his parents to establish a home of his own with his wife.[5] These two persons join sexually to become one; but the separate bodies of the male husband and the female wife indicate that the oneness is within an invisible plane. In a physical sense they are two – biological male/husband and biological female/wife. In a spiritual, mysterious sense they are joined forever as one body, akin to the way in which believers are united with Christ in salvation as one Head and body. Moreover, Genesis 2:24 indicates the monogamous nature of marriage, as the union involves two persons, no more and no less.

Jesus indicated that God is the One joining persons in marriage by virtue of His design for marriage. That is, when there is a heterosexual, monogamous union, one can call the union 'marriage.'[6] This is not cultural, for the appeal is to 'the beginning.' Jesus crosses all time and cultural boundaries to establish that the acts and proclamations at the beginning of the world's history are the objective standard by which to regard the permanency of marriage and of the idea of marriage itself. The creation account pertains to all cultures, not simply those residing in first-century Judea.

---

3. I recognize that the New Testament teaches that death is the means the Lord provides for separating a marital union (Rom. 7:1-3; 1 Cor. 7:39-40).

4. The binary designations reflect anatomy as well as psychology, as Adam cannot procreate without the other biological sex that he recognizes as 'she' in the creation account. However, I wish to separate my use of 'male' and 'female' from the socially constructed baggage they carry. I am speaking of biological distinctions.

5. This truth does not violate any concepts of the ancient Eastern idea of family including one's extended relatives.

6. So-called 'common law,' 'same-sex,' and polygamous unions violate any biblical concept of marriage. As such, they should be thought of as immorality rather than marriage. This remains true whether one views same-sex attraction (SSA) as sin or not. 'Marriage,' biblically, is a heterosexual union.

'Let man not separate' puts divorce outside of God's perfect will for marriage. Later revelation recognizes the fact of divorce among believers without establishing another decree or an exception clause (see 1 Cor. 7:10-11).[7]

Jesus reinforced the permanency of marriage in His response to the disciples' revisitation of the issue. He placed remarriage outside of the bounds of the will of God with His double answer. For both men and women, divorcing one's spouse and remarrying another constitutes adultery. Such a status is only possible if the first marriage remains intact. While one might be free to remarry legally after a divorce, the original mysterious union remains in force in the sight of Jesus. It is dissolvable only by the death of one's spouse. Therefore, remarriage is not an option for believers.[8]

Seemingly, children were bothersome to the disciples, or they may have deemed them unworthy to approach Jesus. Their rebuke provoked the ire of Jesus. Jesus had no

---

7. Some see abandonment, adultery, and abuse as biblical grounds for divorcing one's spouse. As David Schuman writes, 'When someone commits infidelity, they break the bond of their marriage' (David Schuman, 'What 1 Corinthians 7 Says About Desertion and Divorce,' The Gospel Coalition, September 18, 2020, https://www.thegospelcoalition.org/article/desertion-divorce/). See also Joshua Sharp, 'Abuse is Biblical Grounds for Divorce,' Baptist Standard, May 18, 2020, https://www.baptiststandard.com/opinion/voices/ abuse-is-biblical-grounds-for-divorce/.

However, 1 Corinthians 7:10-11 simply speaks about the reality of divorce in the church – that is, there were those in the church in Corinth who were divorced, or contemplating divorce, or trying to understand divorce. For them, Paul simply provides a conditional truth: 'If one divorces, he or she must remain single.' In such a conditional statement, he does not affirm a ground for divorce. He simply recognizes its allowance. The allowance is not limited, for reasons for divorcing are not attached to the conditional statement. Later, Paul will speak of separation and divorce, but not abandonment (1 Cor. 7:12-16; a term for 'separation' is in 7:10).

Paul does not speak directly to the issue of abuse. However, no one should be left in an abusive situation for any reason. But removal of one from a home does not require legal separation, neither do biblical texts assume abuse as a ground for divorce. Again, God's ideal for marriage is permanency, but divorce is a reality permissible by both Moses and Paul.

8. This is consistent with Paul's teaching in 1 Corinthians 7, for there he emphasizes maintaining one's marital status if married or legally divorced but gives to single persons the option to remain single or to marry (1 Cor. 7:8-9, 11-13, 24, 26-28, 36-39). I recognize that there are different evangelical views on divorce and remarriage. See John Murray, Divorce (Phillipsburg, NJ: P&R, 1961) for a different view well-respected by many.

problem with children approaching Him; seemingly they approached Him with faith, as they will be participants in the kingdom.

Jesus' Revelation about the Relationship Between Wealth and Eternal Life Exposes Erroneous Thoughts about Money and Salvation (10:17-31)

Mark's immediate transition to the story of the rich young ruler indicates that the episode with the wealthy leader was related to the ideas addressed in the discussion on divorce. The religious leaders and disciples carried earthly views of marriage and divorce that Jesus corrected. Here, the man kneeling before Him had an earthly view of wealth that Jesus will expose. Both the discussion on divorce and wealth will give way to greater ethics from Jesus. Jesus' teaching on inheriting eternal life revealed the rich man's errors in assuming he had eternal life.

As Jesus and the disciples were departing from the region, the rich man interrupted Jesus before He had made any significant progress. The question came with a sense of urgency as the kneeling would have stopped Jesus rather than allowing for a conversation to have taken place as Jesus walked along. The genuflection here could have denoted worship; at minimum it denoted submission or honor.[9]

The question of inheriting eternal life had an Old Testament background.[10] The hope for the faithful member of Israel was to live forever in the land promised to the patriarchs, apart from the wicked, and with rest from warring with their enemies. Hearing Jesus speak of receiving the kingdom of God and watching Him bless the children rightly provoked a question about the acquisition of the promised life in the kingdom. It was a question about salvation.

By addressing Jesus as 'Good Teacher,' the ruler acknowledged Jesus as a skilled rabbi, one knowledgeable of the Law. But the appellate failed to recognize Jesus' divinity – a truth necessary to have salvation in the Son. Jesus' correction did not deny His own divinity but forced

---

9. Heinrich Schlier, 'Γόνυ, Γονυπετέω,' *TDNT*, 738-40.

10. See Deuteronomy 12:10; Psalms 37:9, 11, 22, 29, 34; 133:3; Isaiah 57:13.

the inquirer and those listening to associate the character of God with the person of Jesus. In absolute character, only God can claim goodness.[11] Jesus made an explicit claim to deity.

The ruler's knowledge of the commandments should be the guide to evidence of eternal life. Jesus speaks of five of the six commandments from the second tablet of the Law, leaving out the command against covetousness and replacing it with a prohibition against defrauding one's neighbor.[12] Luke retains Mark's order and wording, only removing the prohibition against defrauding (Luke 18:20). Matthew has a different wording and order, placing the prohibition against murder first for emphasis, removing the prohibition against defraud, and adding a summary statement for the second tablet related to love of neighbor (Matt. 19:18-19).

The ruler's response made huge assumptions about his own righteousness according to the Law. Without qualification, he affirmed his successful adherence to the standards of the second tablet, having performed the Law from his early childhood. Just as he had missed Jesus' deity, in his hope for eternal life he had missed his own depravity.

Jesus' exposure built upon the man's assumption of righteousness. The editorial comment reveals Jesus was motivated by and carried out love toward the ruler in His response. Among the evangelists, only Mark records both the intensity with which Jesus looked at the young man and the portrayal of love. The loving thing Jesus did was to offer the ruler the opportunity to demonstrate his assumed perfection in keeping the Law, seemingly so that he might see his fault toward the Law, which he did.

The entirety of Jesus' statement overwhelmed the ruler. He was unwilling to sell all he had for giving to the poor and be satisfied with having treasure from God – a treasure currently inaccessible to the possessor of earthly riches. He was unwilling to become a disciple of Jesus.

---

11. See Psalms 34:8; 100:5; 135:3; 145:9; Jeremiah 33:11; Lamentations 3:25.

12. Exodus 20:12-16; Deuteronomy 5:16-20. Edwards suggests the prohibition against defrauding the poor 'may have been added because of its relevance to the rich man, since wealth is often gained at the expense of the poor' (Edwards, *Mark*, 310-11).

Jesus' Teaching to the Disciples on the Difficulty for the Rich to Gain Eternal Life Reveals God to Be Greater than the Impossibilities Posed by Our Relationship with Money (10:32-34)

Jesus then gave a private lesson to His disciples. Having wealth has posed a problem for embracing the values of the kingdom throughout redemptive history. This was evident under the Old Covenant in examples like the attempts by Balak to buy prophetic favor, the necessity of the unnamed man of God to refuse remuneration for his services, and Gehazi's greed.[13] It is evident under the New Covenant in Jesus' words about the inability to serve God and money simultaneously, Paul's statement about the love of money being the root of many types of evil, and in the destruction of Babylon – the whore from whom the kings and merchants of the earth received riches.[14] Jesus indicated that having wealth made the gospel message of the kingdom difficult to receive, for entrance to the kingdom comes through faith in the gospel.

The disciples' astonishment at Jesus' words revealed their worldview as it related to wealth and spirituality. For the disciples, it was shocking to hear that it would be difficult for the wealthy to participate in redemption. The assumption seemed to be that being wealthy was an indicator of favor with God and a sure place in His coming kingdom.

Jesus' Explanation of Servanthood Corrects the Disciples' Views on Exaltation and Provides Service for Bartimaeus (10:35-52)

The disciples' thoughts about reaching Jerusalem concerned exaltation of their Messianic King. Such expectations also fueled posturing, visions of grandeur, and jealousy, even with Jesus right in their midst! The request for seating next to Jesus provided an opportunity for Jesus to teach what kingdom seating – *greatness in the kingdom of God* – is about. In doing so, He corrected the understanding of power in the hands of leadership in four discernible movements.

---

13. See Numbers 22:17-18; 1 Kings 13:8-9; 2 Kings 5:20-27.
14. See Matthew 6:19-24; 1 Timothy 6:9-10; Revelation 17:2; 18:9-17.

First, Jesus stated that the *kingdom is not about getting honor but being able to suffer for the gospel (10:35-39)*. James' and John's request to Jesus reversed the teacher-pupil relationship. By asking Jesus to serve them they were placing Him under them. Jesus willingly entertained their request with, 'What do you want me to do for you?'

In answering their request, Jesus intended for Zebedee's sons to be certain that they knew what they really were asking: *they were asking for Jesus' 'cup' and 'baptism.'* The cup and baptism point to Jesus' forthcoming death foretold in His three passion predictions (8:31; 9:31; 10:33-34).[15]

'Cup' has an Old Testament background.[16] It referred to the punishment of God's wrath upon sinful Israel and the nations. Jesus was looking ahead to when He would bear the wrath of God on behalf of Israel and the nations. 'Baptism,' when used as an image of terror, draws from the images of being overwhelmed by a flood.[17] As it is parallel with cup, it too spoke of the overwhelming nature of God's wrath – and that at the hands of the rulers of Israel and the people of the nations.[18] For Jesus, the path to the kingdom comes through the cross. Jesus foretold the martyrdom of James and the persecution of John: James was beheaded for the gospel (Acts 12:2) and John was exiled to Patmos (Rev. 1:9).

Second, *Jesus revealed that the kingdom of God is not about making requests for exaltation but accepting the sovereignty of God (10:40)*. He explained the different authority between Himself and the Father.[19] Historically this passage has been understood as an expression of Jesus' voluntary submission to the Father in humility to fulfill both of their roles in the plan of redemption.[20] The Father has already prepared the

---

15. Stein, *Mark*, 485.

16. Psalm 75:8, Isaiah 51:17, 22, and Jeremiah 25:15-29.

17. See, for example, Psalms 42:7; 88:10; Isaiah 43:2; Jonah 2:3.

18. Jesus predicts the role of the nations in His crucifixion in Mark 10:33; see also Acts 4:27 and 21:11.

19. Jesus uses 'My Father' in Matthew 20:23.

20. Both the Father and the Son are unified in the plan but have unique roles to various degrees. See Mark 13:32 on the Father's unique knowledge of the timing of the return of Christ, the Father's determination (decree) in the suffering of Christ for our salvation in Matthew 26:39, 42, and the Father's final exaltation above all when all is accomplished in 1 Corinthians 15:28.

seats for certain individuals; Jesus could not play favorites or wrongly judge who should receive them. His service is free from corruption and, likewise, so should ours be *since we cannot affect the decree of God*. Only disciples can be faithful.

Third, *Jesus revealed that the kingdom of God is not about lording authority but serving like our King (10:41-45)*. The indignant response of the disciples to James and John led to instructions on being 'great' and 'first' (vv. 43-44), which is the real issue of desiring seats of exaltation. Jesus said, in contrast, 'But it shall not be so among you.' 'The secular world may think that rulers should be good and fair rather than evil and oppressive, but Christian leadership is far more radical .... It does not involve being *masters* over others at all; instead, it involves being their *servant*.'[21] 'Servant' (Grk. *diakonos*) indicates *someone who waits at tables in service to the one over him* – menial service. 'Slave' (Grk. *doulos*) *referred to someone bound and in compulsory service, totally dependent on his owner*. Jesus made *servant* and *slave* the basic identity of anyone following Him to His kingdom.

The basis for becoming great through service is the sacrificial ministry of Jesus Himself. The one Mark identified as deity from the beginning of his Gospel account (1:1), indicated that He left His pre-existent state to 'come' as a human being (i.e., 'Son of Man,' cf. Gen. 3:15), yet not so that others could serve Him. Instead, He came in order to serve people by giving His life as a 'ransom' on behalf of 'many.' *Ransom* was a payment to secure the release of a slave or captive.[22] Origen (A.D. 182–254) first proposed that Christ paid a ransom to Satan; this is false. In Mark 14:24, Jesus' death seals a covenant with *God*.

'For' (Grk. *anti*) could be translated as 'on behalf of' or 'instead of.' It indicates that the ransom is a substitution in the place of those being ransomed. 'Many' alludes to Isaiah 53:12. The term is not fully inclusive like 'all,' seemingly pointing to the fact that not all in Israel will be saved, but only those for whom Christ died. Keller writes, 'If at the very heart of your worldview is a man dying for His enemies, then the way

21. Stein, *Mark*, 486.
22. See additional uses in Luke 24:21; Ephesians 1:7; 1 Timothy 2:6; Titus 2:14.

you're going to win influence in society is through service rather than power and control.'[23]

Fourth, *Jesus revealed that the kingdom of God is not about people's status, but about opening spiritual sight to Christ (10:46-52)*. Ronald Kernaghan writes, 'Treating people in our congregations with dignity and fairness is commendable. If our congregations are divided along economic, racial and social lines, however, the best we can do is to serve people who are just like us. That is a far cry from the vision Jesus set forth here.'[24] In line with Kernaghan's comments, note that Mark 10:46-52 and 10:35-45 share a verbal link:

> And Jesus said to him, 'What do you want me to do for you?' And the blind man said to Him, 'Rabbi, let me recover my sight' (Mark 10:51).

> And James and John, the sons of Zebedee, came up to Him and said to Him, 'Teacher, we want you to do for us whatever we ask of you.' *And He said to them, 'What do you want me to do for you?'* (Mark 10:35-36).

Jesus asked blind Bartimaeus the very thing He previously asked His two disciples, demonstrating His willingness to serve a blind beggar in the same way He would serve His own. For the reader, one is able to see that if followers of Jesus correctly understand service, they might have the opportunity to see the eyes of the blind opened to Jesus.

From his roadside position, the beggar Bartimaeus correctly identified Jesus as the final, promised Son of David, seeing what many of those with eyesight were unable to see. For him, the Nazarene of whom he has heard is the One with the power of the mercy of God to open the eyes of the blind. It seems that the son of Timaeus had connected Jesus with the prophecies of the coming Lord bringing sight to the blind.[25] More so, Bartimaeus had connected mercy with the Davidic Son, possibly drawing conclusions about the final

---

23. Timothy Keller, *King's Cross: The Story of the World in the Life of Jesus* (New York: Penguin Books, 2013), 149.

24. Ronald J. Kernaghan, *Mark* (Downers Grove, IL, 2007), 206.

25. See Isaiah 35:1-5; 42:6-7.

Son being one who would show mercy to the infirmed in a manner greater than that typified in David's kindness to Mephibosheth (2 Sam. 9).

Reflective Questions

1. How would the ministries, families, and congregations of which you are part change if no one desired to wield power over another and everyone made daily efforts to serve all others without fanfare, recognition, or thanksgiving? Is all your service to others completed with a willingness to suffer on behalf of those you serve, leaving your personal exaltation to the sovereignty of God?

2. Besides pre-marital counseling, what practices are needed in life before marriage to lay a strong foundation for a life-long marriage? What roles could older, mature, married and divorced believers play toward younger, maturing believers to see that all marriages are honoring to Jesus?

12

He Came to Rule and Maximize the Saints' Greater Worship
(Mark 11:1-26)

Martin Kähler described the Gospels as 'passion narratives with extended introductions.'[1] For Mark's Gospel in particular, this description is most apt. The writer uses ten chapters to give the story of three years of Jesus' earthly ministry. Then, in chapters eleven through sixteen, the writer spreads one week of ministry over six chapters. The narrative slows drastically from an average of one-third of a year per chapter to three-fourths of a day per chapter. Rightly, it would seem that the first ten chapters exist to bring focus to the last six chapters. The structure points to the passion narrative as the goal, introduced by ten chapters of previous ministry sped by very quickly.

Chapter 11 marks a turning point in the second Gospel. Three times Jesus had told the disciples of His fate in Jerusalem: *He will be rejected by the Jewish leadership, condemned by them, delivered over by them to the Gentiles, and mocked, spit upon, flogged, and killed by the Gentiles; then He will rise from the dead after three days.*[2] Jesus had not yet told the disciples that the cup and baptism of which He spoke would coordinate

---

1. Martin Kähler, *The So-called Historical Jesus and the Historic, Biblical Christ* (Minneapolis: Fortress Press, 1964), 80.

2. See Mark 8:31-32; 9:31; 10:32-34.

with the Passover, the Feast of the Unleavened Bread, and the weekly Jewish Sabbath. Neither did He mention crucifixion as the means of death. But the arrival in Jerusalem connects the passage to the three death predictions.

How odd it might seem, then, for the initial events in Jerusalem to center on Jesus' rule and worship of Him by some of the people. Jesus' authority was on display with the anticipation connected to the colt, the cursing and withering of the fig tree, and His cleansing of the Temple. With these scenes, those surrounding Him praised Him as the coming King, were astonished by His teaching, and were awed by His power over the fig tree. The Gospel writer connects these two themes to show the reader the relationship between submitting to the rule of Christ and our giving greater worship to Him.

Jesus' Rule Silences Skeptics So His Own Can Celebrate Him as Savior (11:1-11)

As Jesus and the disciples approached Jerusalem from the Mount of Olives, Zechariah's prophecy of the coming day of the Lord's battle against the nations might have been in view for His Jewish disciples:

> On that day His feet shall stand on the Mount of Olives that lies before Jerusalem on the east, and the Mount of Olives shall be split in two from east to west by a very wide valley, so that one half of the Mount shall move northward, and the other half southward (Zech. 14:4).

However, instead of initiating cataclysmic events, Jesus instructed the disciples to find a colt in the next village.

Jesus' rule was evident in His knowledge of the next village, the colt and it being tied, and its innocence as a beast of burden never employed into service. His knowledge of potential questioners and their immediate obedience further revealed Him as One with all knowledge and power to accomplish what He has determined will come to pass.

Naturally speaking, the potential confrontation over taking an innocent colt from another owner without permission might have been scary to the disciples. Yet the disciples obediently followed the command of Christ when they were confronted by those questioning their actions. In doing so they found that the response of the skeptics was in keeping with the words of Christ. Those objecting had no more to say when the disciples followed Christ's commands completely. They allowed the disciples to walk away with a colt that was not theirs so that the Lord's bidding would be done.[3]

As a result of the disciples' obedience to Christ, people would recognize Christ as King as He rode into Jerusalem. First, the disciples had thrown their cloaks on the colt so that Jesus the King did not sit on the bare back of the animal. Second, even though Jesus was not on foot, people laid down their cloaks and leafy branches so that He would not enter by coming on the dusty ground – actions that were 'unnecessary and extravagant.'[4]

Both the coming of Jesus on a colt and the laying of garments for a king had Old Testament passages in mind. When Jehu ascended to his throne, his followers immediately threw their garments on the bare ground to prevent his feet from walking on the ground (2 Kings 9:12-13). The Jewish Messiah was to come riding on a colt.[5] The people recognized Jesus as the One coming to rule over Israel, to vanquish their foes, and to grant to them the promises of God to restore and exalt Israel.[6]

With the establishment of Christ as King by the actions of the disciples and those with branches, an enthronement celebration took place. Crowds going before Jesus and also following Him portrayed a picture of them ascending to Jerusalem to enthrone her King.[7] The shouting of 'Hosanna'

---

3. Royce Gruenler remarks, 'Being unridden, the colt was consecrated to God (cf. Deut. 21:3; 1 Sam. 6:7)' (Gruenler, "Mark," Evangelical Commentary on the Bible [Baker Book House, 1995], 3:788).

4. France, Mark, 433.

5. Zechariah 9:9 with Genesis 49:11.

6. James Edwards, following Morna Hooker, notes that the commandeering of a beast of burden was the prerogative of a king in ancient times. He further suggests that an unbroken beast of burden was regarded as sacred, noting that the Mishnah (m. Sanh. 2:5) indicates that no one else may ride a king's horse (Edwards, Mark, 336; Morna D. Hooker, The Gospel According to St. Mark [New York: Continuum, 2001], 258).

7. See Psalms 24:3-10; 47:5.

from the final Great Hallel Psalm (Ps. 118:25) was a cry for the Messianic King to save Israel, His people.[8] The cry became shouts of praise in the mouths of the ascending throng.

Also taken from Psalm 118, 'Blessed is he who comes in the name of the Lord' was an exclamation of praise to the Messiah coming to rescue Israel (Ps. 118:26). The repeated parallel phrase clarified that the One coming in the name of the Lord would establish the kingdom promised to King David in 2 Samuel 7. That promise included the coming of a Davidic Son whose kingdom would have no end. In the minds of those shouting the Hillel songs on the trek to Jerusalem, Jesus was the final, promised King from the line of David.

To the final 'Hosanna' shout the worshipers added the phrase, 'in the highest.' As an exclamation, Hosanna became the greatest exclamation to the people's King.[9]

Although Jesus' entry into Jerusalem and the Temple portrayed Him as the coming King of Israel, He did not immediately establish His final rule and accept enthronement. He simply observed what was happening in the Temple and departed due to the lateness of the hour. This, too, might have had Messianic Advent overtones in fulfillment of Malachi 3:1.[10]

Quietly, however, Jesus had laid claim to the precinct of the Temple in fulfillment of Malachi 3:1 and would now begin to disclose how He would judge, cleanse, and occupy the sacred space.[11] The first Palm Sunday's celebration ended on a quiet, peaceful note with Jesus among the twelve – twelve who have just celebrated Him as Savior.

---

8. It might be best to understand 'Hosanna' as a phrase meaning, 'O Lord, save us now, I pray.' As Edwards states, 'The shout of "Hosanna" is a transliterated Hebrew word meaning, literally, "Save, I pray"' (Edwards, *Mark*, 336). In addition, *The NET Bible* editors propose 'the underlying Aramaic and Hebrew expressions meant "O Lord, save us …." *Hosanna* is an Aramaic expression that literally means, "help, I pray," or "save, I pray"' (*The NET Bible* (Dallas: Biblical Studies Press, 2005); notes on Mark 11:9.

9. Hooker writes, 'Hosanna in the highest! makes no sense if taken literally; this phrase shows that the word Hosanna had become simply a cry of jubilation' (Hooker, *St. Mark*, 260). Similarly notes Wessel, 'It had become simply an exclamation of praise' (Wessel, *Mark*, 725).

10. This is the suggestion of Gruenler, "Mark," 788.

11. ibid.

Jesus' Rule Condemns Faithlessness So That His Own Can Know Him as Creator (11:12-14)

The Holy Monday episode began with Jesus and the disciples returning from Bethany. The author indicates that Jesus traveled with hunger without relating the hunger to previous evening or morning activities. The simple expectation was that Jesus would find food as He traveled. A fig tree in the distance appeared to be a good candidate for satisfying Jesus' hunger. However, upon arriving at the tree, Jesus found unripe figs. Even though the author notes that it was not the season for ripe figs to be on the tree, Jesus cursed the tree for its apparent fruitlessness. Although the leaves indicated that there might be ripe figs, the tree had not been faithful to produce.

The cursing of the fig tree and its subsequent withering serve as an analogy for Israel and the Temple episode to follow. Four things indicate the pedagogical nature of the incident. First, identifying both Israel's faithlessness (or rebellion) toward God and Israel's judgment with fruitless or sick fig trees was a common device for the Old Testament prophet. For example, Jeremiah writes,

> When I would gather them, declares the Lord,
>   there are no grapes on the vine,
>   nor figs on the fig tree;
> even the leaves are withered,
>   and what I gave them has passed away from them.[12]

Second, the writer specifically notes that Jesus spoke in the hearing of the disciples. Those He previously had sent to proclaim the kingdom of God to Israel, who themselves were expecting the kingdom to come to Israel, and who later became those sent as apostles to proclaim the gospel to Israel, took note of the cursing as an event significant to them.

Third, Mark's sandwich of the story places the Temple incident between the two fig tree scenes. The technique makes the cleansing of the Temple the focus of the sandwich. The Temple's cleansing pertains to the fig tree's (or Israel's) fruitlessness when fruit is expected. What one expected in the

---

12. Jeremiah 8:13. See Isaiah 34:4; Jeremiah 29:17; Hosea 2:12; 9:16; Joel 1:7; Nahum 3:12; Micah 7:1.

Temple – especially with the arrival of the King of Israel – was not what one experienced upon entering the Temple. Israel was faithless toward the Temple activities and thus faithless toward God.

Fourth, immediately following Peter's announcement of the withered fig tree, Jesus used the incident to teach about faith in God. The fig tree pointed backward to the colt incident in which the sent disciples exercised faith in Christ's words. As one continues in the Passion narrative, the reader will discern that the fig tree also signified the faithless hearts of those in Israel shouting 'Hosanna' when Jesus arrived; they later crucified the One they exclaimed as He who brought 'the coming kingdom of our father David.' The lack of faith was evident in the robbery practiced and in the lack of prayer in the Temple.

The analogy of the fig tree and Jesus' words of cursing should not be pressed outside of the canon's theological boundaries, however. Israel was not cursed in such a manner that they become completely useless as the dispersing of Jewish converts to all the earth in the book of Acts readily affirms.

Jesus' Rule Corrects Busyness So His Own Can Be Awed by Him as Teacher (11:15-19)

The Jewish hope was that their King will establish Himself in Jerusalem, fulfill the promises of His kingdom to Israel, and vanquish their foes. Thus, the people of Israel should have been ready to receive Jesus as their King. Yet the people showed that their daily expectation of meeting the King did not have proper daily preparations for meeting the King as ruler over every aspect of their lives.

Jesus' efforts to restore the Temple to a house of prayer for the nations coincided with His coming to be recognized as King. The previous verses reveal this: 'Blessed is the coming *kingdom* of our father David! Hosanna in the highest' (v. 10). The promises to David in 2 Samuel 7 and all prophecies of the coming divine King would be completed in Jesus! God's promises of deliverance, recompense, vengeance, restoration, rest, inheritance, and His very own presence among His people would all be fulfilled in the Son of David. This should have been a cause for contrition, repentance, praise, and celebration by those gathered in the Temple.

However, as the narrative shows, because the individual and corporate focuses in the Temple were wrong, the significance of Jesus coming to meet His people in the Temple was lost. The reader will await the coronation of Israel's Messiah-King, and Mark will take us through Calvary's cross to get there.

The sellers and buyers in the Temple performed commercial activities so that people could obtain items for sacrifice on-site rather than take them from their homes. The money-changers provided a means for people to exchange their currency for the Temple currency for offerings (Exod. 30:13-16), but (wrongly) for a small fee.

The sellers of pigeons were a subset of the sellers who provided a way for those with less means to secure items to offer for sacrifice.[13] Each of the merchants offered a well-intended service: *Make it possible for anyone who comes to the Temple to worship.* Yet, Jesus restricted everyone from carrying any item through the Temple, and He upset the Temple's commercial activities because the activities themselves – not the motives, cheating, or intentions – did not allow for God's purpose for the Temple to be accomplished: 'And he was teaching them and saying to them, "Is it not written, 'My house shall be called a house of prayer for all the nations?' But you have made it a den of robbers'" (v. 17).

When Solomon dedicated the first Temple, he indicated that the Temple was a place for three things. First, it was a place for God's name to dwell on the earth. Second, it was a location to which people of the earth could direct their prayers and have the Lord act on their behalf (1 Kings 8:27-30). Foreigners – people from outside of Israel (i.e., 'the nations') – would be able to pray to the God of Israel and have their prayers answered. This would be possible because, third, the Temple had an evangelistic and missiological intention, making known the Lord as the greatest of all.[14]

Isaiah recognized the evangelistic and missiological purpose for the Temple and Jeremiah rebuked Israel for thinking they could find the safety promised in the Temple

---

13. See Leviticus 1:14; 5:7; 12:8; cf. Luke 2:24.
14. See 1 Kings 8:60; see also 1 Kings 8:43.

without having the holiness required for the Temple.[15] Based on their sinful actions in daily society, the sojourning worshipers of Israel came to God's Temple as robbers – robbers of money concerning the people, and robbers of worship of God concerning themselves.

Thus, Jesus indicated that the problem of the sellers and money-changers was not business; the problem was that the *busyness* inside the Temple prevented the true business of the Temple, and the works outside the Temple negated the worship in the Temple. If God will dwell in His house and be received as King, then prayer should characterize His house as the primary activity, and other things should be cut away so that this can take place. Busyness robbed those approaching the Temple of meeting with God in the way that Jesus would have us meet with God, and have God meet with us.

The chief priests and scribes should have been glad for the cleansing of the Temple in light of the prophecy of Malachi (Mal. 3:1-4). However, as the ones approving of the selling and busy carrying of merchandise through the Temple, they took offense with Jesus teaching a different function for the Temple. If Jesus continued to teach, they would lose the control of the hearts of the people. Thus, motives were in question and revealed: *The leaders of Israel desired busyness to continue because their interest was not in exalting the name of the Lord among the nations. Instead, their interest was in their own exaltation in the eyes of the people.*

The fear of the Jewish leadership revealed that they recognized the authority of Jesus. They did not submit to it, so the fear did not represent a change of heart. In contrast, the crowd marveled at His teaching on prayer and robbery in the Temple. For the crowd, too, the awe did not equal full submission. However, the Lord would have no competitors to His rule. He simply left the city.

Jesus' Rule Commends Faith So That His Own Can Experience His Power as Lord (11:20-26)

The previous evening's departure from the city meant a return to Bethany. This explains the next morning's return

---

15. See Isaiah 56:6-8; Jeremiah 7:5-11.

to the city on a path that passed the previously encountered fig tree.

The withering to the roots rather than of only the leaves and upper branches manifested the rule of Christ. A natural process of withering would have necessitated evaporation of all water from the tree and rotting over a much longer period. The total decay of the tree overnight was supernatural, the significance of which was not lost on Peter. Peter attributes the tree's demise to Jesus' words of cursing. The analogy to the Temple's coming destruction in A.D. 70 is evident.

Jesus, however, did not give an interpretation of the death of the fig tree. Instead, He used the event to commend faith in God to do the impossible. Combined with Peter's connection of Jesus' cursing with the tree's death, 'Truly, I say to you' makes the statement to follow carry the same weight as the cursing. Just as His followers could trust the fig tree to be withered in a night by the Word of Christ, so they could trust God to move a mountain they asked Him to move.

The words of Jesus raise questions about the working of prayer to the contemporary reader, even though those questions are not the concern of the author. He records that Jesus simply proclaimed truth about prayer and then related a parable. The lack of explanation or subsequent discussion by the disciples indicates that they understood the meaning of His words: *the disciples' practice of prayer in submission to God meets conditions to experience the Father's power.*[16]

The promises of Jesus in these words did not amount to *carte blanche* opportunities and self-serving windfalls for the supplicants. If so, the Mount of Olives (*this* mountain) would be removed only once when the first asked for its removal, or it would need to be replaced after the first movement to fulfill similar requests later on. Yet the Old Testament reader knows that the Mount of Olives must be present for eschatological purposes and thus could not be thrown into the sea at the request of a first-century disciple. The saying has inherent

---

16. Although 11:23 is written with the singular 'whoever,' the recipients of Jesus' words in 11:24-25 are described as plural. This does not necessarily mean that Jesus here is commending corporate prayer; He simply is speaking to the entire group rather than holding out a promise to any one person who has faith to speak to the mountain.

hyperbole but does point to the power of God to respond to the prayer of the supplicant submitted to His rule. It is the Father's power that will move the mountain, doing for the disciple that for which he has asked.

Each of the statements in 11:23-25 follows a pattern: 1) A form of request to God (because God always is the object of prayer); 2) a faith action required on the part of the supplicant; and 3) a promise to the supplicant of God's fulfillment of the response to the request made with the faith action (see Fig. 1).

Pattern	11:23	11:24	11:25
Form of Request to God	Truly, I say to you, whoever says to this mountain, 'Be taken up and thrown into the sea.	Therefore I tell you, whatever you ask in prayer	And whenever you stand praying
Faith Action	and does not doubt in his heart, but believes that what he says will come to pass,	believe that you have received it,	forgive, if you have anything against anyone
Promise of Fulfillment	it will be done for him.	and it will be yours	so that your Father also who is in heaven may forgive you your trespasses.'

FIGURE 1 – Pattern of Prayer Instructions in Mark 11:23-25

The pattern manifests the forgiving of trespasses to be an act of faith as much as is speaking to the mountain without doubt. The asking of forgiveness is assumed in forgiving others of trespasses; the disciple seeks forgiveness because the other person is looking to God for forgiveness. All three forms of prayer in the pattern are looking for God to do what only the power of His rule can do.

Conclusion

The relationship between seeing Jesus as ruler and that sight fueling greater worship is not obvious. Commonly, we want to submit to portions of His rule and then worship Him as Lord of all. But this is as incongruent as cluttering the Temple with good intentions only to have the demise of prayer.

When Christ's disciples see His full power over skeptics, faithlessness, and busyness, they will be drawn to even greater worship of their God. God loves for His people to approach Him in prayer as a church. He desires to see fruitfulness from them at all times. He wills to give them favor in the eyes of skeptics. He will gladly move the individual mountains for them.

Reflective Questions

1. To what error does the business in the Temple point toward?

2. If you were to aid your congregation in strengthening prayer during its meeting times, what things would be necessary to do? How would your method of prayer contribute to this strengthening?

13

He Came for Close Encounters of the Elite and Objecting Kind
(Mark 11:27–12:44)

Texts from both James and Paul reveal concerns that the early church had with those of the socially elite class. James asks, 'Are not the rich the ones who oppress you, and the ones who drag you into court?' (James 2:6). Similarly, Paul writes, 'Where is the one who is wise? Where is the scribe? Where is the debater of this age? Has not God made foolish the wisdom of the world?' (1 Cor. 1:20).

In James' inquiry, it is specifically the wealth of persons that brings them into opposition to the church. This does not condemn all persons with great wealth. Instead, it recognizes that for some it is their very wealth that is their cause of conflict with believers. The wealthy are used to being honored for their wealth, whereas following Christ calls for a lowering of oneself, of being aware of greed, and not looking at external matters like riches but matters of one's heart.[1]

Paul's line of questioning concerns intelligent and professional scribes. Their familiarity and debating with texts and ideas gave them an intellectual capacity above many. However, it also often brought with it great pride and a disparaging look upon those without superior intellect and/or rhetorical skills. But following Christ is a calling to humility,

---

1. See John 3:30; Luke 12:15; 1 Samuel 16:7.

courtesy in speech, and the use of one's intellectual capacities to build up people and proclaim the greatness of God.

One might therefore see how those of elite social classes might come into conflict with the church, looking down upon the church as a weaker group, dismissing her message of the kingdom of God as otherworldly rather than pertaining to matters of importance in the present world. The elite might even want to push back against the church's worldview in order to maintain a sense of right about their elitism, honor among people, and control of opinions and philosophies of the day. This is the sort of pushback that brought the Jewish elite into a series of questions with Jesus and His interpretation of the Law and Prophets.

Structure of Mark 11:27–12:44

In theory, Mark 11:27 should form the beginning of a new chapter because the unit of Mark 11:27–12:44 is set apart from both Mark 11:1-26 and Mark 13 structurally. The entering and leaving of the Temple in 11:27 and 13:1 are the first indicators that 11:27–12:44 forms a distinct series of episodes.

Mark 13 then veers from the questions about the teachings of Law and the Prophets into questions related to the destruction of the Temple and accompanying signs (v. 4). It is no longer the Jewish elite who were peppering Jesus with questions about His interpretative views. Instead, now on the Mount of Olives, it was the disciples who wanted to understand Jesus' statement about the stones of the Temple.

The chapter also is bound by Jesus' relentless rebuke and/or condemnation of the Jewish leadership.[2] Pharisees, Herodians, Sadducees, elders, scribes, and rich persons all receive statements of judgment in this chapter, with the scribes taking the most hits. The entire scope of Jewish ruling class stands in stark comparison to the poor widow. Each group approaches Jesus with a question to find error

---

2. See 11:33; 12:8, 17, 24, 27, 37, 38-40 for statements of condemnation and rebuke. Even in the parable, the vineyard owner will destroy the tenants for their obstinance and treachery and will remove the vineyard from them. The term 'condemnation' (Grk. Κρίμα) is a term for legal judgment or condemnation – an unfavorable decision ['κρίμα,' *TDNT*, 942]). The statement, 'For they all contributed out of their abundance' (12:44), has the tone of condemnation when compared to the commendation of the poor widow.

in Him.[3] Jesus responds in ways that prevent Him from being found in error.[4] The questioners then are silenced, or observers respond with awe.[5]

Unity of Ideas in Mark 11:27–12:44

The structuring of Mark 11:27–12:44 points toward the central idea that the author communicates by the words, tone, and theology of this unit. I propose the statement below with an explanation to follow: *Jesus' questioning encounters with the Jewish ruling class and the poor in the Temple on complex interpretive matters in the Law and the Prophets condemned those in error about the Son due to impure motives and commended those who understood the sacrifice required by the Law.* This is the explanation of the statement:

Jesus' Questioning … on Matters of the Law and the Prophets
Each question the Jewish leadership brought to Jesus concerned matters of the Law: the basis of authority (to speak as prophet or teacher),[6] paying taxes to a Gentile government,[7] Levirate Marriage,[8] and the Greatest Commandments.[9] Jesus' rebuke of the scribes looked at the Prophets[10] and the Mosaic

---

3. See 11:28; 12:14, 19-23, 28.

4. See 11:29-30; 12:16, 17, 24-27, 29-31.

5. See 11:33; 12:12, 17, 34, 37.

6. See the reference to John the Baptist being a 'prophet' in 11:32. Like John the Baptist, if Jesus is a prophet, He must have the authority to speak on behalf of God from heaven (cf. Deut. 13:1-5; 18:15-22). The Markan narrative early identifies Jesus as a prophet (Mark 6:4, 15).

7. France comments on the relationship of the question of paying taxes to Old Testament law: 'All Mark's previous uses of ἔξεστιν (2:24, 26; 3:4; 6:18; 10:2) have referred to what is permitted under *divine* law, whether that of the Old Testament directly or that of current scribal interpretation of the Old Testament. When the matter under discussion is one which is not only permitted but mandatory under the law of the Roman occupation, to phrase the question in terms of what is "permitted" is to suggest the possibility of a conflict between divine and human law. It invites Jesus to claim divine sanction for opposing the human government' (France, *Mark*, 468).

8. See Deuteronomy 25:5-10. In His response, Jesus speaks of His opponents not knowing 'the Scriptures' (Mark 12:24), and He quotes the Old Testament in the rebuke (Mark 12:26).

9. Jesus cites commandments from Deuteronomy 6:4-5 and Leviticus 19:18 to explain the greatest commandments to the scribe.

10. Jesus quotes Psalm 110:1.

Law on care of widows.[11] The giving of the widow was on the basis of the Law.[12]

Complex Interpretive Matters

Each of the questions raised by the adversaries or by Jesus was a matter of complex interpretation. On the issue of Jesus' authority, the question hinged on how one interpreted John the Baptist's ministry. On the parable's interpretation, Jesus asked, 'Have you not read?' He then cited Psalm 118:22-23 in conjunction with the understanding of the parable. On paying taxes to Caesar, the Pharisees said the words, 'teach the way of God ... is it lawful,' posing what seems like a conundrum – a 'trap' (Mark 12:13). The Sadducees did not believe in the resurrection and thought that proposing what was absurd would lead to justification of their belief. However, Jesus replied, 'You do not know the Scriptures,' making the issue about interpretation, not simply about differing worldviews. The scribe asked Jesus an opinion about the most important of all of the 613 legal stipulations in the Law. In the resulting dialogue, the words 'you are right' (12:32) and 'answered wisely' were judgments about Jesus' interpretation. Jesus proposes a question about the interpretation of Psalm 110:1, asking, 'How can the scribes say of Psalm 110:1 that it is speaking of Christ?'

Condemns Those in Error about the Son Due to Impure Motives

The first group questioned the authority of Jesus even though they recognized Him as the God-sent son (based upon the parable [12:12]).[13] They wanted the vineyard (e.g., Israel) for themselves and were afraid of the people turning from them.[14] The attempts to trap Jesus and find fault with Him manifested a lack of understanding of His divine Sonship; Jesus demonstrated that the scribes were wrong in not knowing that the Son of David is also David's Lord.[15]

---

11. 'Devour widows' houses' (Mark 12:40) indicates injustice toward widows (cf. Exod. 22:22; Deut. 10:18; 14:29; 24:19-21; Isa. 1:17, 23; 10:2; Ezek. 22:7; Zech. 7:10).

12. See Nehemiah 10:38; 12:44; Malachi 3:10.

13. See also Matthew 21:45 and Luke 20:19.

14. This is evident in 12:7 and 12:12.

15. The questions about the scribes reveal that they err in understanding that the Davidic Son-Messiah is the divine Lord of heaven (cf. 12:37).

Also, Jesus revealed that the rich said their public prayers for 'pretense.'[16]

Commends Those Who Understood the Sacrifice Required by the Law
The scribe who was commended understood that keeping the greatest commandments of the Law is the sacrifice the Lord desires (Mark 12:33). The widow understood that giving her all was the sacrifice required by the Temple authorities to meet the Temple requirements.[17] (In contrast, through the passage, the Jewish leadership believed their understanding of the Law was correct and the rich thought that the appearance of greatness and giving from abundance was pleasing to God.)

The Encounter with Skeptical Religious Authorities (11:27–12:12)
The first encounter involved both a meeting with the Jewish leadership and an interpretation of the encounter by means of a parable. The parable revealed more about the encounter than what was stated explicitly in the exchange.

Encounter (11:27-33)
Jesus' return to Jerusalem brought Him again to the Temple. Unlike the Gospels' accounts of Him cleansing the Temple, Jesus did not provoke an encounter with the Temple populous or authorities.[18] His walking in the Temple was as casual and uneventful as His observatory visit on Palm Sunday (Mark 11:11). It was the Jewish authorities who turned Jesus' visit into a question-and-answer session.

The coming of the elders, chief priests, and scribes together initiated a fulfillment of Jesus' prophetic words about their rejection of Him in Jerusalem.[19] The reader should anticipate an attempt at this scene to hand Jesus over to suffer and be killed. However, Jesus' answer delayed the time of

---

16. From the Grk., πρόφασις, the term means 'to pretend to be engaged in a particular activity' (πρόφασις, *Louw-Nida*, 766), or to do an act 'by subterfuge, for deception' (πρόφασις, *EDNT*, 182).

17. See 12:42 with the commendation in 12:44.

18. Compare with Matthew 21:12-13; Mark 11:15-18; Luke 19:45-47; John 2:14-16.

19. The three are mentioned together in 8:31. The chief priests and the scribes are mentioned together in 10:33 without mention of the elders.

apprehension because God's decree required much more before Jesus drank the Father's cup.

The question the Jewish leaders brought concerned Jesus' authority, and whether that was inherent or conferred. Implicit in the questioning was that Jesus did not have the authority of anyone in leadership in Jerusalem to perform miracles, forgive sins, break the Sabbath and traditions of the elders, cleanse the Temple, and teach what is not the interpretation of the Pharisees and scribes.[20] Both legally and politically, lacking the authority of these three divisions of the Jewish authorities might have presented a problem with Jesus' authority in the eyes of the people. As Kernaghan comments:

> They were the most powerful people in Jerusalem. They controlled the temple, oversaw the resolution of legal disputes and administered the political and financial affairs of the Jewish people. They had not come to conduct a disinterested inquiry about Jesus' credentials. His actions in the temple on the previous day were a direct affront to their leadership. Ultimately, they were the ones He had accused of robbery. A delegation composed of these people indicates how deeply He had shaken things up. Precisely what they hoped to get from Him is impossible to say, but the questions they posed about His authority were not objective theological inquiries. They were legally and politically charged.[21]

The questioning concerned Jesus' right to do His actions rather than the actions themselves.[22] The perception that Jesus was speaking by His own authority was an issue throughout His earthly ministry.[23] Yet if He were to claim that His authority was given by God, He could be accused of blaspheming.

Wisely, seeing the double-dilemma of answering without the authority of the Sanhedrin or claiming the authority of God the Father, Jesus did not answer the question posed. Instead, He offered to answer the question

---

20. On the problem with breaking the tradition of the elders, see Mark 7:3-5.

21. Kernaghan, *Mark*, 224.

22. Edwards, *Mark*, 351.

23. See the concern about 'own authority' in John 5:30; 7:17, 18; 8:28; 12:49; 14:10.

if they would answer one question for Him – literally, 'one word'[24] – on a source of authority. The question pertained to John the Baptist's authority to baptize and preach. The offer to the representatives from the Sanhedrin was legitimate, for either answer would be an admittance of the Jewish leadership's failure to submit to divine authority. A previous failure would imply the possibility of failing to recognize and submit to the divine authority behind Jesus' action.

The chief priests, scribes, and elders discussed among themselves two potential ways to respond. A response that said that John's authority came from heaven would be an admittance that they did not want to do the will of God. It would reveal what the reader already knows based on their previous actions with Jesus: their personal intentions are more important to them than pleasing God. They could not return this answer without condemning themselves.

The alternative response would put the Sanhedrin in direct conflict with those under their rule. The people recognized the Baptizer as a prophet; he spoke as one revealing the oracles of God. To diminish John's authority as deriving from a human source rather than God Himself would bring the ire of the people. The editorial comment about the Jewish leadership's fear of the people demonstrated that their own questioning was a concern about control and power, not about ensuring that both they and Jesus were honoring God. David Garland comments:

> These corrupt leaders do not want to lose credibility with the crowds or alienate them because that may disrupt their scheme to do away with Jesus. Mark's comment that 'they feared the people' (11:32) reveals that their authority derives from humans because they do not fear heaven. These leaders only dreaded losing face before the crowds and will ultimately lose their souls. They may evade Jesus' question, but they cannot evade God's judgment.[25]

---

24. The words translated as 'one question' are ἕνα λόγον, 'one word.' Word has a collective sense here, hence the translation. But grammatically it is significant to later words in the parable. See comments below on 12:6.

25. Garland, *Mark*, 443-44.

The answer that Jesus' opponents gave, 'We do not know,' was calculated, but it was not a lie. Both potential answers revealed that they considered that it was possible that John the Baptist's authority originated with God. To answer such would open the possibility that Jesus acted on the authority of God. Therefore, they delivered to Jesus a non-answer in order to avoid self-condemnation. The ploy resulted in them being the cause of not securing from Jesus an answer to the question they had posed to him.

Parabolic Interpretation of the Encounter (12:1-12)

The 'and' connector in 12:1 ties the parable to the encounter in the Temple. Jesus vividly portrayed the issues surrounding the questioning of the source of His authority by the leaders by means of a story intended to be analogous to the exchange in 11:27-33. The parable placed the exchange in the large context of redemptive history, specifically, 'the perspective of God's long and turbulent relationship with Israel.'[26]

The building of the vineyard, fence (or wall), winepress, pit, and tower was the common practice of preparing a vineyard for the collection of grapes and wine as well as giving protection and shelter for the vineyard owner.[27] The terms also connected the passage to Isaiah 5:1-5 and the song of the vineyard – an allegory speaking of the Lord and His relationship to Israel. The building of the vineyard in Isaiah 5 has a description like the building of the vineyard in Mark 12:1-2, minus the building of the fence around the vineyard. The similarity indicates that Jesus was speaking of Israel by means of the parable, as previous references to Israel being a 'vineyard' would support.[28]

Absentee landlords who trusted rent collection to tenants were known in first-century Israel.[29] Rather than receiving from rent collection, however, this landlord intended to collect produce from the stewards of his own vineyard. If

---

26. Garland, *Mark*, 450.

27. Wessel, *Mark*, 731.

28. See Psalm 80:8-16; Isaiah 5:7; Jeremiah 2:21; 12:10.

29. Hooker, *Saint Mark*, 274.

all factors remained as is, one would expect the tenants to send back produce with thanksgiving and kindness toward the landlord.

Like the allegorical background of 'vineyard,' 'servant' and 'servants,' *being sent* has echoes to the Lord's sending of prophets to Israel. Jeremiah is particularly informative for a background to this parable:

> From the day that your fathers came out of the land of Egypt to this day, I have persistently sent all my servants the prophets to them, day after day. Yet they did not listen to me or incline their ear, but stiffened their neck. They did worse than their fathers. So you shall speak all these words to them, but they will not listen to you. You shall call to them, but they will not answer you. And you shall say to them, 'This is the nation that did not obey the voice of the LORD their God, and did not accept discipline; truth has perished; it is cut off from their lips.'[30]

Jeremiah's condemnation traced the history of Israel's rejection of God's words through His prophets to their earliest identification as a nation. The contemporaries of Jeremiah were guilty of worse obstinance than the earliest generations of Israelites. With certainty, they would treat Jeremiah's words as they had treated the words of the prophets before him. Rejection of God-sent servants characterized the routine of Israel's sojourn with God.

Like Jeremiah's audience, Jesus' detractors did not listen to the Word of God. The nation had rejected the voice of the Lord through Jesus. Even more poignant then would be the actions of the tenant in the parable when the son of the landowner arrived to collect produce. By means of the parable, Mark portrays the Sanhedrin's rejection of Jesus within the history of Israel rejecting the prophets.

The tenants' mistreatment of the vineyard owner's servants was deplorable. The land tenants brutally struck the first servant with blows and sent him back to the owner battered and with no produce in hand. While the empty-handed return could look innocent enough on its own, the

---

30. Jeremiah 7:25-28. See also 2 Chronicles 36:15; Jeremiah 25:4; Daniel 9:6; Amos 3:7; and Zechariah 1:6.

return of a servant at the hands of the stewards would send a message of hateful rejection to the landowner of his request and thus of himself.

Undaunted, the landowner sent a second and third servant. But with each dispatch, the abuse of the servants increased. Mark locates the second's wounding to be directed at his head and to be accompanied by other disrespectful treatment in general. With the third servant, the land renters resorted to murder. The passage does not present any reason on the part of the landowner for why his servants would receive treatment like this.

It is significant that the escalation of the abuse did not result in the death of every sent servant. Some receive maltreatment short of death. But some sent by the owner did pay for their ambassadorship with their lives.

The callousness with which the vineyard workers treated the servants came to a head with the owner sending his son. First, the tenants sent a clear message of refusal to do what the owner had requested and their willingness to resort to violence and murder and to remain unmoved in their hard-heartedness. It was evident that they had regard for none of the servants and that they hated the owner.[31]

Second, it was risky on the part of the owner to send the son into such a hostile environment. The treatment of the servants was not a mishap; it was an established pattern. Many servants came to the vineyard and the tenants' mistreatment did not wane toward any of the servants.

The landowner 'had still one other, a beloved son.' Literally, the Greek order has 'one son beloved.' Edwards suggests that the 'one son' corresponds to the 'one word' of 11:29.[32] As the Jewish leaders rejected the 'one word' of Jesus historically, so in the fictional telling of the owner and his vineyard the land tenants rejected the one son of the owner. For the reader, 'beloved' also ties the parable to the earthly ministry of Jesus

---

31. It seems possible to compartmentalize the treatment of the owner's servants from the tenants' feelings about the owner. However, it is highly unlikely that they would have had favorable feelings toward the owner that did not translate into kind and grateful treatment of the owner's servants. The actions revealed the hearts of the servants toward the owner.

32. Edwards, *Mark*, 351.

as Mark identified Jesus as 'beloved' at both His baptism and the Transfiguration.[33]

It seems right to ask, 'What farmer in his right mind would surrender his son to such tenants?'[34] Yet the owner thought that the tenants would respect the son – the one with legal right to the vineyard as the heir – rather than treat him as a simple representative of the owner. Nothing in the land renters' treatment of the sent servants warranted such thought on the part of the owner. Out of his own hope for a change in the attitudes and actions of the tenants did the owner expect respect for the son he loved.

The owner's sending of the son revealed four things about the stewards of the land. First, the tenants discussed the approaching servant, akin to the discussion that the elders, chief priests, and scribes had over Jesus' question about John's authority in 11:30. Their decision was not haphazard; it was premeditated.

Second, they recognized the servant as the son with the legal right to the vineyard, for they identified him as 'heir' rather than simply as 'son' or even as 'beloved son.' They recognized a significant difference between the previous 'servants' and this one now approaching.

Third, the option chosen for the heir was death. Again, even with the previous escalation of the maltreatment of the servants, all of them were not victims of murder. But beating and suffering shamefully were not an option for the heir, for he was the heir as long as he was alive. Mark's readers, already knowing that the Jewish leadership intends to have Jesus killed, should connect the words of the tenants to the plans of the Sanhedrin council.

Fourth, the words of the tenants revealed the real motives behind their handling of the servants and the son of the owner: *they wanted the vineyard for themselves, taking the prerogative of the owner and the right to inheritance of the son-heir.* Their conclusion was faulty, legally. But they laid

---

33. Wessel proposes that *agapētos* ('beloved') probably means 'only' in this usage, following the LXX of Genesis 22:2, 12, 16 (Wessel, *Mark*, 732). In each of those verses, a form of *agapētos* translates the Hebrew *yâchîyd* ('sole' or 'only').

34. Edwards, *Mark*, 357.

bare their intentions, pointing back to the intentions of the Jewish leaders behind their non-answer to Jesus' question on authority: *they questioned Jesus' right to do as He had been doing because they wanted to have authority in Israel rather than Jesus (and God the Father) having authority.*[35]

The land workers were far from being correct in the predicted outcome of killing the owner's son.[36] What they thought would be a life of gaining produce from the land and keeping it and its profits for themselves turned out to be their own death sentence.

The quotation in verses 10-11 is from Psalm 118, a psalm familiar to Markan readers (and probably Jesus' hearers) as the Psalm from which the crowds shouted 'Save now' in 11:9-10. The idea of salvation in Jesus the Son already swirled in the environment from Jesus' approach to the Temple two days earlier. The quotation is verbatim from the LXX.

---

35. On this verse, Edwards comments, 'If humanity can dispense with God, or even kill God, then humanity can become God' (Edwards, *Mark*, 359).

36. Scholars are divided on how to read the casting of the son from the vineyard within the allegory. France sees 'obvious symbolic significance in relation to the rejection of Jesus,' but he does not see it connecting to Jesus' suffering outside of Jerusalem as in the case of the Matthean and Lukan accounts, it may be that Mark only intends a 'vivid climax' (France, *Mark*, 461).

Wessel is more cautious toward reading the suffering of Jesus outside of Jerusalem into the casting out of the son, suggesting, 'throwing the son out of the vineyard is another detail of the story that should not be allegorized' (Wessel, *Mark*, 732). Yet the casting of the son out of the vineyard is a necessary detail; the writer does not mention the bodily fates of the corpses of the servants. Thus, this detail has significance in the parable and thus in history by way of analogy.

Edwards' proposal may be best: 'The parallel verse in Matt 21:39 alters this part of the parable thus: "So they took him and threw him out of the vineyard and killed him."' Matthew's sequence of events more closely corresponds to the actual passion events, i.e., Jesus was arrested, taken out of Jerusalem, and crucified (so John 19:17; Heb 13:12). Matthew's alteration again argues for Markan priority, for it is easier to explain why Matthew might alter the Markan sequence to correspond to the historical sequence of the passion than to explain why Mark would corrupt an otherwise historical allusion in Matthew. It is possible (though not very likely, in my judgment) that the difference in sequence reflects the Evangelists' understanding of those responsible for Jesus' death: for Mark, Jesus was killed inside the vineyard and then thrown outside, i.e., both rejected and killed by Jews; whereas for Matthew and Luke, Jesus was thrown outside and killed, i.e., rejected by the Jews but killed by the Romans (Edwards, *Mark*, 359). The Jewish leadership's role as (ir)responsible stewards over Israel was removed and transferred initially to the twelve apostles and the Apostle Paul (Matt. 21:43; Acts 13:46; 18:6; 28:28). Their ministry to Israel and the remnant of believing Israel reflects such stewardship.

Psalm 118:22-23 speaks of the rejection of a large stone as useless to the construction of a building.[37] The rejected stone later became a most significant stone in the finalization of the edifice's construction as the 'head of the corner' that held the building together.[38] Coinciding with the use of the parable, Jesus employed Psalm 118:22-23 as support for the parable. Its use was as equally analogous as the parable to the prior discussion on authority. The introduction, 'Have you not read,' required the first-century Jewish reader to share Jesus' understanding that the meaning of the Psalm and the teaching of the parable agree and equally speak analogously.

In Psalm 118, the psalmist's call for Israel and all nations to give thanks to the Lord for His enduring steadfast love recounted the Lord's valiant power as His personal saving refuge in the face of surrounding enemy nations. That call to give thanks also exalted the Lord as the Savior of Israel.[39]

Jesus recognized that the 'stone' of Psalm 118 referred to the individual psalmist who was attacked by the surrounding nations as the discipline of the Lord and who then experienced rescue as he made the Lord his refuge.[40] It was the rejection and exaltation of the 'stone' (the psalmist) that brought salvation to all of Israel. Jesus recognized that no such day had yet fulfilled the words of the psalmist for all nations to

---

37. Wessel is overreading what is behind the text when suggesting that Solomon's Temple is in view in Psalm 118 (Wessel, *Mark*, 732-33). Kerneghan is also overreading what is behind the text when he suggests that the building of the Second Temple is in view (Kerneghan, *Mark*, 227-29). Neither the Psalm's superscription nor any of its verses suggest such.

38. The 'stone' could refer to a cornerstone near the base of a building or the stone between an archway. Either stone position has a place of prominence.

39. Explanation: the psalmist calls for Israel and all nations of the earth to give thanks to the Lord for His enduring steadfast love throughout the psalm (vv. 1-4, 15, 19, 21, 29). 'Recount' is used in verse 17 and is large enough to encompass the activity of the psalmist as he remembers the Lord's victories and communicates them to Israel. The Lord's valiant power (vv. 15, 16) as His personal saving refuge is on display in saving the individual psalmist from the surrounding nations (vv. 10-13) and in saving the psalmist from his personal sins (v. 18). Throughout the psalm the nation of Israel (and the remnant of those who fear the Lord among the tribe of Aaron especially) cry out from her tents and exalt the Lord as the Savior of Israel because she has witnessed the Lord save the psalmist (vv. 2-4, 15-16, 24-27).

40. Wessel overreads the psalm when he views the stone as the nation rather than the individual. It is the psalmist who is surrounded by his enemies and delivered (vv. 10-13) that sets the example for Israel. See Wessel, *Mark*, 733.

offer praise to the Lord for the salvation of Israel. The 'day' of the 'stone's' rejection and exaltation – in which he would live and not die – was forward pointing to a final stone that would make the worship of all nations possible.

The use of Psalm 118:22-23 depicted the Sanhedrin's rejection of Jesus' authority akin to the ancient Gentile nations' attack on the psalmist. The possible ties of the stone to the son by wordplay further supported the parallel between the psalm and the parable.[41] Jesus indicated that His own rejection would lead to His exaltation. The Markan audience should have in mind His three predictions of 8:31, 9:31, and 10:32-33. Figure 2 charts the movement of Psalm 118:22-23 through the historical referent to which the analogy points:

Stone Rejected	Jesus Rejected	Owner's Son Rejected	Stone Rejected
Material stone for an unknown building cast aside as useless.	Son of God for Israel rejected as Messiah with plans for destruction (death), yet with a prophecy of third day rising.	Son of vineyard owner as sent representative and heir cast out.	Son of God – the owner of Israel, rejected and crucified, will rise from the dead.

FIGURE 2 – Movement of Psalm 118:22-23

The additional line in 12:11 from Psalm 118:23 manifested the decree of God in the rejection of the stone and the stone's exaltation. Like the vineyard owner sending the servants and the son, the Father sent the Son in authority to Israel and was completely directing the events for the rejection, crucifixion, resurrection, and final exaltation of the Son. Implicit in Jesus' use of the quotation was His own resurrection: although rejected and eventually killed, Israel will have a day in which they will marvel at Him living, having been rescued by the Lord.

The leaders' decision to avoid arresting Jesus stemmed from the fear of loss of favor and rule of the people. Having

---

41. See France, *Mark*, 463, and Boyer, 'Mark,' on the wordplay of the Hebrew words *bēn* (son) and *'eben* (stone).

realized that the people may have also perceived that the parable was spoken against the chief priests, elders, and scribes, the delegation of the Sanhedrin was hesitant. If the crowd agreed with Jesus, arresting Him would be risky, especially if the expectation was that the stone would bring about the exaltation of the nation. Their leaving only marked temporary strategizing, not a discontinuation of their hopes of destroying Jesus.

The Encounter with the Coalition of Religious and Political Authorities (12:13-17)

Jesus had revealed that the Jewish leadership wanted to kill Him – He will be killed by the stewards of the vineyard. As a result, they wanted to kill Him even more.[42] Yet the Pharisees' and Herodians' joint attempt to trap Jesus on the lawfulness of paying taxes to Caesar trapped them as hypocrites as Jesus instructed them to render to both God and Caesar. Members of both groups left the encounter in awe of Jesus.

The Sanhedrin were strategic in sending the joint delegation of the Pharisees and Herodians to trap Jesus. The two groups have had conversations about destroying Jesus since the incident of healing the man with the withered hand in Mark 3:6. The content of the plans seems to have three parts.

First, they have discussed paying taxes to Caesar. The Herodians were the pro-Herod sympathizers who supported his regime and wanted to keep the Roman authorities from entering into the affairs of Herod and the Jews.[43] Part of their philosophy was for Jerusalem to be at peace with the Empire in order to appease Rome.[44] The Pharisees, on the other hand,

---

42. The reader should understand 'arrest him' and 'trap him' in light of previous revelation about the leadership's desire to kill Jesus in Mark 3:6 and 11:18, and of Jesus' own predictions of the intent of the Jewish leadership to kill Him in Jerusalem in 8:31, 9:31, and 10:33.

43. Edwards indicates that the Herodians' inclusion means the opposition to Jesus is 'political' as well as religious. Edwards, *Mark*, 102.

44. France is correct in stating, 'Our very limited information about the Ἡρωδιανοί [*Herodianoi*) does not allow us, however, to reconstruct their specific interests with any confidence' (France, *Mark*, 467). However, Edwards understands them to have been 'sympathizers and supporters of Herod's cause and the Herodian dynasty' (Edwards, *Mark*, 102). Hoehner proposes that the relationship was stronger than sympathy and support of Herod – that they were adherents of Herodian rule, specifically that of Herod Antipas at this point in Jesus' ministry. They were those

as followers of the Mosaic Law, would pay taxes to the Temple for the work of God.[45] To give money to Caesar, in some sense, is to affirm that Caesar is Lord.

Second, they have had conversations about their mutual disregard for Jesus. This may seem a strong statement with respect to the Herodians, but not in the Markan narrative, as they previously 'held counsel' with the Pharisees on destroying Jesus.[46] They agreed with the Pharisees to trap Jesus rather than simply coming by themselves and asking Jesus for insight.[47] Also, Jesus' response to both groups was that they both were hypocrites.

Third, they came to an agreement that this approach would be a good means for showing that Jesus was either anti-Temple or anti-Caesar, or anti-both.

The concern of the two groups was to condemn Jesus legally so that He would be executed (Mark 3:6; 12:12; 14:1, 55). The legal question – legal with respect both to Roman law and the Jewish Mosaic Law – would appear to put Jesus in a double-bind. It seems that the leaders of the two sects had bet on Jesus being pro-Temple and anti-Caesar, which would satisfy both groups' longings to kill Him,

---

who 'preferred [Herod Antipas's] rule to the direct rule of the Roman prefects' (H. W. Hoehner, 'Herodians,' *The International Standard Bible Encyclopedia, rev. ed.*, Wm. B. Eerdmans Publishing, 1979–1988, 698). What we know related to the Herodians is that the Herod family appointed the High Priests before A.D. 6 and after A.D. 37 (France, *Mark*, 151). Further, Edwards suggests that the coalition of the Herodians and Pharisees was 'at best an awkward alliance, forged more by a common enemy in Jesus than by any agreement among themselves' (Edwards, *Mark*, 362). Significant, therefore, to our understanding of the Herodians and their alliance with the Pharisees is the comment by Wessel: 'Collaboration in wickedness, as well as goodness, has great power' (Wessel, *Mark*, 733).

45. The Pharisees thought that Jesus misinterpreted the Mosaic Law and the Herodians felt that their mentor Herod Antipas should rule and have tribute money for the Roman coffers (Hoehner, 'Herodians,' 698).

46. At Mark 3:6, the Greek συμβούλιον ἐδίδουν (*symboulion edidoun*) denotes 'to engage in joint planning so as to devise a course of common action, often one with a harmful or evil purpose – "to confer, to consult, to plot, to make plans against"' (συμβουλεύομαι, *Louw-Nida*, 358). 'Conspired' in the NRSV and 'plotting' in the CSB capture the sense of the idiom.

47. On 'trap' ('catch' in the NIV), Edwards notes, 'The Greek word for "catch," *agreuein*, occurs in the New Testament only here and connotes violent pursuit' (Edwards, *Mark*, 362). The word has the sense of 'to hunt, catch' in contexts of those pursuing animals for food (France, *Mark*, 467; see also ἀγρεύω; παγιδεύω; θηρεύω, *Louw-Nida*, 329).

for He would be found guilty of treason. As usual, Jesus flipped the script on those bringing a question to Him. Jesus compelled the two groups to recognize two domains that must be satisfied rather than merely one.

Some contemporary writers use 'render to Caesar the things that are Caesar's' to speak of the relation of religious institutions, beliefs, and mandates to the institutions, beliefs, and mandates of the State.[48] Although this sub-unit within Mark 11:27-44 should contribute to any Christian theology of Church and State, Jesus' teaching here was narrower than a theological examination of politics and believers. I will explain this by considering the significance of this sub-unit in light of its central idea.

Contemporary society has no Pharisees and Herodians with which followers of Jesus could argue about paying taxes. However, there are *religious legalists* like the Pharisees and *pro-government loyalists* like the Herodians who have questions over the Church, Christian institutions and other non-Christian religious institutions paying taxes to a secular government of a sovereign nation. This holds true even though submission to governing authorities and paying taxes are part of believers' obedience to Christ and witness to the world of our obedience to Him.[49]

In the first century, as followers of the Mosaic Law, Jews were to give a portion of their wealth toward the work of the Temple and to offer various other sacrifices and vows. In the theocracy prior to Gentile rule, this would have sufficed for State taxes also. However, under Gentile rule, there was a responsibility to give to both the Temple and State coffers.

Finding itself in submission to the rule of various sovereign nations, the Church pays taxes to those nations as required. Such giving should flow from one's acknowledgment of the grace of God in Christ working in their lives, as the only prescriptions for giving in the New Testament have to do

---

48. Immanuel Wallerstein, 'Render Unto Caesar? The Dilemmas of a Multi-cultural World,' *Sociology of Religion* 66 (2005), 121. See also Lynn H. Cohick, '"Render unto Caesar:" The Christian's Call to Action or Retreat?' *Comment* (Fall 2012), 62-69.

49. See Matthew 23:1-3; Romans 13:1-6; 1 Peter 2:18–2:25.

with placing our treasures in heaven, supporting the work of the Gospel, and helping the needy.[50]

The Pharisees' and Herodians' joint attempt to trap Jesus on the lawfulness of paying taxes to Caesar trapped them as hypocrites as Jesus instructed them to render rightly to both God and Caesar and left them in awe of Jesus. I would suggest that the passage speaks to religious and political attempts to question both the Church's loyalty to the government and righteousness before God in the matter of paying national taxes. Such attempts should be met with wisdom from the Church that shows the questioners to be hypocrites and makes them stand in awe of the Gospel as we maintain our responsibilities to both the State and God (e.g., taxes and tithes).[51] That is, believers should not try to escape paying taxes or supporting the government financially. Those with religious and political attempts to question the church's loyalties and righteousness might view such actions as anti-patriotic, subversive, anarchist, selfish, and/or greedy. The message of the gospel could then seem like the message of the miser.

Also, believers should give faithfully to support one's local church, missions, and the relief of the poor (Rom. 15:25-28; Gal. 2:10; Eph. 4:25-29; Phil. 4:10-20). Otherwise, the church could stand accused of fearing and trusting the government more than the Lord, and believers would appear to be those who only give when they can maintain a certain amount of wealth for themselves.

The Encounter with the Sadducees over Marriage and the Resurrection (12:18-27)

Having witnessed the failure of the two combined groups to entrap Jesus in His teachings, the Sadducees approached Jesus without a coalition. The Sadducees sought for Jesus to admit that there is no resurrection based on an absurd application of the Mosaic Law of levirate marriage to the resurrection. The editorial comment on the Sadducees' disbelief in the

---

50. Matthew 6:19-24; Acts 2:45; 4:32-35; 11:28; 20:35; Romans 15:26-29; 1 Corinthians 16:1-2; 2 Corinthians 8:3-7; 9:3-5; Galatians 6:6-10; Ephesians 4:28.

51. The use of 'tithes' here is generic, speaking of giving to God. It is not intended to mean '10%' vs. so-called 'free-will giving.'

resurrection of the dead exposes the insincerity of their motives in approaching Jesus. They did not wish instruction from the teacher on that which they did not believe would occur. This is Mark's only direct reference to the Sadducees.

The scenario the Sadducees proposed stemmed from the law on levirate marriage. In levirate marriage, a man was legally required to marry the widow of his brother to provide care and protection for the widow, build up the name of his brother by guaranteeing the continuance of his line, and keeping the brother's inheritance within his family line. Moses prescribed it by law in Deuteronomy 25:5-6, and he wrote in Genesis 38:8-10 of a failed example in practice before the giving of the law.[52]

The focus of the question centered on the failure of each successive brother of the deceased to build up the family's line through the provision of children – the intent of the levirate marriage law. Each brother enters into his legal responsibility in good faith, but each died without success in building up the line, causing the need for another to then build. The childless widow's death followed the deaths of the six male siblings of the first husband, eliminating the need for a near relative to make another attempt to provide an offspring.

However, the Sadducees created the story to ask a question about the resurrection, which was not the intent of the law, but a creative suggestion of the significance of the law to the afterlife. They thought that proposing seven legitimate marriages ended by death would mar the resurrection with an absurdity because it would disagree with any supposed logical appropriation of the law.

Jesus' reply immediately designated the question as erroneous. He gave two categories of reasons for their error: their line of questioning revealed that they did not understand the Scriptures, and it revealed that they did not know God's power. Like other religious heretics, the Sadducees were distorted on the nature of salvation – in this case, on the glorification of believers. Jesus explained the two errors the Sadducees had made.

---

52. Edwards also describes levirate as 'a compensatory social custom designed to prevent intermarriage of Jews and Gentiles' (Edwards, *Mark*, 366).

First, in terms of the power of God, they failed to understand that the translation from this age to the next will render marriage unnecessary. There will be no need for resurrected persons to have offspring (as intended by levirate marriage), and thus, to have married. The earthly conceptualization of marriage for individuals will not be carried over into the cosmic conceptualization of the great mystery of the marriage of Christ to His bride. 'For Jesus the taxonomy of earthly realities is insufficient to explain the life to come; an entirely new category, "like the angels in heaven," is necessary to fathom resurrected existence,' writes Edwards.[53] Similarly, Hooker comments, 'What He is rejecting is therefore the notion that this social contract continues in the resurrection life.'[54] Edwards provides an important perspective to respond to heretics that misunderstand the glorious hope of believers' future bodily existence:

> God's power to create and restore life bursts the limits of both logic and imagination. The glorious realities of the life to come can no more be accommodated to the pedestrian routines of earthly life than can butterflies be compared to caterpillars. Present earthly experience is entirely insufficient to forecast divine heavenly realities: we can no more imagine heavenly existence than an infant *in utero* can imagine a Beethoven piano concerto or the Grand Canyon at sunset.[55]

In terms of the error of the Sadducees' knowledge of what the Scriptures teach on the resurrection of the dead, Jesus appealed to the Pentateuch, a source trusted by the Sadducees. The appeal to 'the book of Moses' in 12:26 corresponded to the Sadducees' statement, 'Moses wrote,' in 12:19. Jesus countered their selective use of the Torah by an appeal to other words from Moses, demonstrating their lack of knowledge of what Moses had taught.

---

53. Edwards, *Mark*, 367.

54. Hooker, *Mark*, 284. Hooker elaborates: 'The implication is perhaps that the limitations of this bond will be removed in the age to come, allowing a wider and deeper experience of human relationships in an existence which will be very different from that of this present age. Jesus rejects materialistic notions of the resurrection life: its nature will be quite different from life in the present age.'

55. Edwards, *Mark*, 367-68.

Jesus referred to Exodus 3:6 to reveal that the patriarchs were alive at the time God appeared to Moses at the burning bush. The fact that God, as the 'I am,' identified Himself according to the patriarchs meant that death was not the end of their existence. As much as God is alive as their God, they are alive. Jesus taught the Sadducees that God would not be the God of the patriarchs if their existence had ended. For Jesus, a living God maintains the life of each of His subjects past their earthly death.

Jesus previously said that the Sadducees had been misled (by their own interpretations).[56] The repetition of the same verb with the qualifier 'quite' emphasized the magnitude of their error. They were very wrong on their theology of the resurrection and their ability to read Scripture.

All heretics on the final glorification of the believer err to the degree of the Sadducees. Moreover, there are skeptics who doubt the resurrection of the dead based on the resurrection's perceived inability to address marital problems created by this life. Such Sadducee-like concerns are nullified by an explanation of the difference between what God does for marriage in the next life in comparison to this life. One also dispenses with such concerns by explaining God's role in giving life to the dead according to the Scriptures.

The Encounter with the Scribe Close to the Kingdom over Monotheism and Love (12:28-34)

Previously, along with the delegation of chief priests and elders from the Sanhedrin, the scribes raised the questions of Jesus' authority and right to proclaim His message and perform the powerful acts that constituted His earthly ministry (Mark 11:27). This expert in the Law posed his question in response to the dispute over the law of levirate marriage, having heard Jesus' interpretation of two passages in the Torah and His ability to proclaim that the Sadducees read the Law erroneously.[57] If Jesus could not answer this question

---

56. Mark 12:24, in which the tense of the verb translated '[are] wrong' (πλανᾶσθε, 2nd pers., pl., pres. pass. indct. of πλανάω, to wonder), would be rendered better by the passive 'led astray.' Jesus repeated the same verb in 12:27.

57. The proposal that Mark and Luke disagree on this incident is without merit, for the incidents are not the same. The incident in Luke occurs shortly after Jesus

to the satisfaction of the scribe, His ability to interpret any part of the Law would be in jeopardy.

Given the importance of each of the codes of the Decalogue and of the entirety of the 613 commandments and prohibitions, singling the most important of them all – and that as interpreted by the scribes – would be a large task. With great wisdom, Jesus proclaimed that prominence belongs to the beginning of the Shema (Deut. 6:4-5), words that the Jews spoke daily in their recitation of Deuteronomy 6:4-9.

Jesus' answer affirmed the monotheism and exclusivity of the Jews' belief about God, and He affirmed the covenant relationship of the Jews with the Lord ('our God'). The affirmations are unique to the Markan version of the incident, further strengthening Jesus' reference to Exodus 3 in the prior exchange with the Sadducees. Jesus indicated that His answers flowed from a proper theology of God and the Hebrews' relationship with God as His chosen people.

The second part of Jesus' reply followed the LXX of Deuteronomy 6:4 with an addition and a change. The Hebrew of Deuteronomy 6:4 has 'heart … soul … and strength.' The LXX follows with the Greek words for 'heart' (καρδίας), 'soul' (ψυχή), and 'might' (δύναμις). But Jesus added the word for 'mind' (διανοίας) and changed 'might' to 'strength' (ἰσχύος). The use of 'mind' gave 'heart' an emotional sense, and the use of 'strength' brought in the use of one's body. This second part of the answer made one's love for the Lord with one's full being part of the most important commandment.

Jesus went beyond the question asked by the scribe and added His idea of the second most important commandment. The addition and ranking of a 'second' commandment and the later statement 'no other' (v. 31) demonstrates that Jesus was thinking of priority of importance and not simply a common idea undergirding the Law.[58] Coupled with one's full

---

sets out on His journey toward Jerusalem (Luke 10). Luke's Triumphal Entry into Jerusalem is much later in Luke 19:28-40. Seemingly Luke does not need to include the second encounter with a scribe as the discussion in question from both scribes is the same.

58. This is contra Hooker, *Mark*, 287. Even with the difficulty of the grammar of coordinating the masculine noun for 'commandment' with the female modifier for 'all,' France concludes 'it seems clear that Jesus is being asked to identify a "first commandment"' (France, *Mark*, 479).

love for the Lord, one's love for all persons is next in rank. The two are inseparable although differing in priority. One must love the Lord more than one loves people, lest one makes a person an idol, thereby breaking the commandments and showing one does not love the Lord with all of one's being. However, to lack in love for any person would be to ignore the commandment Jesus quoted from Leviticus 19:6. This would be as disobedient as breaking any other commandment and also demonstrating that one lacks love for the Lord with one's full being.

Instead, love for the one covenant-keeping God who is Israel's Lord should spawn love for all people. This requires one to see love as more than emotions and sentimentalism, but inclusive of these. Love involves emotional, soulish, cognitive, bodily activity toward the Lord. Actions and acts of love, therefore, seem implicit in love for people. Christian ethical behavior is more than cognitive agreement and it is no less than feeling a warmth toward others that pursues their good. Jesus made faith in the Lord and ethical treatment of others the priority commandments without making them the only commandments.

Like his unique insertion of the opening words of the Shema, Mark alone records the scribe's words of agreement with Jesus' reply. The teacher of the Law agreed with Jesus' understanding of monotheism and the exclusivity of the Lord as God. He further agreed that the two love commandments are greater than bringing an offering before the Lord.

The second Gospel's description of Jesus' rejoinder to the scribal agreement does three things. First, it identifies the scribe as one with wisdom. He was unlike the Sadducees who erred, and the elders, chief priests, and scribes who lived in fear of the people, and the Herodians and Pharisees who unnecessarily put at odds concepts pertaining to obedience to God and the State. 'Wisdom' indicates he was acting in fear of the Lord.[59]

Second, it reveals that there was one scribe within proximity of the kingdom of God. This, along with seeing

---

59. See Job 28:28, Psalm 111:10, Proverbs 1:7, 9:10, and 15:33 for this understanding of wisdom.

him exercise wisdom, paints this one scribe in a positive light. But Jesus' words did not confer eternal life on this scribe, for he did not yet obtain entrance into the kingdom. His monotheistic, exclusive belief combined with his full love for the Lord and love of neighbor showed wisdom. But only faith in Jesus would provide salvation.

Third, Jesus' approval of the scribe's faith as 'near' the kingdom brings an end to the Temple inquisition. Hearing that Jesus did not toss away the faith and practice of the scribe as insignificant gave the listening Jewish audience the freedom to stop questioning the truthfulness of Jesus' Jewish understanding of following the Law. Similarly, if we can have the grace to say one's monotheistic belief combined with love for God and love of neighbor are close to salvation, people can cease speaking of possible other issues with the Christian faith. Rather than continuing in hostility akin to that of Jesus' detractors in the Temple, one outside of Christ, bringing an interpretation of faith in God from some knowledge of the Christian Scriptures, might cease opposing the faith and give a hearing to the gospel. This is not guaranteed. Yet affirming one's religious efforts when they are very similar to the practices of the Christian faith and affirming of monotheism could allow those affirming to build bridges to explain the gospel. The scribe who was not far from the kingdom did not get into the kingdom on the basis of right answers; he only showed a heart questioning of Jesus that was heading in the right direction. He still needed faith in Christ.

The Encounter with the People on the Sonship of Christ and the Empty Religion of the Scribes (12:35-40)

Jesus has encountered the scribes twice in this Temple episode. As copyists and interpreters of the Law, the scribes' understanding of a passage was weighty in the eyes of the Jewish people. Therefore, it was noteworthy that Jesus moved from being questioned by the scribes and a scribe, to affirming the nearness of one scribe to the kingdom, to now inviting the people to consider scribal interpretation of a Messianic passage. What the scribes said about the Messiah was held by the people as the correct teaching on the Messiah.

Therefore, Jesus had to clarify the connection between the Messianic lineage of the Son and the divine identity of the Son. Contemporary Christian preaching and teaching must do the same.

The words of Jesus' question, 'How can the scribes say,' invited the audience to evaluate the teaching of the scribes. Their teaching was not incorrect. The Davidic covenant promised the rule of a son to come who would build God's house and have a kingdom without end.[60] The cry of blind Bartimaeus evidenced the acceptance of this belief among the Jews.[61] However, although the scribes' interpretation was correct, it was incomplete. For their concept of a Messianic son did not include divine Lordship. The promise of the Davidic covenant included God's pronouncement, 'I will be to him a father, and he shall be to me a son.'[62] The scribes had not discerned the divinity of the Son within these words, even though His throne would be forever.

Jesus turned to Psalm 110:1, noting both the human and divine nature of Scripture as He did so. The words are both the declaration of David and given by the working of the Spirit in David to give us the words. The prophetic oracle of Psalm 110:1 is the first part of the psalm's assurance of victory for David's 'Lord.'[63] The psalm's speaker identified 'my Lord' as the recipient of words from 'the Lord.' The Hebrew of Psalm 110:1 has the sovereign Lord speak to one also identified as 'Lord.' Both titles are divine.

The scribes rightly had equated the Messiah with David's 'my Lord.' But they had not connected the sonship of the

---

60. See 2 Samuel 7:12-16.

61. See Mark 10:47-48 for Bartimaeus' cries to Jesus as the 'son of David.'

62. 2 Samuel 7:14; 1 Chronicles 17:13.

63. For more on the Messianic interpretation of Psalm 110:1, see Victor d'Assonville, '"The perpetuity of Christ's reign ..." Calvin's interpretation of Psalm110:1,' Bulletin for Christian Scholarship 87.1 (2022); Barry C. Davis, 'Is Psalm 110 a Messianic Psalm?' BSac 157 (2000): 160-73; Matthew Emadi, The Royal Priest: Psalm 110 in Biblical Theology, Downers Grove: IVP, 2022; idem., 'You Are Priest Forever: Psalm 110 and the Melchizedekian Priesthood of Christ,' SBJT 23.1 (2019): 57-84; Elliott E. Johnson, 'Hermeneutical Principles and the Interpretation of Psalm 110,' BSac 149 (Oct 1992): 428-437; Ian J. Vaillancourt, 'The Multifaceted Saviour of Psalms 110 and 118: A Canonical Exegesis,' Hebrew Bible Monographs 86 (Sheffield: Sheffield Phoenix Press, 2019).

Davidic covenant with the Lordship of David's divine Lord.
Jesus focused on the use of 'my Lord' in Psalm 110:1 rather
than the entirety of the verse's proclamation of victory over
all of the Messiah's enemies.

No figure in the crowd responded to Jesus' question. But
they heard a preaching of the Messiah's sonship that was
connected to the divine Lord and responded with gladness.
The hope intimated by Jesus is that the Lord Himself is the
Messiah, and as a human son of David He would come and
defeat the enemies of Israel. The question to the crowd invited
them to think of the possibility of a divine Messiah coming
in incarnate form as a Davidic son.

The questioning of the scribes' interpretation quickly led
to a warning about the scribes themselves. The cautionary
words speak of six ills of the scribes. Jesus desired that those
who revered the scribes and their interpretation would see
through to the true character of the scribes and the danger of
following their teachings.

First, the scribes wore long robes in order to give a display
of religious success by '[distinguishing] rabbis and scholars
as men of wealth and eminence.'[64]

Second, they enjoyed 'greetings,' what Ben Witherington
identifies as 'the deference they received from the common
people.'[65] This might have included 'being addressed by the
honorific titles "Rabbi," "Father," and "Master."'[66] Modern
church leaders who need superlative titles like 'apostle' or
'presiding prelate' to demand more respect from parishioners
than those titled 'pastor,' or who must wear badges to identify
themselves as an officer within a local congregation, often have
the same motives as the scribes, and their church members
should heed the words Jesus speaks about the scribes.

Third, the scribes sought seats in the front of the
synagogues that faced the congregants sitting on the floor.
The elevation in seating communicated an elevation in status,
akin to special seating in churches for officers, prominent
families, or wealthy givers.

---

64. Edwards, *Mark*, 378.

65. Witherington, *Mark*, 334.

66. Wessel, *Mark*, 739.

Fourth, as with the synagogue seats, they would sit in prominent places at banquets, probably closest to the hosting patron. Each of these first four items contributed to a flamboyant display intended to gain honor for themselves from those who should have been giving glory to the Lord.

Fifth, their oppressive treatment of the widow's property showed complete disregard for the law's emphasis on the care of widows. Those displaying piety in dress and positions were callous toward those without representation to defend themselves.

Six, their prayers were only for show, just like their clothing and seats. There was no love of God in their prayers or love of neighbor in their treatment of widows. Kerneghan's extended comments on injustices of the scribes toward widows are important for modern discussion disconnecting individual faith from social structures and justice:

> What is described in Mark 12:40 is not a few isolated instances in which one or two people trapped in poverty lost their homes, but an entire set of legal practices like foreclosing the mortgages of widows who could not repay loans their husbands had taken out. Jesus viewed these practices as a form of oppression that was enabled and justified by the keepers of the law. It was perfectly legal, and it was systemic. Devouring widows' homes was embedded in the economic fabric of the social order.
>
> Of particular interest is the combination of personal sin and systemic evil. Typically, we think of personal sins as a discrete category of wrongdoing, and if we confess our sin when we worship God, personal transgressions are the things we specify. In Jesus' denunciation of the scribes, however, personal sin was inseparably connected to social evil. In failing to love God with all their heart, soul, mind and strength, the scribes had created a platform for oppression. In this Gospel, faithful love of God is inseparable from faithful love for one's neighbors. It is the foundation for social justice.
>
> True piety also requires the love of justice. To love God is to do more than create a level playing field, where everyone starts with an equal opportunity. The most gifted and cunning have a permanent advantage. If their love of God is mingled with the love of success and social prominence, then the emergence of disenfranchised people is inevitable. To love justice is to

make the commitment that there will be no disenfranchised underclass. A lack of concern for justice demonstrates a failure to love our neighbors as ourselves, and it is a sign that our love of God is fatally flawed.[67]

The words to follow eternally condemn the scribes as a whole for their pride, hypocrisy, and injustice. For the audience in the Temple, the scribes were not simply wrong in their interpretations; they were also wrong in thinking that they were pleasing God and would experience His salvation. They will not, and those following them would have been wise to turn away from honoring the scribes after hearing Jesus' prophetic woe towards them.

The Encounter with the Rich and Poor Giving to the Treasury (12:41-44)

Immediately following the reference to widows, Jesus and His disciples experienced a living object lesson that placed an exclamation point on His rebuke of the Jewish elite. In the Court of Women, across from the treasury box in the Temple where worshipers placed their offerings, Jesus carefully watched the givers. The rich did not keep the amounts of their giving private. Much like the public displays of greatness made by the scribes, the large contributions to the Temple by the rich were for all to see.

In contrast to the wealthy, a poor widow approached the treasury to give. The difference between the 'large sums' and the two pennies that the widow gave is magnified by the recognition that she gave everything on which she had to live. She was a visible example of loving the Lord with all and of loving as herself her neighbors who had duties to the Temple. The scribes, the rich, giving in order to receive honor, do not love the Lord or neighbor; they love themselves.

The widow gave more in the eyes of Jesus because of the measure of her giving in comparison to her ability to give. The rich were not making sacrifices, for they had abundance. But the widow made a total sacrifice before God. The widow's example demonstrates that some might have faith in God

---

67. Kernaghan, *Mark*, 242-43.

correct without looking as polished as some wealthy or upper crust religious adherents who actually have no love for God.

Reflective Questions

1. What is the contextual usage of 'render unto Caesar that which is Caesar's?' How have you seen it divorced from its context in discussions about politics?

2. Who have you seen live a life that is characterized by the sacrificial life of the widow who put all she had into the treasury? What decisions would you need to make to receive from Jesus a commendation similar to that made about the widow?

14

He Came to Exhort Us to Be Wisely Awake for Coming Troubles

(Mark 13)

After a long day at work, it can be difficult for one to fight off sleepiness during evening activities. Care of the home, helping children with homework, enjoying meaningful time with a spouse, grading a student's work or getting on a call to do business in a later time-zone might require us to down a strong cup of coffee, vigorously exercise for a short period, or even skip dinner to have the strength to stay awake. We will do whatever it takes to remain alert until completion of the last duty allows us to close our eyes and relax fully.

Jesus' exhortation to His disciples called for similar wakefulness surrounding the events associated with the destruction of the Temple and the return of the Son of Man. As I will explain in the exposition below, the concept of staying awake in this discourse means three things: (1) be watchful for deceivers, (2) be prepared for persecution, and (3) be faithful until the return of the Master. The concept of 'awake' summarizes four verbs in the passage, translated in the English as 'leads you astray,' 'be on your guard,' 'keep awake,' and 'stay awake.'[1]

---

1. In 13:1, the writer uses the Greek ἴδε to indicate 'Behold!' It includes a sense of amazement or wonder. English translations render it as 'Look!' in

- See that no one leads you astray (*planaō*, 13:5).[2]
- But be on [your] guard (*blepō*, 13:9, 23, 33).[3]
- Keep awake (*agrypneō*, 13:33).[4]
- Stay awake (*grēgoreō*, 13:34, 35, 37).[5]

The structure of this passage has eight discernible subsections: vv. 1-2; 3-4; 5-8; 9-13; 14-23; 24-27; 28-31 and 32-37. The passage has a clear distinction from Mark 12 as Jesus and the disciples leave the Temple in 13:1 and observe items outside of it. The imperative 'stay awake' in 13:37 closes the repetition of 'be on guard' and 'stay awake' throughout the section. In the Greek text, Jesus begins the discourse with a verb for seeing and ends it with a verb related to seeing for 'stay awake.'

One faces many interpretive issues in Mark 13. Robert Stein outlines them well (and I quote him selectively):

Other more specific exegetical issues encountered in 13:5-23 are: What do 'come in my name' (13:6) and 'endures to the end' (13:13) mean? What does the 'abomination of desolation' refer to? Is the appearance of the abomination of desolation in 13:14 the 'sign' referred to in 13:4? Should the expression 'has not been from the beginning of the creation that God created until now, no, and never will be' (13:19) be interpreted literally? Is this expression used elsewhere in the Bible? If so, is it used here as exaggerated language to emphasize the horror of the coming 'holocaust' of A.D. 70?

13:1 and 21 (2x). In 13:14, 26, and 29 the writer uses a form of ὁράω (*horao – to see*) to describe simply seeing with one's eyes.

2. The Greek πλανάω (*planao*) means 'To mislead people as to proper views which they should have may often be expressed idiomatically, for example, "to twist people's thoughts," "to cause what is false to seem like what is true," "to make a lie appear true," "to dig away the truth," or "to cover the eyes with lies"' (Louw-Nida, 366). It is used again in 13:6 to speak of those who have been misled.

3. The Greek βλέπω (*blepo*) means 'to see, to become aware of, to notice, to glance at' (Louw-Nida, 277). In 13:2, Jesus replies to the disciple with a form of βλέπω (*blepo*) in response to the disciple gazing at the wonder of the buildings. In 13:5, Jesus combines βλέπω (*blepo*) with a form of πλανάω (*planao*) to give a sense of using one's eyes to help comprehend potential deception.

4. The Greek ἀγρυπνέω (*agrupneo*) means 'to make an effort to learn of what might be a potential future threat – "to be alert, to be on the lookout for, to be vigilant"' (Louw-Nida, 332).

5. The Greek γρηγορέω (*grēgoreo*) means 'to be in continuous readiness and alertness to learn – "to be alert, to be watchful, to be vigilant"' (Louw-Nida, 332).

As to 13:24-27, should this language be understood literally or symbolically? Is such cosmic language found elsewhere in the Bible? If so, how is it used? Is the coming of the Son of Man in these verses referred to elsewhere in the Bible? Was the coming of the Son of Man from heaven a familiar teaching to Christians at the time Mark was written? If so, how would Mark's readers have been inclined to interpret this passage? How should the temporal sequence in 13:24, 'But in those days, after that suffering,' be understood? Is 'in those days' a technical term?

In 13:28-31, does Mark understand the fig tree blossoming as indicating the time of Jerusalem's destruction or the Son of Man's coming? Should 'these things' in 13:29a and 'all these things' in 13:30 be interpreted in light of the use of these same two expressions in 13:4? And how should Jesus' emphatic statement 'Truly … this generation will not pass away until all these things have taken place' be interpreted?

For 13:32-37, does Jesus, as the Son, truly mean that He did not know the day that the Son of Man would return? What are the theological implications of this?[6]

I will attempt to address some of these issues in the commentary below.

Wisely Awake Involves Not Measuring Fading Beauty (13:1-2)

After the incessant questioning of the Jewish leaders, one might think the departure from the Temple would end questions to Jesus temporarily. But the passion narrative has Jesus' proclamation of His coming suffering, death, and resurrection as the wind in its sails.[7] Events must turn to make Him the victim of the evil of His opponents. Mark 13 will attach itself to the predictions with Jesus' revelation of the coming suffering, death, and resurrection of the disciples.

One unnamed disciple called Jesus' attention to the stones and building of the Temple complex. The exclamatory phrase was not a statement of opinion as much as it was inviting a response. In Luke 13:1, the crowd proposed a similar

---

6. Robert H. Stein, *Jesus, the Temple and the Coming Son of Man: A Commentary on Mark 13* (Downers Grove, IL: IVP Academic, 2014), 48.

7. See Mark 8:31; 9:31; 10:32-33.

statement of fact without the form of a question. Yet Jesus responded as if asked a question because those reporting the events were expecting a judgment from Him; they were not sharing general information. The judgment the disciple sought was agreement on the greatness of the stones. Old Testament history evidenced the people's enamor with Solomon's Temple.[8]

Jesus' reply intentionally turned the gaze of the disciples away from the architectural wonder to a vision of the eschaton. While Mark 13:2 foreshadowed the destruction of the Temple in A.D. 70, it was not completely fulfilled in the first century. Fulfillment is limited to the end times because the Wailing Wall still exists. This means (1) A.D. 70 falls in the type of this passage but is not in this passage, and (2) all that follows concerns the end times even though it anticipates A.D. 70. It was still a warning; when the disciples (and those who had heard or read the second Gospel) were in the events of A.D. 70, these words would have been in their minds.[9]

---

8. See Ezra 3:12; Psalms 74:7; 79:1; and Jeremiah 7:4. James Edwards explains the disciples' enamour well: 'In Jesus' day the temple had already been under construction fifty years and was still unfinished. At no place was Herod the Great's obsession with grandeur and permanence more apparent than in the Jerusalem temple .... Herod enlarged Solomon's temple to an esplanade measuring some 325 meters wide by 500 meters long, with a circumference of nearly a mile. The immense thirty-five-acre enclosure could accommodate twelve football fields. The southeast corner of the retaining wall hung some fifteen stories above the ground that sloped down to the Kidron Valley. The blocks of stone used in construction were enormous; Josephus (JW 5.189) reports that some were forty cubits (approximately sixty feet) in length. No block that size has been found in the existing foundation, but stones north of Wilson's Arch measure forty-two feet long, eleven feet high, fourteen feet deep, and weigh over a million pounds. The magnitude of the temple mount and the stones used to construct it exceed in size any other temple in the ancient world. And this was merely the retaining wall. Above, on the south end of the esplanade, perched the gleaming Royal Portico, "a striking spectacle," to quote Josephus .... The figures Josephus gives for the blocks of stone in the sanctuary exceed in size even those of the foundation (JW 5.222–24). A vast and stupendous complex it was. No wonder the disciples were overwhelmed!' (Edwards, Mark, 387).

9. To say that Jesus used hyperbole here is to make His words mean less than what He intended by them. Hyperbole occurs when words exceed the limits of reality for the specified context, as in the phrases, 'I am so hungry, I could eat a horse,' or 'My feet are killing me.' No human being has the capacity to eat an entire horse in a meal. One's feet do not grab weapons or poisons to attack the rest of the body. Even if a person uses the phrase to speak of gangrene of the feet, it is still a figure of speech, for it is the disease contracted by the feet that leads to the person's death. It was very possible for an event to happen that would destroy every

The admonition here warns against contemporary marveling over edifices of worship as a measure of success. Like the disciples concerning the Temple, believers must bear in mind the destruction of this present world as foretold in Scripture and the coming judgment of God that will go beyond outward appearances.

Wisely Awake Means to Question the Coming Apostasy (13:3-8)

Just across the Kidron Valley, opposite the Temple, the disciples and Jesus paused to sit on the Mount of Olives. The addition of Andrew indicates that at least the two sets of brothers were present. Moreover, it expanded the inner circle to which the reader has become accustomed.[10] Unlike the Transfiguration account, a fourth set of ears gained unique instruction. The disciples did not ask a question about the sign of the return of Christ as in the parallel passage (Matt. 24:3). They asked a question about the time and sign of the coming destruction of the Temple.

Jesus' strong warning to the disciples invited them to use their eyes to avoid deception about the timing of the destruction. The words undercut being trapped by apocalyptic date-setters and doomsayers. The coming deception is twofold, with one required response for the wise, and two pieces of reasoning.

The first deception will be the claim by some to be the long-promised Messiah. History gives witness to the attempts of many to assume this role among a following remnant.[11] The dating of 'The time is at hand' was unspecified but concerned the destruction of the Temple. The prophets associated the return of the Messiah with cataclysmic events, including the

---

stone of the entire Temple complex. The decimation of buildings or cities was not unknown to the ancient world. An equal error would be to make the words mean more than what the writer said, such as to make 'temple' here refer to a spiritual temple rather than a material temple made of physical stones.

10. Mark 5:37; 9:2; also 14:33. The presence of Andrew also means that this discourse was not a private concoction made in the aftermath of the Transfiguration. Four disciples were present, not just the three of the inner circle.

11. An infamous modern example is that of James ('Jim') Warren Jones and The Peoples Temple and the suicide massacre in 1978. See 'Jim Jones,' *Encyclopedia Britannica*, 14 Nov. 2022.

movement of the Mount of Olives, which could cause the destruction of the Temple mount.[12]

The second deception would be personal and interpretive – what to make of hearing about wars – real or only rumored. The self-deception would be to take what one heard and allow it to lead one to fear of near proximity of cataclysmic destruction. Again, the speculative, the cynical, the nihilistic, and the suspicious can take the reality of one war or potential war and forecast warring that would involve the whole world. But the disciples' hearing of wars was not to lead to alarm. Consistent with this idea, Paul later admonished the Thessalonians against being alarmed by a false report of the coming of the Day of the Lord (2 Thess. 2:2).

The necessity of the coming of false messiahs and proclamations about wars reveals the working of divine sovereignty in human history.[13] The Lord's decree is moving history toward the end, but the messianic claims of deceivers and the hearing of wars did not mean that the end associated with the destruction of the Temple was near.

Similarly, history continues to contain wars between sovereign nations, movements of seismic plates, and absence of food in some regions. This is part of human history. Analogously, they are like initial labor pains that point toward more birth pains long before there is enough dilatation for the birth of a child (or enough time passing without a natural birth to require a C-Section). Wars, earthquakes, and famines are only signposts *en route* to the day of destruction. They do not indicate nearness of that day.

The same is to be said for the threats of end-times' deception that the church faces in every age. Global disasters are only signposts of coming apostasy to the church and the hope of a new creation.[14] Modern disciples, like our forebears, should discern false messiahs and not give way to the fear that people without hope of the resurrection have when wars and other regional disasters happen.

---

12. Zechariah 14:4.

13. The Greek word 'δεῖ (*dei*) in the New Testament is normally an expression for the decree and esp. of the plan of God' (δεῖ, *EDNT*, 279). For a different view, see P. Smit, 'Questioning Divine δεῖ,' *NovT* 61 (2018): 40-54.

14. Romans 8:18-25; 2 Thessalonians 2:1-3.

Wisely Awake Requires Enduring without Anxiety (13:9-13)

Literally, Jesus warned, 'See to yourselves,' giving all disciples personal responsibility to be prepared for forthcoming persecution. 'Hand you over' often carries the idea of betrayal or being given to an authority (for legal judgment).[15] Jesus foretold the disciples' religious trials, floggings, and trials before Gentile authorities. Both the Book of Acts and the New Testament letters attest to the fulfillment of these prophetic warnings.[16]

Jesus explained 'for my sake' by the words 'to bear witness before them.' The disciples were to be prepared for persecution that would take them before human authorities in Jewish religious settings and secular legal courts for the purpose of giving testimony to the death and resurrection of Christ.[17] The call to 'be on your guard' did not intend to make the disciples hesitant to live out their faith in the face of persecution or to withdraw from society; instead, one outcome of being awake is the proclamation of the gospel to powerful earthly authorities. Such authorities need the message of salvation as much as those over whom they rule.

The good news of the kingdom will be proclaimed to all nations surrounding the events of the final destruction of the Temple. Jesus is the Abrahamic offspring through whom 'all nations' will be blessed; the proclamation to all nations (or all people groups) corresponds to that promise of blessing. Sandwiched between the forewarnings about standing before authorities and the coming 'trial[s]' (v. 11), the proclamation of the good news of the kingdom to the authorities was part of the means by which the gospel will go to the nations.

---

15. For example, see the use of παραδίδωμι (*paradidomi – to hand over*) in Matthew 17:22; 24:10; 26:46; and John 6:71; 18:36. Jesus used the term in Mark 9:31 and 10:33 to speak of His fate at the hands of the authorities. Mark will return to the use of this verb to demonstrate the fulfillment of Jesus' predictions in 14:10, 11, 18, 21, 41, 42, 44; 15:1, 10, 15. By means of association, the reader should hear the potential for martyrdom in Jesus' predictions for the disciples.

16. Acts 4:1-22; 5:27-32; 7:54–8:3; 9:13, 21; 12:1-3; 14:19; 23:33; 25:6; 2 Corinthians 11:23-25.

17. This is not an attempt to read Acts 1:8 into Mark 13. Instead, I am considering the promise of the resurrection in Mark 8:31, 9:31, and 10:32-33.

Standing before those with human authority over life and death is daunting even for those innocent and righteous according to human laws. Any authority can yield to concerns about keeping the favor of constituents and/or prefer a bribe over doing what is just.[18] Even if innocent, the gospel is of such offense that it creates enemies in legal settings – enemies with the power to call for one's execution. It would be tempting to adjust the content of one's speech to be as inoffensive as possible – which, in the case of the good news, would result in the dumbing down of the message of Christ such that it becomes useless.

Jesus instructed His disciples to refrain from fear of potentates and religious authorities. Searching for the right words in order to craft a speech pleasing to authorities would be unnecessary. Part of the ministry of the Holy Spirit will be to give disciples the words to speak when on trial for the gospel. The Spirit sees the disciple on trial, speaks through him when he speaks, and provides the words of defense that are necessary.[19]

The coming persecution for Jesus' sake will be legal, religious, political, familial, and final (for some). Jewish disciples might have heard a corporate identity in the word 'brother.' But in this string of enemies, it is a familial term like 'father,' 'child,' 'children,' and 'parents.' The presence of Andrew in the private discourse means two sets of brothers heard Jesus speak of brotherly betrayal, adding to the significance of what Jesus said in their hearing.

Even a close familiarity as brothers and fathers will be so offended by the message of the kingdom that they will betray (or hand over) to the authorities their Christ-following family members. The common love between parents and children will fail when it comes to giving deference to Christ's disciples. Those who find disciples to be intolerant of a message of salvation other than the gospel will prove to be the most intolerant of religious pluralism; they will seek the deaths of their own.

---

18. For example, see 1 Samuel 15:24; Matthew 14:5; Mark 6:26; 11:46; 12:12; Luke 22:2; Acts 5:26; 24:26; 25:9.

19. See examples of this working of the Spirit in the lives of Peter and Stephen in Acts 4:48 and 6:8, 15.

This hatred in the courts and homes will encompass all segments of society. Everyone who is not a disciple of Christ will hate those who are His followers.[20] Yet such widespread, pervasive hatred does not call for retreat or resignation from society. Christ's followers should persist in following Him in the face of persecution until 'the end' spoken of in 13:7. For some this will mean enduring until martyrdom; for others it will mean enduring until Christ's return[21] – the time associated with the complete destruction of the Temple, the proclamation of the good news of the kingdom to all nations, and societal rejection of the gospel and its followers on a scale larger than anything seen in history.

Perseverance in the face of the coming persecution will result in salvation for Christ's followers – not on the basis of endurance meriting salvation, but on the basis of endurance evidencing the working of salvation by the Spirit (v. 11) in the elect (vv. 20, 27). Freedom from anxiety, reliance on the Holy Spirit, and endurance until the end are simple faith responses, in keeping with the meaning of Mark's Gospel. The endurance until the end will save people unto the kingdom. Those acting for Christ's sake are those called to discipleship like His. Christ's discourse was His servant ministry to the disciples in Mark 13.

Wisely Awake Includes Being Discerning and Taking Jesus' Warning Seriously (13:14-23)

Jesus again exhorted the disciples to use their visual faculties to make note of a particular future event. 'The abomination of desolation' echoes the language of Daniel 9:27, 11:31, and 12:11. Lexically, it refers to a sacrilegious desecration that causes people to desert.[22] Historically, the reference is to

---

20. Garland writes, 'They will be loathed by everyone (13:13). Tacitus's account of how Nero tried to pin the guilt for the devastating fire in Rome on the Christians describes them as "a class hated for their abominations ... by the populace ...." The antagonism will be so intense that family members will even turn on other family members because they passionately hate the gospel or are desperate to escape persecution themselves' (Garland, Mark, 494).

21. While the disciples do not ask for signs of Christ's return in the Markan discourse, Christ does speak of His return after the time of the aforementioned tribulation in 13:26.

22. Kernaghan, Mark, 255, with Wessel, Mark, 748.

Antiochus IV Epiphanes' sacrifice of a pig on the Temple altar in 167 B.C., the event that sparked the Maccabean Revolt. 1 Maccabees 1:54 uses similar language as Daniel to record the desecration under Antiochus IV.

Jesus' use of Daniel's language recalled the historical event 'as a prefigurement or symbol of something equally outrageous and cataclysmic to occur in the future.'[23] Commentators vary on the object of the prefigurement, proposing Caligula, Titus, the Zealots' installation of Phanni as high priest in 67–68, or the final Antichrist.[24]

Mark's cryptic use of 'standing where it ought not to be' differs from Matthew's direct reference to the Temple, 'standing in the holy place.' As an aside from the writer for those reading a written copy of the second Gospel, 'let the reader understand' refers to Mark's use of the masculine 'standing' with the neuter 'where it ought not to be.' The reader would know that the lack of matching of the phrase points toward a male desecrator standing somewhere that would be unholy for him to do so. The language only requires a reference to the Temple if one reads the Matthean parallel into Mark.[25] A reference to the coming man of lawlessness would fit the final referent.

The sacrilege will take place in Judea which, again, does not limit the timing of the event. However, the haste with which the residents of Judea must flee and the location of safety goes beyond the ability to flee Judea when it was surrounded by the Roman army. Grabbing household goods or a cloak for warmth would be useless when the desecrating one appears. Pregnant women would have great difficulty fleeing from Judea with the envisioned haste. Winter would make crossing water-filled wadis extremely difficult, slowing the pace of the fugitives.

---

23. Edwards, *Mark*, 396.

24. See Edwards, *Mark*, 395-400 for extended discussion on the options. Robert Stein proposes the Zealot priestly installation as an option (Stein, *Jesus, the Temple*, 85-93).

25. Mark's language is broad and vague. Many places could provide fulfillment of 'where.' This vagueness allows for the possibility that this is not referring to the Holy Place, and neither is it limited from being an eschatological event. The initial readers and hearers would have associated Jesus' words with the destruction of the Temple. But readers since A.D. 70 have no reason to question a future event being prefigured.

This tribulation will be the greatest ever. Thus, this is not an A.D. 70 event, unless the events of A.D. 70 are greater than the final tribulation upon the earth. Nothing in history of this magnitude had occurred prior to Jesus' proclamation. Nothing in history future to the proclamation anywhere in the world could match the persecution to follow the advent of the desecrating one. Jesus' hearers would have thought that the events of A.D. 70 met that description even as those witnessing World War I thought no future war would be as great as that one. But as history witnessed the eclipse of greatness of WWI by what happened in WWII, so unspecified later readers of Mark's Gospel will witness a persecution unparalleled in history anywhere in the world.

'No human' and 'the elect' broaden the final participants beyond that of Jewish worshipers in the Temple. Israel were the chosen people of God.[26] But 'the elect' is a term inclusive of Gentiles for whom Christ died.[27] God's mercy decreed the shortening of the period of this great tribulation in kindness toward His own so that their time of suffering is reduced.

The seeing of the Antichrist (and antichrists) with discernment ('let the reader understand') should make disciples wisely alert of an increase in persecution, false messiahs, and false prophets. Claims of the appearance of the Messiah will abound, but Christ's followers should not be fooled. Nevertheless, the deception of those with powers to perform signs and wonders will be so powerful that those chosen for salvation will be tempted to believe that forerunners of Jesus have appeared. The 'if possible' reveals the gracious keeping of the believer's perseverance by the Lord so that salvation will be fulfilled for His own without them having abandoned Christ.

Jesus' words of warning dropped with weightiness. The foretelling of the tribulation events was kindness. They were and are words to be taken with the utmost sincerity by His followers.

---

26. See Deuteronomy 7:7; Psalms 33:12; 105:6, 34; 106:5; 135:4; Isaiah 41:8.

27. See Luke 18:7; Romans 8:33; 11:7; 2 Timothy 2:10; Titus 1:1; 1 Peter 1:1. Jesus assumed 'the elect, whom He chose,' included terms that would be understood without explanation by the disciples.

Wisely Awake Hopes for the Age of Suffering to Give Way to Christ's Coming (13:24-27)

The times of the cataclysmic post-tribulation events will reveal two things: (1) the powerful and glorious return of the Son of Man and (2) His angelic gathering of His elect from the whole world to heaven. That 'time' is the subject of this section is evident in the contrasting phrase, 'but in those days,' and the time marker, 'after that tribulation.' The first phrase immediately connected the times of the greatest tribulation, persecution, deception, and the Temple's complete destruction to the advent of the Son of Man.

The darkening of the sun and the dimming of the moon's light simultaneously make sense in a scientific age, as the small luminary body only reflects the light of the larger one. But Jesus' words were more than scientific realities. He spoke of the changing of the ordering of the cosmos with the death of stars. He borrowed the language of Isaiah 13:10 and Joel 2:10 (even though Joel 2 describes a different event).[28] France proposes 'such "cosmic" language conveys a powerful symbolism of political changes within world history, and is not naturally to be understood of a literal collapse of the universe at the end of the world.'[29] Yet one should see 'the powers' (literally 'the ones in the heavens') shaken back and forth because the Son of Man comes 'with great power' so that He might gather the elect even from 'the ends of the heavens.' The use of cosmic language for political upheaval in a different context does not mean that every use of cosmic destruction is doing the same thing. Jesus' vision was looking at contrasting powers that appear in the sky.

The coming of the Son of Man will bring a visible display of the glory of God in Christ. In this way, the persecution that Christ's followers will experience at the hands of family

---

28. Joel 2 describes a locust plague without precedent in size and power, spoken of in terms descriptive of an Ancient Near Eastern army. The cataclysmic terms in Joel describe the appearance of the sun and moon and sky when distorted by a locust plague. Also, Hooker proposes 'the four parallel lines in vv. 24f. seem, indeed, to be a composite quotation from Isa. 13:10 and 34:4' (Hooker, *Mark*, 318).

29. France, *Mark*, 533.

members, politicians, courts, etc., will give way to the goal of their hope. 'The elect' no longer will suffer or face the temptation of deception by false messiahs and prophets because the truth will stand before them.[30] Jesus will gather His own 'after that tribulation' – a period that is not descriptive of A.D. 70, but of a period yet further in the future.[31]

Wisely Awake Requires Discerning and Enduring Patiently (13:28-31)

The disciples' certainty of the nearness of Christ's return requires discernment with patience. Jesus launched into the first of two parabolic statements that offer encouragement in the face of the coming persecution and end of the present order.

Inserting a lesson recalls the instruction in 13:14 for the reader to understand – to be discerning. This is the nature of a 'parable,' which is a better translation than 'lesson.'[32] The analogy between the fig tree's tender sprouting of its leaves indicating the nearness of summer corresponded to 'these things taking place' as indicating the nearness of the advent of the Son of Man. The fig tree developed its sap and then sprouted leaves in the spring. Jesus' hearers and Mark's readers would have been familiar with the pomology of the fig tree and its cycle of seasons.

Even as the disciples could use the fig tree to discern the coming of summer, so they must use all that Jesus said in 13:5-23 to discern the nearness of the advent of the Son of Man. In summary, this meant taking note of the combination of nine things that together will point toward the nearness of Christ's return:

1. Many will claim to come with Jesus' authority and lead many astray (vv. 6, 22)

---

30. The term 'his elect' is broad enough to encompass the remnant of Old Covenant Israel and the faithful of the New Covenant church. It need not speak only of the church *militant*, but also of the church *triumphant – the church invisible, universal.*

31. Therefore, I disagree with Kernaghan, who gives an extended discussion to the idea that 13:24-27 describes the gathering together of the church into a new community to proclaim the gospel (Kernaghan, *Mark*, 262-70). This gathering occurs at the destruction of the old order.

32. Jesus uses the Greek term παραβολήν, 'parable.' See the translation in the NASB, NET, and NKJV.

2. The reality of wars and rumors of wars between nations (v. 7)

3. Earthquakes and famines (v. 8)

4. Religious and legal persecution, inclusive of the followers of Christ standing in the presence of world leaders to proclaim Christ (v. 10)

5. Empowerment by the Holy Spirit to speak as witnesses for Christ before courts and councils (v. 11)

6. Martyrdom for following Christ, with deathblows arising from within one's own family (v. 12).

7. Universal hatred of Christ's followers (v. 13)

8. The revealing of the final abomination of desolation figure (v. 14)

9. Tribulation on the grandest scale ever (v. 19)

No one thing in this list alone points toward the nearness of the advent of Christ, neither do only a few of the items. 'These things' looks back at the entirety of the elements that precede 'but in those days, after that tribulation' (v. 24). While many of these elements appear throughout church history, the universal hatred of believers, the revelation of the final antichrist, and the grand tribulation are events still future. Yet the discourse had meaning to the first-century hearers and readers. They would have been 'keeping awake' for these elements during Caligula's attempt to profane the Temple, Claudius' expulsion of the Jews from Rome, the Neronian persecution, Titus' destruction of Jerusalem, and the persecution under Domitian.

The combination of the events preceding the nearness of the advent comes without a direct time reference. Date-setting is not possible; only discernment is possible.

The truth statement of Jesus provided assurance as He spoke directly and firmly to the disciples. Their discernment would require them to give proper placement to the continuing presence of wicked people who will do violence toward the elect. 'This generation' points toward those who will rise against believers, and not to the living generations of Jesus' day.[33] Such evil persons will continue to present themselves in the future. Their presence does not point toward the return of the Messiah, so the disciples must be discerning.

Jesus equally assured the disciples that all He has taught them will carry the authority of God's voice for all eternity. Discernment also requires the disciples to hold to Jesus' words even as the world plunges into chaos around them.

Wisely Awake Sustains Wakefulness Faithfully (13:32-37)

The hour of the return of the Son of man was hidden from all but the Father. This called for Jesus' disciples to stay awake like a faithful house steward under a suddenly returning master. Jesus turned to the discussion of the timing of His return seemingly in anticipation of questions in response to His words about the nearness of the advent.

All beings in both terrestrial and celestial realms are excluded from knowledge of the time of Christ's return. Christ's inclusion of Himself in this absence of knowledge reveals His choice of humility toward God the Father in the plan of redemption. While being fully God, within His humanity only the Son has chosen voluntary ignorance of this one fact in His voluntary submission to the Father.[34] He is consistent in saying that the Father, by His own authority, has set the time and dates related to the end.[35]

The lack of a definitive date for the return of the Son encouraged faithful readiness. The fact of the Son's coming

---

33. I agree with Susan Rieske's conclusion drawn from Matthew's use of 'this generation': 'This γενεά (*genea*) refers to the persecutors of the elect of the time of Jesus Himself within the nation of Israel, who are not in the elect seedline, and consequently, not the true children of the Father. As murderers of the Messiah, this γενεά represents the full flowering of the non-elect seedline, that seedline that has opposed and persecuted the elect and the prophets throughout time' (Susan M. Rieske, *A Tale of Two Families: 'This Generation' and the Elect in the Book of Matthew*, Ph.D. Diss., Wheaton College, 2018, 329). See also, Susan M. Rieske, 'What is The Meaning of "This Generation" in Matthew 23:36?' *BSac* 165 (2008): 209-26.

34. On the divinity of the 'Son' in this verse, Edwards comments, 'The "Son" is properly understood as Son of God rather than Son of Man since the latter does not occur in the Gospels in an absolute sense (i.e., "the Son"), whereas "Son of God" is used absolutely (e.g., Matt 11:27//Luke 10:22). "The Son," which stands correlative to "Father," means "the Father's Son," or the Son of God' (Edwards, *Mark*, 407).

35. See Acts 1:7.

and the elect's gathering was established. One might wonder then why there was a need for one to be ready for the return. The inference of the judgment of the faithfulness of the disciples became explicit in the parable.

The 'it' refers to 'the time' of the coming of the Son. In a second parable, Jesus compared the readiness needed for His return to the readiness a doorkeeper needs as a steward watching for the return of the master of the house. In the parable, each servant has an authoritative task within his or her realm of stewardship.[36] However, the doorkeeper has only one task in the parable: stay alert for the return of the master of the house.[37] If he is awake to the return at all times (discounting required times of sleeping, which should be assumed in a human context), he would always ensure that all stewards had been faithful to their various charges in the house, which meant that at all times they were prepared for the master to return and find his house cared for, as he had charged them. Thus, the parable taught that the steward was expecting his faithfulness to come into judgment. The disciples' readiness for the return of Jesus is 'like' this stewardship. The readiness for the return only matters if judgment of faithfulness is on the table.

Making allegorical use of the parable, Jesus inserted Himself into the parable as 'the master of the house.' Speaking directly to the disciples, He told them to 'stay awake.' But the reasoning concerned the return of the master of the house in the previous parable. The master was not now returning from a journey; that was the task of the fictional master in the parable. This master could come at evening, midnight, rooster crow time, or in the morning – all time references of the four Roman watches in the first-century world.[38] Even as the master in the parable could return at any watch to

---

36. The Greek for 'charge' is ἐξουσίαν (*exousian*), a word for 'authority' or 'power.'

37. The Greek ἀγρυπνεῖτε (*agrupneite*) differs from the other words used for wakefulness in this discourse. It carries the idea of vigilance, like those alert for spiritual warfare (Eph 6:18) and faithful leaders who care vigilantly for the souls of the members of the flock under their care (Heb 13:17).

38. Hooker notes that Mark mentions three of the four watches as his narrative moves toward the crucifixion, that three of the four disciples addressed here are again commanded to watch, and Jesus returns to find them sleeping rather than

measure the work of his servants, so Jesus can return at any time to measure the faithfulness of His servants. 'He ... find you asleep' inserted each of the disciples into the parable as the doorkeeper, allegorically, for only the doorkeeper was commanded to stay awake.

Even as the master in the parable could return suddenly, without warning, so Jesus' return will be without warning, suddenly. Like the doorkeeper, at any moment the disciples of Christ must be ready for His return to His 'house' to measure the stewardship of His doorkeeper.

Jesus widened His responsible audience to 'all.' The readers would have found and, even now, should find themselves within the admonitions in the discourse and the lessons of the two parables. Jesus began this discourse with the charge against being led astray.[39] He will end the discourse with the charge to stay awake.[40] The inclusion places emphasis on the watchfulness needed by all of Jesus' disciples.[41]

Reflective Questions

1. How does the contemporary church's polarization over social and political issues prime her for being deceived rather than wisely awake?

2. How should one understand Christ's deity and His lack of knowledge of His own return?

---

awake (14:34, 37, 38, 40, 41) (Hooker, *Mark*, 324). Importantly, Edwards adds that the disciples were 'reprimanded five times for failure to watch' (Edwards, *Mark*, 409).

39. βλέπετε (see) is the first word in Mark 13:5 as Jesus speaks.

40. The last word Jesus speaks in Mark 13:37 is γρηγορεῖτε (*gregoreite – Watch*).

41. As Hooker writes, 'The warning to keep watch, however, is not meant for the disciples alone: the final words of the discourse – And what I say to you I say to all – remind Mark's readers that the warning is addressed to them also' (Hooker, *Mark*, 324).

15

He Came to Expose Intentions and Hostile Opposition

(Mark 14)

There are many intentions surrounding the choices people make about embracing or rejecting Jesus amid opposition; some intentions are good and others are evil. Believers must have the right intentions in following Jesus in difficult settings so as to experience God's blessings from such encounters. What should motivate right intentions is our confidence that what Scripture says about Jesus' work as the Son of the Blessed will be fulfilled. Others will be condemned for being ashamed of Him as Scripture moves toward fulfillment.

Intention, Atonement, and Pleasing Hostile People (14:1-2)

In Jewish counting, Mark 14 opens the Wednesday of Holy Week. One of the three annual feasts that the Jewish people were to celebrate in Jerusalem was upon them (Exod. 23:13-17). As Passover and the Feast of the Unleavened Bread were back-to-back celebrations, the people would have been in Jerusalem for Passover. Already concerned about Jesus' following (John 11:48), the Jewish authorities sought for a way to have Him legally charged and condemned to death.

Their efforts to condemn Jesus needed to go without notice. This would appear to be a mammoth task when one considers the popularity of Jesus among the people and the sizes of the crowds that followed Him. The Jewish leadership showed their true motivations: they could condemn Him if the condemnation was separated from the celebrations in Jerusalem. The simultaneous feasts could provide an occasion for revolt against the leadership and attract attention from Rome if the people did not agree with the leadership's actions. However, in the decree of God, they will condemn Jesus during the celebration of the Feast of the Unleavened Bread, allowing for the completion of the Passover.

In the vein of the Jewish leadership, some still attempt to separate the death of Jesus from the need for an atonement (e.g., Passover). The account reveals the motives of such attempts, especially in the hearts and minds of those who attempted to do so quietly. But those who proclaim Jesus but see no need for humankind to have an atoning work are simply people-pleasers, for that type of 'Jesus' gives no cause of offense.

Monetary Intentions, Worshipful, Misguided, and Selfish (14:3-11)

On the Wednesday of Holy Week, Jesus went to the home of a healed leper named Simon. Simon must have been healed previously, or Jesus and the other guests could not approach him. The scene was one in anticipation of the meals to be shared during the feast as Jesus enjoyed fellowship with those there. It seemed like a simple gathering of enjoyment, maybe shared with friends and family of Simon, and with some of them following Jesus.

The appearance of a woman interrupted the meal. This was a very different woman from Lazarus' sister, Mary, for her anointing of Jesus took place four days prior to this one, before the Triumphal Entry (John 12:1-3, 12). This woman also differed from the 'woman of the city' who appeared in the home of a Pharisee in Nain early in Jesus' ministry, even though the Pharisee shared the name 'Simon' with the host in the Markan passage (Luke 7:26-50). This woman was neither Mary nor a woman known for vices. She simply was a woman with a very expensive jar of ointment.

The purity of the ointment, its value, and the pouring of it over the head of Jesus bring allusions to the anointing of the priest and tabernacle for service before God, and of kings being anointed for service to Israel.[1] The high aromatic ointment would have filled the room with its scent, and the visual display of the oil running down Jesus' hair and clothing would have been in vivid contrast to the appearance of others reclining at the table. All focus would turn to Him (and the woman) as she made an embodied picture of Jesus being anointed as the Messiah.

Yet it was not the woman's recognition of Jesus' priest-king-presence-of-God Messianic identity that was of concern to the observers; that significance was lost on them. Instead, they devaluated Jesus in their indignance, granting to Him less honor than the poor. Their concern about waste revealed hearts driven by monetary priorities. The conversation they had among themselves bubbled over into condemnation of the woman's actions.

In opposition to those scoffing and the woman's choice to sacrifice her item of great cost on Jesus – in preparation for His burial – He commended her and condemned the troubling actions of the observers who were scolding the woman. Implicit in Jesus' rebuke of the observers and commendation of the woman was His acceptance of (1) actions that recognized His Messianic identity and (2) the use on Him of what could have helped many poor. In the eyes of Jesus, the woman had done a good thing rather than something for which she needed to be corrected.[2]

Mark previously recorded Jesus' care for the poor and affirmation of the poor.[3] The clause, 'For you always have the poor with you,' therefore should not be taken as Jesus' dismissal of the poor. Instead, Jesus was comparing the concern about spending wealth on Him as He goes to His death versus spending wealth on the poor. The woman's focus was on Jesus' death (which would be followed by a burial). What revelation gave her knowledge of His impending substitutionary work is not made clear. By whatever means

---

1. See Exodus 27:20; 29:7; 30:22-33; Leviticus 8:10-12, 30; 1 Samuel 10:1; 16:33; 2 Samuel 2:4; 5:3; 1 Chronicles 29:22; and Psalms 45:7; 89:20; and 133:2.

2. The Greek word that the ESV translates as 'beautiful' is *kalon* which means 'good.'

3. Mark 10:21; 12:42-43. See also Matthew 11:5; 19:21; Luke 14:13, 21; 16:22.

she learned of His death as the coming king-priest, she made a value judgment: Jesus' death was worth sacrificing this pure nard for. Those who wanted to help the poor had plenty of time to do so.[4] But this was the hour to weigh Jesus' death over other monetary options.

The commendation of the woman also recognized her intent: she wanted to do something good toward Jesus before He died, but the only thing of value (or the most valued thing) that she had was the nard. Rather than keeping the nard as an asset or security for a time of financial hardship or shortfall, she determined that the dead body of Jesus would do well to have it. So instead of waiting until His death, she performed an act foreshadowing her hope. Later, several women will attempt to anoint Jesus' dead body with fragrances (Mark 16:1).

The prophetic-promise in verse 9 continues the words of commendation of the woman. With an emphatic truth statement, Jesus promised the remembrance of this story wherever the good news is preached. His words are fulfilled in the capturing of the story in the Gospel accounts. The story was attached to the good news of the kingdom – the message Jesus had preached throughout His ministry and the reason for which He came. The story will reach people in 'the whole world,' having a ministry greater than those who heard Jesus speak these words.

Since Mark 3:19, the reader has anticipated the revealing of Judas as the betrayer. The motive and means of betrayal have been hidden until this chapter. But the woman's choice of spending her wealth on Jesus and His commendation of her turned Judas from being among Jesus' followers to becoming a betrayer. His actions began the fulfillment of Jesus' predictions in Mark 8:31, 9:31, and 10:33. Judas went to the chief priests to gain authority by Jewish legal code to turn Jesus in as a blasphemer. Even the chief priests will need Rome to declare Him a treasonous threat to Caesar, worthy of death.[5] The chief priests' gladness and monetary offering to Judas exposed their intentions. Whatever it took to arrest

---

4. A different word in the Greek, *eu*, meaning 'beneficial,' is behind 'good' in verse 7.

5. See Matthew 27:1-2; Luke 23:1-2, 13-16; John 18:30-31; 19:12.

Jesus, they would do; a follower volunteering eliminated the problem of a potential uproar.

The giving of money to Judas kept the focus of the passage on monetary intentions surrounding Jesus. The woman found Jesus' impending death worthy of a large financial sacrifice, because she had faith to see Him as her king-priest Messiah. The observers did not think Jesus was of as much worth as giving to the poor; they pitted giving to the poor against giving to Jesus. Judas saw Jesus' death as an opportunity for financial gain and the chief priests were willing to give money if it meant getting rid of Jesus. Only the woman received commendation.

The gospel is not something to be juxtaposed against compassion to the poor; Jesus' care for the poor was evident before this episode. One should not see Jesus' death as a means to advantage oneself financially. Yet with money in hand, Judas needed to finish the job for which he had contracted himself.

Intentions, Word, and Sacrament (14:12-16)

It was now early Thursday, the day of the Passover slaughter.[6] The Passover was attached to the Feast of Unleavened Bread and considered its first day. The preparation day was Nisan 14, which was Thursday, following the instructions to sacrifice the Passover offering in the evening at sunset (Deut. 16:6). The verses focus on preparing the Passover (i.e., 'Passover' in verses 12 (2x), 14, 16, and 'prepare'/'prepared' in verses 12, 15, 16).

In preparing for the Passover, Jesus instructed two of the twelve concerning two men in the city. The men who appear here with one-hit-wonder roles in redemptive history have precedent in Scripture, as similar appear-once figures occur in the lives of Joseph, David, and the disciples.[7] Although foils in the narrative, they are significant to the story of redemption for their obedience to Jesus and service to the disciples. The first man came to the disciples; he would be identified specifically by him carrying a jar of water. Jesus' knowledge

---

6. Exodus 12:6, 18; Leviticus 23:4-8; Numbers 9:1-5; 28:16.

7. Joseph (Gen. 37:15-17), David (1 Sam. 30:11-15), and the disciples (John 6:9).

of those details showed His exhaustive foreknowledge, describing location, events, persons, materials, and contents with exactness without waiting upon the free-will decision of persons to reveal God's decree.

Upon following the identified man, the disciples were to speak to the house master. That person knew Jesus as Rabbi, and had had previous discussion about a guest room and about its use for Passover. He was awaiting the arrival of Jesus. The disciples' trust in those exact details took faith in what Jesus said. They needed to trust the words of God for their Passover instructions if they were to enjoy the Passover with proper order. Jesus' words came true in every detail. The disciples prepared the memorial to Israel's deliverance from Egypt, only this time they would celebrate a greater deliverance.

In the New Testament, believers have instructions on how to receive the Lord's Supper within a local congregation, but few words on preparation for the meal in comparison to the lengthy discussion of Passover preparation in the Old Testament.

1. We must cleanse out (the old leaven of) evil and malice from within and among us (1 Cor. 5:7-8).

2. We must flee from all forms of idolatry (1 Cor. 10:14).

3. We must examine ourselves for selfishness and/or lack of love toward members of the body (1 Cor. 11:21, 27, 28).

4. We are to be reconciled to offended brothers and sisters prior to participating in this act of worship (Matt. 5:23-24).

5. We must give thanks for the bread (1 Cor. 11:24).

6. We should break the bread (1 Cor. 10:16; 11:25).

7. We should bless the cup (1 Cor. 10:16).

As our Passover Lamb has been sacrificed for us once and for all (1 Cor. 5:7-9), we are to share in remembrance of His atoning work when we gather. In Mark 14, the Lord was revealing the power of obedience to His commands in the disciples' enjoyment of the meal with Him; now believers do similar, for we enjoy the meal most when we are living in obedience to His Word – e.g., 'Word and Sacrament.' Jesus intends our obedience to His Word as we approach the sacrament of the Lord's Supper. He expects our obedience as much as He fully expected two disciples to go ahead to a city and await an unknown man with a jar of water to lead them to the place where another unknown man would show them the place prepared for them to eat the Passover with Jesus.

Intentions and Apostates (14:17-21)

Thursday evening of Holy Week found the disciples enjoying the Passover meal with Jesus at the prepared location. 'The twelve' informs the reader of the presence of Judas. One still should be anticipating Jesus' predicted betrayal, especially since the time Judas secured a reward for his offer to the chief priests.

In similar fashion to the experience of the meal at Simon's home, Jesus interrupted the memorial meal with a startling revelation. He pointed the finger toward an unknown betrayer among them – one who, rather than following Jesus in sincerity, would set in motion Him being handed over to His opponents.

'One who is eating with me' reveals how much a betrayer might blend in with the disciples. Judas Iscariot was appointed as one of the twelve by Jesus, designated 'apostle' like the other eleven, was sent out to proclaim the good news of the kingdom of God with the others, and had similar authority over demons (Mark 3:14-19). He looked the part of a faithful disciple and apostle. There was no reason to suspect him until the betrayal happened. In the New Testament, apostates blend in with the elect, looking similar to believers in their experiences.[8] It is only the actual departure from the faith into evil or sin that reveals an apostate's true identity as one unredeemed (Heb. 6:6-9).

The notification of a betrayer brought both sorrow and introspection from each of them. Such personal examination was appropriate, as was sorrow over the presence of a defector.[9] Yet after each had made inquiry, Jesus gave more revelation, repeating that He was speaking of 'one of the

---

8. Matthew 13:30; Acts 20:29-30; 2 Corinthians 11:15; Hebrews 6:4-5; 2 Peter 2:1; Jude 1:4.

9. 1 Corinthians 11:28; 2 Corinthians 13:5; Galatians 6:4; 2 Peter 1:9-11.

twelve' who looked as much like a committed follower as all the others. Jesus had full knowledge of the betrayer and again revealed His exhaustive foreknowledge of what would happen. But the eleven could not discern the betrayer for his participation among them seemed genuine; it mimicked the confession of Christ made by the others, until it didn't.

Jesus dipped His bread into a bowl of sauce used in the Passover meal.[10] The dipping of the bread brings an echo of Psalm 41:9, 'Even my close friend in whom I trusted, who ate my bread, has lifted his heel against me.' Judas fell into the pattern of David's close friend turned enemy. Now, to the promised Davidic Son, Judas will be the greatest betrayer in the history of the world.

The events leading up to the departure of Jesus to the cross, including the fellowship meal with an intimate friend sharing bread with Him, were foretold in the Hebrew Canon. The delivering up of God's Servant was foretold by Isaiah. There is little doubt that Doeg the Edomite, Absalom, and Joab each foreshadowed the betrayer.[11] Jesus pronounced strong condemnation upon the betrayer – one that indicated the betrayer would perish. The fate of the betrayer is of sufficient woe that he would wish life in this world had never come to him. The finality with which Jesus spoke shows that Judas was beyond repentance.

Intentions and the Power of the Bread and the Cup (14:22-25)

During the Passover meal, Jesus instituted the Lord's Supper. His institution of the Supper with the disciples during Passover revealed the symbolism of His body and the covenant blood for the atonement of the remnant. It inaugurated the New Covenant and pointed to His participation with us in the kingdom of God.

Mark's telling of the institution of the Lord's Supper does not include a reference to the bread representing a body that suffers on behalf of the people. However, Mark includes (1) God's invitation to the meal in the words of blessings, (2) the sharing from one loaf that is broken, and (3) the partaking of

10. Wessel, *Mark*, 759.
11. Doeg (1 Sam. 21:7; 22:9, 22); Absalom (2 Sam. 15:1-14), Joab (1 Kings 2:5-6).

the meal as symbolic of being united into Jesus' body and of His presence among them.

The shared partaking of the cup manifested (1) God's invitation to the meal in the words of thanksgiving, (2) the sharing from one cup that is drank, and (3) the partaking of the meal as symbolic of Jesus' death cutting the covenant and providing a ransom. 'Blood of the covenant' borrows the language of Exodus 24:8, where the Old Covenant (Law) was instituted by blood: 'And Moses took the blood and threw it on the people and said, "Behold the blood of the covenant that the LORD has made with you in accordance with all these words."' Although Mark does not use 'new' to modify 'covenant,' the infusion of Jesus' life and death into the meal indicated that more than a memorial of the Exodus was taking place. A new thing would take place in Jesus' death that would not be part of the Old Covenant.

In addition to Exodus 24, the taking of the cup draws upon the Servant's sacrifice for the remnant in Isaiah 53:12: 'Therefore I will divide him a portion with *the many* and he shall divide the spoil with the strong, because he poured out his soul to death and was numbered with the transgressors; yet he bore the sin *of many*, and makes intercession for the transgressors.'

The Lord's Supper has been practiced in the church since its inception.[12] In His death, Jesus fulfilled the Passover so that the Lord's Supper became the memorial meal for Christians (1 Cor. 5:7-8). Yet the meal, as symbolic, also points forward to the return of Christ. All of Jesus' disciples look forward to sharing a fulfilled meal with Jesus in the kingdom of God. The meal here is not the final hope but only points to it – to the New Covenant's promise for sin to be forgiven forever and for the knowledge of God to be full and internal (Jer. 31:33-34). The meal is powerful for the remnant.

Intentions, Allegiance, Shame, Grace (14:26-31)

The Mount of Olives, which looks out over the Kidron Valley, has a special place in the passion narrative (Mark 11:1). The Temple mount would have been visible from it (Mark 13:3)

---

12. Acts 2:42, 46; 20:7, 11; 1 Corinthians 5:7-8; 10:16-17; 11:23-27; see also Acts 27:35.

and the promise of the Messiah's return was associated with it (Zech. 14:4). Every visit to the mount carried the hope of the Messiah's victorious return to establish the kingdom promised to Israel. As the Hillel Psalms and Great Hillel were sung during the Passover, the disciples may have sung one of them between the meal and the mount.[13]

Jesus' insertion of Zechariah 13:7 brings the Word of Scripture to the forefront of the passion events. God's own voice has decreed the events ahead and has determined the path before the disciples and Jesus. All eleven of the disciples will flee in those coming events.[14] They are connected to the words in Zechariah 13:7 as Jesus assumes the role of 'the shepherd' and thusly identifies His followers as 'the sheep.' The striking which Jesus mentioned found reference in His betrayal and arrest.

With another reference to His own resurrection, Jesus communicated grace towards the failing disciples. Despite their scattering away from Jesus, He will meet them as His own in Galilee. Rather than experiencing wrath for their lack of allegiance, the disciples experience the grace of Christ's power and presence. Even though Jesus has spoken the words breathed out from the mouth of God through Zechariah, Peter will speak to counter what the Lord has spoken, as he has done previously.[15] Even though Peter's intention is good, zealous, and spoken with sincerity, they are arrogant and ill-informed. They also miss the grace guaranteed in the words, 'I will go before you.'

Peter set himself above the other disciples by rejecting the possibility that he could be scattered by fear of seeing the shepherd harmed. In response to those words spoken in the absolute, Jesus directed His words to Peter, speaking with absolute certainty to reveal his arrogance and error. The reply of Jesus had three elements, each related to a numerical exactness spoken with emphasis: (1) The same night (literally 'Today, this night'), (2) before 'twice' (in

13. The Hillel Psalms (113–118) were sung during the Passover. The Great Hillel (Psalm 136) was sung during the Passover Seder.

14. Mark 14:50. Judas had defected and will die; he will not be present. John also fled initially, but then turned to follow Jesus (John 18:15).

15. See Mark 8:32-33.

position in the clause in front of 'the rooster crows'), and (3) 'three times' (spoken first in this clause). The last clause says literally, 'three times me you will utterly disown,' looking ahead to when Peter would use foul language to disassociate himself from Jesus and His followers. Peter will not be above the other disciples; more than simply scattering like the others, Peter will actively distance himself from any knowledge of Jesus.

Still having good intentions but being unwilling to yield to the Word of God, Peter retorted with great insistence that he would choose death before denial.[16] He had interpreted 'scattered' as total apostasy, whereas Jesus only viewed the scattering as a turning away in fear that will later see the disciples coming to Him in Galilee. The words from the mouth of God will rule in grace over the good but misinformed intentions of Peter and the disciples.

The disciples all placed their allegiances to Jesus to the point of their individual deaths. But they will run away when it looks as if they will be arrested with Jesus. Prideful allegiance has no place in following Jesus. All believers have moments of lapse in which they intend to be unwavering in commitment to Christ, but fail to make their allegiance known in the face of hostilities or potential hostilities directed toward Christ. Thankfully, grace will rule over believers' lives in the same way as it did for the disciples.

Intentions, Temptations, Watching, Praying (Mark 14:32-42)

The Garden of Gethsemane was part of the Mount of Olives. Jesus instructed eight disciples to remain closer to the entrance than to where He took the three of the inner circle. They were to wait while He prays, without any reference to what He will be seeking in prayer. He commanded them to pray because they would be facing great temptation and fear once opposing forces came to arrest Jesus.

The choice to take Peter, James, and John should conjure for the reader the hope of a miracle like that of the raising of Jairus'

---

16. The word behind 'emphatically' means a degree which is considerably in excess of some point on an implied or explicit scale of extent – 'very great, excessive, extremely, emphatic, surpassing, all the more, much greater' (Louw-Nida, 687).

daughter (Mark 5:37) or the Transfiguration (Mark 9:2). Their presence will give them unique experiences needed for their roles in the church. In this incident, they will witness Jesus' approach to the temptations associated with the sorrows of Gethsemane. Jesus became deeply emotionally and mentally stressed. His entire being anticipated the coming of the cross and seeing His transformation to this disposition would have been a first for the disciples.

Jesus was poignant about His distress: His death has brought about this major shift in His outlook; sorrow now overwhelmed Him. What He intended to do to address His sorrow required the disciples to stay alert for the coming of opponents. While the other disciples prayed, they had the more practical task of being ready to alert Jesus to the coming of those who will bring about the events of His death. In keeping with the story since 8:31, readers should be looking for Jesus to be betrayed into the hands of the Jewish authorities so that He would go to His death.

Jesus' steps of sorrow brought Him to the ground. But rather than being overwhelmed without recourse, Jesus turned to prayer. Even the distresses of Gethsemane – the sorrow of the coming cross – did not deter Jesus from seeking the Father. Instead, His approach to the greatest experience of emotional and mental anguish known to the world was to look to the Father in prayer. The second Gospel does not contain teaching on the Lord's Prayer, but in the record of the prayer, the church hears words that are reminiscent of this episode: 'Father ... lead us not into temptation but deliver us from evil.'

Mark frames the content of Jesus' prayer before giving the words of the prayer. From the ground, Jesus was invoking the Lord's mercy. 'The hour' referenced was His death; within the depths of His distressing sorrow, He asked for a means to avoid the death, for His death meant drinking the cup of God's wrath (cf. Mark 10:38-39). Jesus sought possibilities as one feeling emotionally and mentally overwhelmed; He was not demanding to avoid the cross.

After framing the content, the writer gives us the words of Jesus' request in four parts. First, Jesus' vocative address used the Aramaic 'Abba,' a term of intimacy, but not to be equated with the English term, 'Daddy.'[17] The Jews never addressed God the Father in this manner, for fear of showing disrespect to Him. Jesus' use of the term 'provides crystal clarity into Jesus' consciousness of being God's Son, and of His willingness to drink the bitter cup of suffering as an ineluctable consequence of His complete trust in the Father and obedience to His will.'[18]

Second, Jesus recognized the absolute power of God over all things real and potential. Even in His emotional distress, Jesus held to the truth about the character of God in hope.

Third, His request asked for the object of distress to be removed. Jesus asked to have the wrath of God removed, which is to ask not to die a substitutionary death for humankind. He faced wrath for the sake of sinners. An answer to this request, however, would mean the perishing of all.

Fourth, the request yielded the wishes of Jesus to the Father. The Son subordinated His desires to the decree of God. What the Son desired mentally, emotionally, and in His soul, was to avoid the sorrow of the cross. But Jesus yields to whatever the Father has determined for His own glory.

Jesus left the three with a command to watch for the betrayer. One might wonder how they failed to stay at their posts. The significance of the statements about the cross had not affected a change in their behavior. Thus, finding them sleeping rather than watching, Jesus spoke directly to Peter – the one who was adamant about his loyalty to Jesus. Peter should have been able to watch for people approaching the entire time Jesus went away to pray, even if Jesus had departed for an hour.

The admonition to be watchful and prayerful was also for Peter's sake. Peter (and James and John) needed to seek

---

17. France comments, 'The much-discussed contention of J. Jeremias that an address to God as Ἀββά is unparalleled in Jewish literature, and marks a unique sense of intimacy with God, remains valid, even if the issue has been clouded by the frequent assertion by preachers that this familiar term equates to the English "Daddy". J. Barr's argument that "Abba is not Daddy"[16] is well taken, in that there is nothing childish about the special relationship implied (it was also used, for example, by disciples addressing their rabbi), but that was not Jeremias's point. The term conveys the respectful intimacy of a son in a patriarchal family' (France, *Mark*, 584; he references J. Barr, 'ABBĀ ISN'T "DADDY,"' *JTS* 39 [1988], 28-47).

18. Edwards, *Mark*, 434.

the Father for help with the trials they would face. The impending death of Jesus would bring temptations for the disciples; being alert for coming challenges would keep them from overreacting to a startling event. Prayer would allow the Father to strengthen Peter's inner-person so that he would not weakly yield to coming temptations.

Jesus repeated His previous prayer, saying exactly the same words without concern about being repetitive. The temptation and distress were so great that Jesus cried out to the Father a second time for a possible means to avoid the cup of His wrath.

The cycle of finding them sleeping a second and third time indicates that Jesus went away to pray a third time. The previous repetition of the prayer suggests a pattern of words Jesus would have repeated during His third session of prayer. Jesus returned from that session to find the three with heaviness of eyes.[19] They had yielded to the temptation to sleep rather than pray. Yet Jesus did not excuse their lack of prayer on the basis of their tiredness, as evidenced by the loss of words to His inquiry by the disciples.

More than enough time had passed for the disciples to have both rested and prayed; but they had chosen to continue to rest. Their lack of alertness and prayer would bring them to the hour of Jesus' betrayal without preparation of their inner being; soon they will find that their weakness in their physical bodies involved more than sleepiness.

The Daniel figure, 'The Son of Man,' again tied Jesus' identity as deity to the work of the atonement. The One who will come in the clouds with power now experienced betrayal by one of His own. As He moved toward His own death, He was forging the path to His own glorious return. The path was one in which sinners would mistreat Him. Yet, always in control of His situation, by yielding to the will of God, Jesus rose to face the betrayer as the will of God for Him. Having turned in prayer to His Father, He was prepared for the temptations to come, whereas the disciples were not.

---

19. The writer uses the word *katabapynō* – to be heavy or weighed down, or burdened.

Intentions, Wrong Responses, and the Fulfillment of Scripture (14:43-52)

The cohort led by Judas had been *en route* to arrest Jesus during His sessions of prayer. While He was chastening the disciples for their lack of prayer, Judas and the crowd appeared. In this episode, Jesus' reply to Judas and the delegation's capture by betrayal will allow for wrong approaches to Him – to the Son of Man who will die for sinners (v. 41) – so that Scripture might be fulfilled. Mark shows six incorrect responses surrounding the betrayal of Jesus: (1) Judas pretended to love Jesus only to have Him captured. (2) The guards laid hands on Jesus and seized Him. (3) A disciple attempted to defend Jesus although that disciple was weak in his body. (4) The crowd did not seize Jesus in the Temple due to fear. (5) The disciples all fled. (6) A young man fled naked.

It is important to the writer of the second Gospel to distinguish Judas as 'one of the twelve.'[20] The betrayal was an inside job, from someone who was present when Jesus cast out unclean spirits, calmed the storm on the sea, healed a hemorrhaging woman, fed four thousand to ten thousand people on separate occasions, and healed lepers and people of various infirmities. That Judas had been in close proximity to Jesus and had seen evidence for His claim to be God the Son made Judas' betrayal a sin of the highest order.[21]

The delegation with Judas came prepared for a difficult arrest, armed to fight anyone who would attempt to prevent Jesus from being captured. They had the authority of the Jewish leadership, and the identity of those authorizing reminds readers that the story still heads toward the fulfillment of Jesus' words in 8:31, 9:31, and 10:32.

Judas prearranged a signal to pinpoint Jesus to the arresting delegation, as He might not have been known to them. With a kiss that would normally be for a friend,[22] Judas gave away Jesus to be grabbed and transported like a criminal.

---

20. Mark 14:10, 20, 43.

21. Judas is sinning according to the Mosaic Law – Deuteronomy 19:15-21; Proverbs 17:15; 18:5; 28:21.

22. One should compare Mark's use of *phileo* (kiss) to his use of the intensified compound, *kataphileo* (kiss) in Mark 14:45.

The greeting of 'Rabbi' was intended to make the approach seem pleasant. However, when he kissed Him, those grabbing Jesus forcefully revealed the true intentions of the greeting. Judas was an apostate, too cowardly to simply look Jesus in the eye and say that he had come to arrest Him.

Only the fourth Gospel identifies Peter as the one who drew a sword and struck the earlobe of the high priest's servant and cut it off. Associating the servant with the high priest indicted the Jewish leadership in the betrayal and raised the stakes of the arrest. The word of the servant's injury at the hand of one of Jesus' disciples would have made its way back to the high priest (even as it made it into the record of all four Gospel accounts). The lashing out by Peter manifested the weakness of his tired body to think wisely, not give into fear or unrighteous anger, and not return evil for evil. Intending to be faithful to his stated loyalty, Peter created a crisis situation in which those with the swords and clubs now could come after him and the disciples.

The Markan account does not mention the healing of the servant's ear (Luke 22:51), which gives great tension to the scene. The servant had been attacked and was bleeding, and his companions were armed with swords and clubs that could be used in response. Jesus used the attack on the servant to point out the hypocrisy of the arresting throng. A thief or armed anarchist would deserve the approach they have brought to Jesus. But Jesus was not deserving of such an approach, even if only speaking of Him as a human. Certainly as the coming substitutionary sacrifice He was not deserving of being accosted like one guilty of crimes. The failure of those like the delegation to apprehend Jesus while He was among the crowds in the Temple showed what was in the hearts of those authorizing the arrest (and not only of those carrying out their orders): they wanted to rid themselves of Jesus without losing the favor of the people.[23]

The entirety of the activities in this betrayal scene are in concert with what the Lord had spoken in Scripture. Psalms 41:9 and 55:12-13 are among Scriptures in which the experiences of the Old Testament speakers go beyond that

---

23. See comments on Mark 14:1-2.

of their immediate human setting to find completion in the experience of Jesus in Gethsemane. This will lead to scores of Scriptures related to the work of God in salvation being fulfilled as Jesus is beaten, deprived of justice, sacrificed in death, and raised victoriously in three days.

Also immediately fulfilled are the words of Zechariah 13:7 quoted in Mark 14:27: all of the disciples deserted Jesus when He was betrayed. Their loyalty was limited by the threat of death at this point in their walk with Christ.

The odd scene of the fleeing young man falls into the pattern of the disciples and the betrayers. Everyone in this scene responded incorrectly to Jesus' heading toward His death. The betrayer was an apostate to Jesus and the Mosaic Covenant. Peter and the eleven temporarily deserted Christ as betrayers of the truth about His identity as Israel's long-awaited Messiah. The unnamed figure falls into this pattern. In Christ, love accepts that there are moments in the lives of believers in which some will flee temporarily from being associated with Jesus in order to preserve their lives, however unfaithful such fleeing is.

It would be wise to assume that Mark, the author of the second Gospel, was the young man. Otherwise, one would need to ask how the incident was known and who would have told it to the writer without shame. The details of 'young man,' 'but a linen cloth,' 'left the linen cloth,' and 'ran away naked' are words of eyewitness detail. When he was seized like Jesus, rather than joining Jesus in His suffering, like the disciples his following of Jesus was limited by the threat of (in)justice at the hands of the authorities for associating with Jesus. His fleeing showed partial fulfillment of Amos 2:16: '"And he who is stout of heart among the mighty shall flee away naked in that day," declares the LORD.'

Intentions, and Silence to Unrighteousness (14:53-65)

Various hypocritical religious responses now came to Jesus as He stood before the high priest. Following His initial silence to false accusations, these responses are met with Jesus' revelation of His identity as the Christ. Eventually, the episode will see Him condemned as deserving death without regard for Him as a prophet.

The throng had to take Jesus to the chief religious authority for judgment. Jesus' predicted cast of characters were present, bringing further fulfillment of the words He spoke in Mark 8:31, 9:31, and 10:32. In great contrast, Peter did not stand by Jesus' side as one willing to die. He traveled behind Jesus at a distance that he thought would disconnect him from any associations that could have him arrested. He was in the courtyard of the one who should have stood as a mediator for Israel. But both Peter and the mediator failed Jesus at this hour. Peter sat with those working for the high priest in order to gain warmth when he could have gained warmth in the house with Jesus.

Mark condemns the entirety of the Jewish leadership. They were guilty of seeking false witness against an innocent person.[24] But Jesus' words and life stood up to the religious scrutiny of those deceitful men. They had no words for which to condemn Him to death; the words of the false witnesses were conflicting because Jesus had complete integrity.[25]

The council welcomed the testimony of false witnesses who twisted the words of Jesus in an attempt to have Him condemned. The claim they made against Him did not come from words recorded in the Synoptics, but only in John 2:19. The repetition of the claim in Mark shows the veracity of the words as Jesus' own.[26] Yet the words of Mark 14:58 differ from what John records Jesus as saying, for Jesus did not speak of 'not made with hands' toward the new edifice. The exaggeration seems to have been an attempt to discredit Jesus. But the false witnesses did not speak in unison on what Jesus reportedly said. He could stand up to their religious attacks.

Even though it was evident that the witnesses were false because they could not agree on what is true, the high priest still examined Jesus. The focus made him the chief opponent of Jesus in verses 60-64. His question attempted to lure Jesus into self-incrimination, but Jesus again stood up to this scrutiny with His silence, as foretold in Isaiah 53:7. He had no need to answer false accusations about statements related to

---

24. Exodus 20:16; 23:1; Proverbs 24:28; 25:18.
25. There is a fulfillment of Psalm 27:12 in this scene.
26. See also Mark 15:29.

the Temple, for statements interpreted as blasphemy against the Temple would be heard as blasphemy against God.

The second question from the high priest went directly to the identity of Jesus, equating the Messiah and the divine Sonship of Jesus.[27] Jewish belief did not separate deity from Messiahship; it knew God to be the promised Servant of Israel. Jesus therefore broke His silence to agree with what was true, in great contrast to the false witnesses. He is the Messiah, and He is the divine Son of God the Father. He is Daniel's figure who will approach the Ancient of Days and take the seat of the Vice-Regent of God to rule with dominion on behalf of God the Father.[28] As the Son of Man, He will return in the clouds of the skies – a symbol of the approach of God borrowed from Old Testament imagery.[29]

Jesus' testimony of righteousness and hope of exaltation were the needed reply to the high priest. They should have established His innocence and the unjust religious trial should have ended with His words. However, the high priest was not convinced or silenced. In tearing his clothes, he graphically expressed his belief that Jesus had uttered blasphemy. Yet the tearing profaned the priest from performing his duties in the Temple (Lev. 21:10). Unlike Jesus, who was silent in the face of hearing unrighteous words toward Him because He was righteous, the high priest spoke in the face of hearing what he perceived to be blasphemy while standing in unrighteousness in his torn clothes.

The high priest's dismissal of a need for witness removed both the problem of a lack of two or three witnesses to agree

---

27. On 'Son of the Blessed,' France notes, 'The use of εὐλογητός in place of θεός reflects the Jewish avoidance of direct use of the name of God. In this context where "blasphemy" is at issue, the usage is important.... ὁ εὐλογητός alone as a title for God (as opposed to the frequent adjectival use, "Blessed be God ...", Luke 1:68; Eph. 1:3; 1 Pet. 1:3, etc.) does not occur elsewhere in biblical literature' (France, *Mark*, 610). James Edwards similarly comments, 'In the original Greek the wording is put in the form of a statement with a question implied ("You are the Christ, the Son of the Blessed One?"). The "you" is emphatic, and "the Blessed One," a Jewish circumlocution for God's name, means none other than "God's Son." The effect is to put a full christological confession into the mouth of the high priest!' (Edwards, *Mark*, 446.)

28. See Daniel 7:13-14. 'Of Power' is an additional Jewish circumlocution for God's name.

29. Exodus 40:34-38; 2 Samuel 22:21 (Psalm 18:11); Job 22:14; Psalms 97:2; 104:3; Isaiah 19:1; Nahum 1:3.

on charges against Jesus and the reception of false testimony. His invitation for the council to offer a statement of legal judgment effectively condemns the council in unrighteousness as they spoke against Jesus. Their judgment accomplished the requirements for death according to Jewish law, but Roman judgment was needed for Jesus to be put to death.

The actions that followed the adjudication were heinous. The spitting and mocking were intended to degrade and demean Jesus as a sinner. 'Some' and 'blows' portray to the reader how many members of the council engaged in dehumanizing Jesus. They would have Him prophesy about who hit Him even though He could not see them, to prove that He was a prophet. But Jesus had prophesied before them about His return in power. They were only mocking Him. The guards' bludgeoning of Him showed that all participated in the working of false witnesses.

Intentions, Potential Hostility, and Denial (14:66-72)

Casually Peter stood in the courtyard as if he belonged there – as if he was only another bystander in the courtyard of the high priest. As he stood near a fire to keep warm, the light of the fire allowed someone present to look closely at him.[30] Peter's identity was betrayed by a servant, not a delegation from the council. He was outed by a woman, not by one of the twelve.

Other than a Gentile, a Jewish female servant was the person of lowest rank who could identify Peter. Her testimony almost was negligible when she placed Peter with Jesus. Peter could have brushed her words aside as that of a female servant. Instead, he denied having been with the man from Nazareth, and claimed to have no specific knowledge about His identity and no ability to comprehend that of which the servant spoke. He did not deny belief in Jesus' Messianic qualifications; he only sought to escape the trial(s) associated with Jesus' claim to be the coming Son of Man.

Peter moved away from the fire's light to the vestibule area so as not to be seen so easily. It was then that a rooster

---

30. The Greek has two words: *idoūsa* ... *embléphasa* ('perceive with the eye ...' 'see up close').

crowed.[31] The crowing should have warned Peter that his following of Jesus was in jeopardy of becoming the prophesied triple denial, but it did not. He continued to stay near the courtyard area.

The servant girl did not need the light of the fire to identify Peter a second time, having already recognized him. With confidence she pointed out Peter to others in the courtyard and said he was 'from' the group of Jesus' disciples.[32] Mark records Peter's second denial without giving the contents of his speech. He had denied any knowledge of Jesus, and now denied being one of His followers. His denials increased so that he might continue to benefit from the resources of those around him who were not followers of Jesus. He did not want trouble from them, or to be told to get away from the fire's warmth and stand in the cold alone.

The words of Peter's identity spread among the bystanders. Having heard his denial, they did not need the fire or the servant girl to associate Peter with Jesus and His followers. The bystanders confronted Peter directly on his identity as a follower of Jesus. They were certain of his identity based on his Galilean dialect.[33] Being caught by multiple witnesses, Peter resorted to the use of an oath combined with cursing to distance himself from Jesus. The sense of the words seems to be that first he invoked damnation upon himself,[34] possibly like, 'May I be anathemized if it is not true that I don't know this man.' Second, he provided an oath formula before his words, '[I swear before God that] I do not know of this man of whom you speak.' Even 'this man' and 'you speak' were attempts to show that he had no knowledge of Jesus and the bystanders were inventing his association. But neither Peter's nor our identities as followers of Jesus can be hidden. Peter was a follower, as his presence and weeping show. Judas was an apostate, as previously shown.

---

31. There are difficulties associated with 'the rooster crowed' being the preferred reading, but I think it is the more difficult reading and should be retained.

32. The Greek has *ek autōn*, 'from them,' referencing the followers of Jesus.

33. Edwards, *Mark*, 451. See Matthew 26:73 in which Peter's accent is said to give him away. Hooker proposes, 'There must have been plenty of Galileans in Jerusalem at festival time but not, presumably, inside the high priest's house' (Hooker, *Mark*, 364-65).

34. 'Curse' is a form of *anathema* (cf. 1 Cor. 12:3; 16:33; Gal. 1:8, 9).

As Peter cursed, Jesus' prediction of the cock crowing twice came to fulfillment. Peter's remembering meant that he heard the first crowing and had disregarded what Jesus had said. But the Word of God will not fail. That same Word speaks on the shame that deniers of Christ will experience before the Father.[35] Only election, repentance, and the grace of Christ's restoration separated Peter from Judas.[36]

As if a burden too great for him to lift had been laid on him, Peter fell down emotionally under the crushing weight of his sinful denials, crying aloud with sorrow. Seemingly, in redemptive history, this episode in the life of Peter would foster humility in him about his own abilities, commitment, and convictions. He would be sympathetic to those struggling in the faith after seeing his own role in sending Jesus to the cross. Shame is a powerful tool of God in the lives of believers.

Reflective Questions

1. To what does the 'cup' of the Lord's Supper point, and what does it reveal? Why is it important to follow the apostolic formula of participating in the Lord's Supper?

2. Where is grace evident throughout Mark 14? What does one learn about the grace of God for us by all that transpires in this chapter?

---

35. See Mark 8:38; Luke 9:26; Romans 1:16; Philippians 1:20; 2 Timothy 1:8; 1:12; 2:16.

36. On election, see John 6:44, 45, 65, 70-71; 13:18, 17:12. On repentance and restoration, see John 21:15-19 with Mark 14:28.

16

He Came to Show Us How to Suffer Unjustly as a King

(Mark 15)

Don't you hear the hammering?
Don't you hear the hammering?
Don't you hear the hammering?
Surely He died on Calvary.[1]

He would not come down from the cross
*   just to save himself,*
He decided to die just to save me.[2]

These words of two African American spirituals highlight the injustice of the cross for Jesus. The very God who gives us the power to use a hammer saw sinners use that power to crucify Him as a criminal, and the one who came to save us from the wrath of God did not choose to save Himself, though innocent, so that salvation could be accomplished. Jesus was brutally mistreated, yet did nothing to stop it. He did not reply to the accusation of the Jews, He did not accept wine as a sedative, and He did not rescue Himself. The release of Barabbas and the mocking that Jesus endured took place without Him speaking up or using His divine power to stop the injustice.

---

1. 'Calvary, Calvary,' African American Spiritual, Public Domain.
2. Donald Vails, 'He Decided to Die,' *He Decided to Die*, Savoy Records, 1990.

In accepting the greatest abuse ever leveled at a person in history at His crucifixion, Jesus showed His disciples an example of how to handle their own crucifixion(s) – that is, their own persecution for following Jesus. Jesus underwent the *most unimaginable, unbearable, unjust, unrelenting, undeserved, and seemingly unendurable trial* while also revealing His identity as our King. He now invites us as believers to reveal Him as King when we face similar trials. This chapter shows us how.

Let Your Silence Speak When You Are Wrongly Accused (15:1-5)

The chief priests wasted no time in proceeding from their religious trial conclusions toward their final goal. When morning broke, they consulted with the full Jewish leadership on their next moves. They needed Roman approval for their involvement in Jesus' death lest they be found guilty of murder resulting from an inner-religious squabble. They bound Jesus like a criminal and handed Him over to Pilate as Jesus prophesied in Mark 10:33. Pilate was the Roman prefect of the jurisdiction of Jerusalem from A.D. 26–27; he had authority to execute criminals.

Pilate's question indicates that the charge brought by the Jewish leadership was that Jesus claimed to be King of the Jews. As in the previous chapter, Jesus will affirm the truth. But His affirmation indicates that Pilate, a Gentile ruler, recognized Jesus' identity as the Messianic ruler. Mark does not specify the contents of the 'many things' of which the Jews accused Jesus. The false witness of the religious trial might offer insight; Luke 23:2 states one accusation made against Jesus. Whatever accusations they made were false, and Jesus gave no answer to them.

Jesus did not act as a person charged typically would, going back and forth with his accusers over his innocence. So Pilate was moved to ask Him about His silence toward the accusations, especially as they increased.

Jesus' limited answer to Pilate's examination of the charges against Him revealed Him as King of the Jews, to the amazement of Pilate. Jesus affirmed He was King; He did not need to speak further or to justify Himself against false accusations. His presence as a King stood despite Him being bound. As Jesus showed, there are times when silence speaks appropriately and loudly in the face of unjust accusation.

Watch Your Innocence Stand When Leaders Play Politics (15:6-15)

The feast in question was the Passover. To appease those under his rule, in an effort to maintain favor among his constituency, Pilate released a prisoner annually. Mark describes Barabbas with words in great contrast to the accused King of the Jews; Barabbas was a prisoner, rebel, murderer, insurrectionist. Jesus had freed people from sin, had been a peaceful citizen, had offered life, and had not even spoken against Rome.

The Passover crowd desired their annual gift, and it was politically wise for Pilate to grant what they wanted. Yet his question to the largely Jewish crowd made sense. An innocent King of the Jews should be released, and releasing Him might gain Him favor above that of the religious leadership. The leadership was envious of Jesus' popularity and acceptance among the people.[3]

Perceiving Pilate's ploy, the chief priests worked the crowd so that they spoke against his intentions. In doing so, they sought to have a guilty person freed and an innocent man condemned, in contrast to the stipulation of the Mosaic Law (Exod. 23:7). Their need to work the crowd indicates that the crowd had not perceived a reason for the King of the Jews to be condemned.

Pilate asked the crowd directly about their desired fate for Jesus. His inquiry indicated that the Jewish people claimed that Jesus was their King. If He is their King, what is His fate since they were calling for the release of a prisoner. They could have called for Jesus' release. But they did not; they called for Him to be nailed on a cross like a criminal – the place Barabbas rightly deserved to go as an insurrectionist, and that the Jewish leaders deserved to go as those working to undermine Pilate's political ploy.

Pilate's next two questions repeat the Markan portrayal of Jesus' innocence. Pilate had found no evil worthy of sending Jesus to death. As if the crowd was an accusing attorney, he

---

3. See Matthew 21:46; John 3:26; 12:19.

asked them to explain their reason for condemning the man
he found free of charges of wrongdoing. But the crowd did
not answer the question. As Wessel rightly comments, 'The
crowd, now a mob, ignored his question (v. 14). They had
reached a stage where they were beyond reason. No death for
Jesus but crucifixion would satisfy them. They wanted Him
to suffer the full ignominy of the cross.'[4] They were willing
to send Jesus to His death without reason. The ironies here
are multiplied.[5]

For the sake of political expediency Pilate arranged for
Jesus to be crucified and released Barabbas. Pilate had Jesus
scourged (or flogged) before being taken to Calvary. Flogging
was a brutal act:

> The prisoner was stripped and bound to a post and beaten with
> a leather whip woven with bits of bone or metal. No maximum
> number of strokes was prescribed. The scourging lacerated
> and stripped the flesh, often exposing bones and entrails.
> One of its purposes was to shorten the duration of crucifixion,
> but scourging was so brutal that some prisoners died before
> reaching the cross.[6]

Nevertheless, the scourged Jesus left the scene as innocent
as He entered. But being innocent does not necessarily spare
one from the brutalities of politics, whether governmental,
ecclesial, occupational, or judicial. Pilate gave the innocent
Jesus over to be crucified.

Expect Minimization of Your Beliefs Even If They Reveal the True King (15:16-20)

The scene shifted as the soldiers moved Jesus from the exterior
of the palace (or praetorium) to the interior.[7] The soldiers put

---

4. Wessel, *Mark*, 775.

5. Edwards writes, 'In the trial scene, as elsewhere in Mark's Gospel, ineluctable ironies confront us. Pilate, who begins by seeking amnesty for Jesus, ends by seeking it for himself. The Jewish subjects, on the other hand, whose duty it is to obey, assert their will and win the day. The governor is thus strangely governed. The free sovereign ... loses his freedom to forces he presumes to control, whereas Jesus, the silent prisoner who has no control, remains true to His divinely ordained purpose, and thus alone remains truly free' (*Mark*, 464).

6. Edwards, *Mark*, 464.

7. See John 18:28-29, 33, 38; 19:4-5.

out word to assemble the battalion (or Roman cohort) of local guards – about six hundred men. Inside the praetorium, Jesus faced mocking before hundreds of Gentile military men who had no regard for the Jews, and certainly not for one who claimed to be the Jews' King. The motive they had was to make sport of one perceived to be helpless before Pilate, and to belittle the Jewish people by dashing any hopes of them having a king who could liberate them from Rome.

The soldiers made several attempts to belittle Jesus. First, purple was associated with royalty, but the cloak was not the attire of a true king. Second, rulers would have worn a crown, but they would not have been made of materials as cheap and harmful as thorns. They did not go to a skilled workman; instead, they fashioned together Jesus' crown with their unskilled hands. By His attire, Jesus made a poor specimen for King of the Jews in the eyes of His detractors. By using thorns, the soldiers intended to inflict pain.

Third, the soldiers offered a salute in mimicry of the respectful salute given to a king. The saluting came from those fully loyal to Caesar. To the soldiers, Jesus was not a real king. They distanced themselves from Him as part of the mocking: He was not worthy of being a king in their eyes. Mark does not say how many soldiers gave this mocking salute.

Fourth, in a series of actions that have Old Testament allusions, the soldiers hit Jesus, spat on Him, and knelt before Him. In striking Him, the most immediate thought is Jesus' words in 14:27 that quote Zechariah 13:7: 'Strike the shepherd.' A better referent would be Moses' striking of the Rock.[8] The spitting fulfills Isaiah 50:6: 'I did not hide my face from ... spitting.'[9] The kneeling looks back to the words in Isaiah 45:23, 'every knee shall bow;' the soldiers' bowing falls within the pattern of the future submission of all to Christ as the *entire* battalion is present. The stripping of the robe is reminiscent of Genesis 37:23 where Joseph is stripped of his coat when his brothers initially had it in their hearts to kill him. Every Old Testament allusion in this scene shows that Scripture is

---

8. The Greek of Exodus 17:6 does not match the Greek wording in this verse. This would be a conceptual echo, if it is one, with knowledge that the Rock that was struck was Christ (1 Cor. 10:4).

9. Job 17:6 and 30:10.

being fulfilled as God brings about the redemption He has promised. Every Old Testament allusion points to Jesus as the King of the Jews despite the dishonor and harm shown by the large number of soldiers before whom He stood.

The soldiers were responsible for their actions. They led Jesus out even as they led Him in. They led Him there only to make sport of Him *en route* to crucifying Him. In returning His clothes to Him, the soldiers revealed what they really thought about the claim that Jesus was a King.

Endure Persecution for the Faith to Rebuff Cheapening of the Cross (15:21-32)

In 15:21-32, with a concentration of wrongs greater than that in the scene of the battalion, the criminal, degrading, cheapening treatment of Jesus as He was crucified revealed Him as the Christ – as the King of the Jews, in fulfillment of Old Testament Scriptures. The reader witnesses the people unleash an all-out assault on 'the King of the Jews,' a term now used for the fifth time in this chapter.[10]

The conscripting of Simon of Cyrene reflected the authority of soldiers to compel civilians to carry their wares for a Roman mile. Simon might have been a Roman, or he could have been a Jew in Jerusalem for the feast. He was from the north coast of Africa, which, as Edwards notes, 'may indicate that Simon was a man of color.'[11] The reference to 'Alexander and Rufus' was for the original recipients, suggesting further that Mark wrote to believers in Rome, if Rufus was the same person identified in Paul's greeting to the Romans (Rom. 16:13). Simon, a simple visitor to the city, carried Jesus' crossbeam, which led to him becoming the first to follow Mark 8:34 and take up his cross to follow Jesus.

---

10. Mark 15:2, 9, 12, 18, and 26. Also, Mark 15:32 uses the synonymous 'King of Israel.'

11. Edwards, *Mark*, 470. Edwards' comments are much more gracious that Wessel's, who writes with absolute certainty, 'Simon was no doubt a Jew (not an African black as some have suggested) and was on his way to the city of Jerusalem for the Passover celebration' (Wessel, *Mark*, 778). Wessel's comments do not reflect scholarship, but bias and insensitivity, as the words, 'as some have suggested' reveal. His entire parenthetical statement is unnecessary, and his argument for Simon's Jewish heritage could have been made without it.

The King of the Jews did not go to the Jewish Temple or to a king's palace. Instead, He went to a place associated with the skull of a corpse.[12] They offered Him a sedative – an echo of Psalm 69:21 – but He refused to deaden His sense of the full force of the wrath of God, or even possibly take a poisonous mixture that could end His life quickly. Either outcome would minimize the cross, so Jesus refused.

While Jesus was suffering on the cross, the soldiers gambled over who would have His clothing as keepsakes. Even as God directed the affairs of history to bring about the crucifixion of the Son of God, so the dividing of the garments fulfilled the words of Psalm 22:18. To the soldiers, the garments were more important than the One on the cross. But Jesus did not come down to confront the soldiers for this belittlement.

Mark states the time, allowing the reader to calculate how long the King of the Jews hung on the cross. Jesus was placed on the cross at 9 a.m. The placard with the charge revisits the title most often used for Jesus in this chapter – 'The King of the Jews.' The placard itself is full of irony for the reader because the inscription 'The King of the Jews' was not a charge; the inscription did not indicate that Jesus made this claim, which would have been read as treasonous (John 19:21-22). Instead, the sign rightly indicated that Jesus had gone to the cross because He is the King of the Jews. His Messiahship did not come without suffering on behalf of His people. The Jews who cried, 'Crucify him!' were complicit with Rome in placing their King on the cross. His identification as 'King of the Jews' cannot be minimized, despite all efforts to do so by the characters in Mark 15.

The placing of the King of the Jews among thieves gave to onlookers the idea that Jesus was a common criminal rather than a king. They may not have seen the total depravity of two thieves mocking the one who was their only hope. They may not have seen that He did not save Himself so that He might be a substitute for others, or that the decree of God delivered Him up for us (Acts 2:23).

The placement between two robbers fulfills Isaiah 53:12, although Mark does not give a fulfillment formula or reference

---

12. The origin of the name 'Golgotha' is unknown.

to that passage. While being portrayed as a criminal, Jesus shone forth as Isaiah's Servant.[13] Where one would expect cherubim to flank each side of the King, only criminals were found.[14] Even James and John were not found on Jesus' 'right' and 'left' as they had asked (Mark 10:37). One should not assume people understood salvation when looking at Jesus and His cross.

Even common people passing those crucified specifically directed derision at Jesus. Their head wagging and 'Aha' words fulfilled multiple Old Testament Scriptures regarding the enemies of the Messiah.[15] The Scriptures foretold of the enemies of Christ and their mocking centuries before the act occurred. God saw the attempts to cheapen the work of the cross in redemptive history ten centuries prior to Good Friday. Jesus' enduring of the slurs showed His power as King and His ability to give His own people the power to endure the lesser slurs they receive for following Him as Lord.

This is the second time Mark's Gospel reports of Jesus' speaking of destroying the Temple and rebuilding it in three days, even though such words are not recorded in the mouth of Jesus in this Gospel account. Evidently, the words were accurate, and were very significant to the Jews and their feelings about Jesus. Their reasoning was from lesser to greater: One who claimed to have the power to tear down a temple and then rebuild in three days what originally took forty-six years to build would have had the power to remove nails and come down from a cross (John 2:20). But in His failure to do so, the passers scoffed at both the figure on the cross and His claim about the Temple. Their misunderstanding about both Jesus and the Temple masked what the readers know to be true: the King of the Jews will rise three days after the temple of His body was destroyed.

The author ties the chief priests and the scribes into the group of those mocking. Rather than being above the

---

13. Isaiah 52:13; 53:11; see also Isaiah 42:1, 19; 43:10; 44:26; 49:3, 5, 6, 7; 50:10; Matthew 12:18; Acts 3:13, 26; 4:30.

14. See Exodus 25:19 and 37:8 for the placing of the cherubim with respect to the ark and the mercy seat.

15. Psalms 22:7; 35:21, 25; 40:15; 70:3; 109:25.

crowd as leaders, they were as sinful as the people in their disregard for the King. The mention of the chief priests and scribes brought all their confrontations to consummation. The chief priests were at the fore of the opposition in the passion narrative. Mark had insight into the words of intra-communication of the chief priest and scribes.

Within the intra-communication was more unintended recognition of the Messiah. 'The King of Israel' is synonymous to 'The King of the Jews,' but it has an echo to Isaiah 44:6 that 'of the Jews' does not have.[16] The irony of the chief priests and scribes' challenge for Jesus to come down from the cross is that coming down would empty out the goal of belief; there would not be a substitute to atone for sin. Thus, belief would have no object for salvation. Jesus did not provide them with the sign they wanted to see.

The two thieves flanking Jesus, though justly suffering themselves, joined the injustice by mocking the Savior. Whatever they said to Him in reviling Him, Jesus was on the cross because of those words too.

Interpret Suffering as Part of God's Plan of Redemption (15:33-41)

Darkness was a response of God to the crucifixion of His Son. God was not pleased with the darkness of the land – the darkness of humankind's sin. The forbidding feeling displayed the very wrath of God and forsaking of the Son. Stein notes, 'This real darkness at the crucifixion is a proleptic experience of the judgment that was coming upon Israel in A.D. 70.'[17] It was utter darkness for three hours. Christ had hung on the cross for six hours by the time of His death.

Jesus' interpretive response explained the darkness. He had been forsaken by God legally and covenantally. As Cranfield wrote, 'The burden of the world's sin, His complete self-identification with sinners, involved not merely a felt, but

---

16. 'Thus says the LORD, *the King of Israel* and His Redeemer, the LORD of hosts: "I am the first and I am the last; besides me there is no god."' See also Isaiah 6:5; 33:17, 22; 41:21; 43:15; Jeremiah 10:10; 23:5; 46:18; 48:15; Ezekiel 20:33; Zechariah 14:9, 16, 32; Malachi 1:4.

17. Stein, *Mark*, 2008, 715.

a real abandonment by the Father. It is in the cry of dereliction that the full horror of man's sin stands revealed.'[18]

The Father must judge sin and He must allow a breech between Himself and the Son similar to that of His breech with Israel.[19] It is here that the promised Genesis 3:15 deliverer received the wounding of His heel from the evil one. Jesus cried into the darkness loud enough for all to hear that He had been forsaken.[20] The words of Psalm 22:1 have always pointed to one who would yet declare God's name to His brothers in victory after suffering at the hands of His enemies (Ps. 22:22, 31). Here the words found completion in the loud cry of Jesus. Mark interpreted the cry so that non-Jewish readers would not mistake how Jesus viewed Calvary from the cross.

Those nearby misinterpreted what was happening to Jesus at Calvary. They heard 'Elijah' in 'Eloi.' They did not connect the crucifixion to Psalm 22. They thought Jesus was calling for the prophet to rescue Him. This is the fourth word of the seven sayings of Jesus from the cross and the only one repeated in two Gospel accounts.[21]

Having endured the wrath of God, Jesus was free to quench His parched lips and mouth with sour wine – one of a taste like vinegar.[22] The kind bystander would have had to stretch the reed high to reach Jesus – to serve the King exalted above the earth. The act of mercy also looked for Jesus to survive long enough for a possible rescue by Elijah. However, the person with the sponge was confused, also misinterpreting the events of Calvary. The cross was not about quenching of thirst or the return of a prophet. It was about One forsaken by God as a substitute for others.

With similar volume as used in His cry of abandonment, Jesus gave a guttural scream of words unknown to us.[23] It was

---

18. Cranfield, *St. Mark*, 1959, 458.

19. See Hosea 1:9 in which the Lord indicates He breaks the marital bond forged with Israel. Similarly, see Jeremiah 3:8.

20. Mark uses *phonē magále*, from which the modern reader can see the resemblance to 'megaphone.'

21. Also in Matthew 27:46. The other six sayings in order may be found in Luke 23:34; 23:43; John 19:26-27; 19:29; 19:30; and Luke 23:46.

22. Hans Wolfgang Heidland, Ὄξος, *TDNT*, 288-89.

23. Mark uses *phonèn megálen*. See comment above on Mark 15:34.

a cry of great anguish.[24] It would be His last sound before drawing His last breath. His cry and breathing showed He was a person – a divine King in a human body. The strength to do this after His degree of suffering pointed to *divine* power. Jesus' acceptance of unjust treatment as He was crucified affirmed His identity as the Messianic King of the Jews.

The tearing of the inner veil from top to bottom was the working of God.[25] Had it been from bottom to top, one may have considered it a human act. But from above it was torn; God no longer wanted the way to Him veiled. What stood between God and man was removed in the death of Christ. The way is now available for all to approach God through a greater High Priest. For God, what took place on Calvary answered the darkness the earth deserved. There now is a way to God.

The response of the centurion were the words of one who may have seen hundreds or thousands of crucifixions. A unique individual standing in a unique position made an unusual statement of certainty. The centurion was looking directly at Jesus, not looking casually at all three being crucified. He observed Jesus' cries from the cross, His sip of wine, and His last breath. In comparison to all other crucifixions he had seen, he was able to conclude about this death that it was like no other: *This one who died was God's very own Son.* What the reader has known since the opening verse of the second Gospel, a Gentile character finally stated explicitly. One sees the work of the King of the Jews – the King of Israel – blessing one outside of Israel, in fulfillment of the Abrahamic Covenant promises.[26] This polytheistic,

---

24. It is possible that the cry in Mark 15:37 was the same as the words in John 19:30. If so, then it was a cry of victory and not of anguish.

25. I agree with Robert Plummer, who writes, 'The lexical evidence for καταπέτασμα and ναός is inconclusive' (Robert L. Plummer, 'Something Awry in the Temple? The Rending of the Temple Veil and Early Jewish Sources that Report Unusual Phenomena in the Temple Around A.D. 30,' *JETS* 48 [2005]: 303). However, in mild disagreement with him, I think it is important to identify whether it is the outer curtain of the veil that was torn, or whether it is the inner one that was torn (and not two tearings, because the evangelists describe one). I find Daniel Gurtner to be correct in saying, '[The] term, as used in the New Testament, most certainly refers to the inner veil before the holy of holies' (Daniel M. Gurtner, 'The Veil of The Temple in History and Legend,' *JETS* 49 [2006]: 97. See also, Daniel M. Gurtner, 'LXX Syntax and the Identity of the New Testament Veil,' *NovT* 47 [2005]: 344-53).

26. Genesis 12:3; 18:18; 22:18; 26:4; 28:14; Acts 3:28; Galatians 3:8.

military man, who several hours previously participated in the massive group mockery of Jesus by the soldiers (the entire battalion was there), had no framework for monotheistic belief. His conclusion revealed that he had processed all that had been said about Jesus in his hearing and combined it with what he saw at Golgotha. He reasoned that the cross had witnessed the dying of the Son of God. He was certain of it (i.e., 'surely').

The presence of the women – both named and unnamed – showed their belief in Jesus' identity as Israel's King. They followed Him to the cross, having served Him in the past and seen up close that He had the words and character of the promised Messiah. Each name mentioned matters greatly in redemptive and church history.

Mary of Magdala was a woman of great means. She remained loyal to Jesus through to His resurrection. Mary, the mother of James the younger, is introduced to the Markan reader in this scene. She too was faithful in her service to her King. Salome also will be faithful through to the resurrection.

The three women served Jesus when He was in Galilee. They were among many women who had been served faithfully by Jesus, found Him to be a King who used His power to serve, establishing the dignity of both men and women, and had followed Him from Galilee to Jerusalem. They seem to have anticipated His enthronement as King of the Jews. Their loyalty spoke of their faith in His royalty. They gave witness to His identity after His death.

Jesus' acceptance of unjust treatment as He was crucified gained respect in His death through the women who followed Him faithfully.

Live in Light of His Death for Us in Ways to Garner Respect for Jesus (15:42-47)

Joseph showed respect for Jesus. If Jesus were not the King of the Jews, it would not have been the task of such a well-respected member of the Sanhedrin to ask for His body. Joseph sought to ensure that Jesus' crucifixion did not fall into Jesus becoming a curse for hanging on a tree.[27] Joseph had

---

27. Deuteronomy 21:23; Galatians 3:13.

hope in Jesus establishing the kingdom of God – a work of One who was King of the Jewish people. In the face of all that had transpired since Gethsemane and knowing Jesus had been crucified as a criminal under Pilate's authority, Joseph summoned courage to ask Pilate for Jesus' body. Joseph put himself at risk of being associated with Jesus but did so to give the King of the Jews a proper burial.

Pilate was surprised to hear that Jesus had already died. It took those crucified hours to die, usually much longer than it took Jesus. His inquiry to the centurion verified that Jesus had expired. By going through Pilate, Joseph gave respect to the prefect while also showing honor to the body of Jesus.

'Linen' has associations with ruling attire, the tabernacle, and the priesthood. Linen could make it appear that Jesus was wrapped in materials for death that were removed from the Levitical High Priest upon his death.[28] Twice the writer tells us the materials to draw our attention to them. Joseph spent of his own money to bury Jesus. He purchased uncommon materials and placed Jesus in a rock-hewn tomb. Joseph, by rolling the stone in front of the tomb, does not allow for anyone to access the body of Jesus. The burial was honorable.

With Mark 8:31, 9:31, and 10:33 in mind, the reader would have faced the dilemma of what should be done with the stone across the entrance of the tomb. Jesus had been handed over into the hands of people to die, as predicted. To move this stone, however, anticipates a visible, powerful display of the divine authority of He who is the King of the Jews. The stone prevented anyone from tampering with the body. But it did not prevent the King from bringing His kingdom – the kingdom He had proclaimed from the outset of His ministry.[29] Two of the ladies reappear. The location of the King's burial was known by them with certainty. Jesus' acceptance of unjust treatment as He was crucified gained further respect through the actions of Joseph of Arimathea.

---

28. Numbers 20:28; Exodus 28:5, 8, 15, 39; 29:29; Leviticus 16:4, 23, 24, 32. Also, see Leviticus 21:1-2, 10-11.

29. Mark 1:15.

Reflective Questions

1. What are some non-political reasons why believers in Western nations experience less death threats for their faith than those in non-Western nations?

2. What does Jesus' experience during the three hours of darkness say to us? How should His experience fuel both our worship of Him and our witness for Him?

17

He Came for You to Fearlessly Proclaim the Empty Tomb
(Mark 16)

Much contemporary Christian music sung to the Lord in worship is creative, beautiful, and inspiring to sing, and much of it is written to address God in the third person:

> Oh, that with all the sacred throng
> we at His feet may fall!
> We'll join the everlasting song
> and crown Him Lord of all.
> We'll join the everlasting song
> and crown Him Lord of all.[1]

> O the love of my redeemer,
> Never failing come what may
> *He* has purchased my forgiveness,
> and has washed my sins away.[2]

> Christ alone; cornerstone
> Weak made strong in the Savior's love
> Through the storm, *He* is Lord
> Lord of all.[3]

1. Edward Perronet, 'All Hail the Power of Jesus' Name' (1780). Public Domain.

2. Josh Caterer, 'Oh, the Love of My Redeemer' (2007).

3. Eric Oskar Liljero, Jonas Carl Gustaf Myrin, Reuben Timothy Morgan, 'Cornerstone,' *Hillsong Live,* Hillsong Music and Capitol CMG Publishing (2012).

When Darkness seems to hide *His* face
I rest on *His* unchanging grace
In every high and stormy gale
My anchor holds within the veil.[4]

While the third person nature of such singing gives us the truth of God and a means for making the Word dwell in believers richly, it also allows the worshiper to remain one step removed from even greater personal and emotional engagement with the Lord. A different engagement occurs when one addresses the Lord in worship in the first person – that is, when 'He' becomes 'You,' and when 'our God' becomes 'my God.' The use of the first-person forces one to speak directly to Jesus rather than act as if He is an artifact in the room or is not in the room at all. *It is to speak to Jesus as alive rather than absent.*

Much of the joy we as believers could have in the Christian walk would overtake us in so many areas of life if we would participate in corporate worship as if Jesus is alive rather than absent. Those gathered should think of Jesus as living and present as they enter the house of worship, as they greet and embrace those for whom He died, as they come to the table of His Supper, as they hear His Word, and as they pray to Him. One grand change that would begin to take place is that believers would overcome fears to tell others that He is alive because the fact of His resurrection would be more of a reality to us.

In Mark 16, the reader encounters *the women's hope to anoint the dead Jesus, without obstacles after the Sabbath had passed on the first day of the week, when the sun had risen.* That hope turned to both alarm and silencing of saying anything to anyone, even when those obstacles were removed. This occurred despite the young man's reassurances that Jesus was alive. It occurred despite His charge for them to tell Peter and the disciples that they will see Jesus as He had promised. These final eight verses are about *those believers' failure to honor the Lord Jesus as alive.*

The Problem of the Ending of Mark 16
Before going further in Mark, one should recognize that at the end of Mark 16:8 there is a note regarding what scholars

---

4. Edward Mote, 'My Hope is Built on Nothing Less' (1834). Public Domain.

have read in the Greek texts explaining why some question
the length of the ending of Mark's Gospel account: '[Some of
The Earliest Manuscripts Do Not Include 16:9–20].' There are
many textual issues surrounding the ending of the second
Gospel, including the appearance of several new words not
found anywhere else in Mark's Gospel. Many scholars have
given detailed efforts to resolving the concerns.[5] Briefly, the
concerns surround endings found in manuscripts containing
the Gospel of Mark.

The 'Undisputed' Ending of Mark 16:8
Those opposing reading Mark 16:9-20 as Scripture typically
end Mark at 16:8. However, even verse 8 is not without concern
because of its contents and because it ends with the word 'for'
in the Greek text.

Longer Ending of Mark 16:9-20
Mark 16:9-20 is missing from Codex Sinaiticus, the only uncial
manuscript with the complete text of the New Testament.
Uniquely, Codex Sinaiticus is the only extant manuscript
written in four columns per page. It also is missing from
Codex Vaticanus, a manuscript that contains the full text of
both the Septuagint (LXX) and the Greek New Testament.
Although written in the fourth century, it resembles a second-
century papyrus.

5. J. D. Atkins, 'The Earliest Evidence for the Longer Ending of Mark.' Paper
presented at the Annual Meeting of the Evangelical Theological Society. Atlanta,
GA. November 17, 2015; David Alan Black, ed., *Perspectives on the Ending of
Mark: Four Views* (Nashville, TN: B&H Academic, 2008); Peter M. Head, 'A Case
against the Longer Ending of Mark: An Argument that Mark 16:9–20 is not Original
and so not Inspired Scripture,' Text and Canon Institute Blog, June 14, 2022, https://
textandcanon.org/a-case-against-the-longer-ending-of-mark/ (last accessed
April 25, 2024); Nicholas P. Lunn, *The Original Ending of Mark: A New Case for the
Authenticity of Mark 16:9-20* (Sisters, OR: Pickwick, 2014); Mina Monier, 'Mark's
Ending in the Digital Age: Paratextual Evidence, New Findings and Transcription
Challenges,' *Postscripts* 12 (2021): 75–98; Kara Lyons-Pardue, *Gospel Women
and the Long Ending of Mark* (New York: Bloomsbury, 2021); Jeffrey T Riddle, 'The
Ending of Mark as a Canonical Crisis,' *Puritan Reformed Journal* 10, no. 1 (2018):
31–54; James Snapp, Jr., 'A Case for the Longer Ending of Mark: An Argument for
Mark 16:9–20 as the Original, Canonical Ending, Written by Mark but Added by his
Colleagues,' Text and Canon Institute Blog, June 1, 2022, https://textandcanon.
org/a-case-against-the-longer-ending-of-mark/ (last accessed April 25, 2024);
Robert H. Stein, 'The Ending of Mark,' *BBR* 18 (2008): 92-93.

Codex Alexandrinus from the fifth century has the longer ending. More than 1,200 manuscripts of the Byzantine text-type of Mark have the longer ending.

Freer Logion of Mark 16 Inserted Between 16:14 and 16:15
Codex Washingtonensis, also known as the *Washington Manuscript of the Gospels* and *The Freer Gospel*, contains the four Gospels (fifth century). It also contains an ending of Mark different from that in all other manuscripts:

> And they excused themselves, saying, This age of lawlessness and unbelief is under Satan, who does not allow the truth and power of God to prevail over the unclean things dominated by the spirits. Therefore, reveal your righteousness now – thus they spoke to Christ. And Christ responded to them, The limit of the years of Satan's power is completed, but other terrible things draw near. And for those who sinned I was handed over to death, that they might return to the truth and no longer sin, in order that they might inherit the spiritual and incorruptible heavenly glory of righteousness.

The manuscript containing these verses inserts them between verses 14 and 15 of the longer ending.

The Shorter Ending of Mark 16 with No Verse Number
The NRSV includes an unnumbered verse between 16:8 and 16:9, known as 'The Shorter Ending': 'And all that had been commanded them they told briefly to those around Peter. And afterward Jesus Himself sent out through them, from east to west, the sacred and imperishable proclamation of eternal salvation. Amen.' This reading first appears in the third century.

Note of Grace on the Endings of Mark
Although extant manuscript evidence favors the ending at Mark 16:8, it is wise to admit that we do not have full certainty on the ending of Mark. J. D. Atkins is one who has demonstrated that the early church cited words from the longer ending of Mark, giving early attestation to that ending.[6]

6. Atkins, 'The Earliest Evidence.'

Fearless Proclamation Because the Stone Is Rolled Away (16:1-4)

In Mark 16:1-8, two of the Marys and Salome went to see who they thought was a dead Jesus. It is extremely significant that Mark includes three women in the initial visit to the tomb. The writers of the Gospels were selective, including only the most significant and well-researched materials.[7] The second Gospel seems to have been written to give the early believers the core of the Gospel story. It is absent of a genealogy for Jesus, miraculous birth stories, many of the Synoptics' parables, miracles, and discourses, and it is missing a post-resurrection appearance of Jesus, His commissioning of the apostles to the world, and ascension. Yet the writer found the presence of women to be important both to the core story of the gospel for the early church and the historical witness to Jesus' resurrection.[8] Mark repeats his emphasis on the women and their role in the history of redemption, giving them worth that should have been esteemed by the early recipients.

The women were committed disciples and Jesus was very dear to them. They ministered to His provisional needs over the course of His earthly ministry and were standing in the distance when He was crucified (Mark 15:40-41). Also, both Marys went to the tomb and saw exactly where Joseph of Arimathea had buried Him; they had watched the stone roll over the door of the tomb (Mark 15:47).

The women's concern now was to honor Jesus with spices that would show His worth and limit the smell of

---

7. Luke 1:1-4; John 20:30-31.

8. Edwards notes, 'The listing of proper names – so unusual for Mark – certifies on the basis of eyewitnesses the veracity of the events described. More remarkable is the repetition of the list, and even more so that they are the names of *women*. Jewish opinion of women, especially in religious matters, was not always positive .... [It] attests to the veracity of the resurrection narrative, for had early Christians fabricated the resurrection story, the testimony of women (in all four Gospels!) was no way to go about it .... The witness of Mary the mother of James and Joses, Salome, and especially Mary Magdalene (v. 1), whose name heads the resurrection witnesses in all four Gospels, endows the resurrection narratives with the highest degree of probability. Unless women were actually present at the tomb, the early church would scarcely have placed them there since Judaism did not accept the testimony of women' (Edwards, *Mark*, 491-92).

decomposition.[9] Their only obstacle, they thought, was the large stone rolled in front of the tomb. Both the spices and the tomb show that they regarded Jesus as dead – this was so despite their hearing of the predictions of His resurrection, the passing of the Sabbath, and the sun now risen on the first day of the week – the third day after His death. They were going to honor a seemingly dead Jesus on the first Easter Sunday, when the focus on the paschal lamb was behind them. They were not even beginning to think that He was alive, or that they could approach the tomb with such expectation. However, three things happened that would change their perspective.

The first is that they encountered the stone rolled away from the tomb. Miraculously, the huge stone that blocked entrance to the sepulcher was moved out of the way! This was a clue that something different had taken place with the death of Jesus. It should have been a reminder of His predictions of returning to life after three days.[10] It certainly should have given them reason to worship at the tomb, for all thanks should go to God for removing this obstacle.

In addition to saying on Easter Morning, 'He is risen,' and repeating the catechetical response, 'He is risen indeed,' believers should remember that we have every assurance that Jesus walked out of His tomb alive and is among us because that stone was moved. The women gave witness to the resurrection in all four Gospels, with Mary Magdalene being named in all four accounts.[11]

Fearless Proclamation Because an Angel Confirmed Jesus' Rising (16:5-6)

The second miraculous detail that the women experienced was that an angel in the tomb told them that Jesus had risen.

---

9. Wessel comments, 'The anointing was not for the purpose of preserving the body (embalming was not practiced by the Jews) but was a single act of love and devotion probably meant to reduce the stench of the decomposing body' (Wessel, *Mark*, 786).

10. Mark 8:31; 9:31; 10:34. His resurrection is inherent in the predictions of His meeting with the disciples in Galilee and of His return in 13:26-27; 14:25, 28, and 62.

11. Matthew 28:1-10; Mark 16:1-8; Luke 24:1-11; John 20:1-2, 11-18.

The white attire indicates a heavenly being and sitting on the right side is a specific given by an eyewitness. In fact, he told them several things. First, *they should not be alarmed by not finding Jesus there.* Angels are God's ministering spirits, and they were on standby to come to the Garden and destroy Jesus' enemies if He had wanted them to do so (cf. Matt 26:53). This angel's presence confirmed that God was in the tomb, and that it was the right tomb. The alarm of the women was one of fear and awe.[12] They were not expecting a heavenly being and their response to him was appropriate.

Second, *they were seeking Jesus of Nazareth.* In Mark's Gospel, *Nazareth* was the place with which the demons associated Jesus 'the Holy One of God' (1:24), and *Nazareth* was the place with which blind Bartimaeus associated Jesus 'the Son of David' (10:47-48). *Nazareth* was the geographical place that made Jesus a Nazarene. But a *nazīr* in Hebrew is a *branch*, and in the Gospels *Nazareth is the redemptive place that makes Jesus the branch of Jesse who will save Israel.*[13] They should have expected the One they were seeking to be alive so that He would perform His Messianic decree to save David's people.

Third, *Jesus was crucified.* Jesus did as He had intended; the women's eyes were not deceiving them when they saw Him on the cross. He had paid the ransom price for the sins of many, as Isaiah's Servant was to do. He satisfied the debt due for sins. As prophesied, the dead Jesus could not stay dead, for He had to deal a deathblow to the evil one after receiving His minor wound (Gen. 3:15).

Fourth, *Jesus had risen and vacated the tomb.* If all the rest was too much for the women to believe, the angel offered to let them investigate the tomb to make sure that Jesus was not hidden within it. No, He was not there! He had defeated death and His payment was acceptable to God. So having life in Himself , He walked out of the tomb *alive* and remains alive to this very day.

---

12. Mark uses the Greek word, *ekthambeomai.* It is found only in Mark (9:15; 14; 33; 16:5, 6).

13. Isaiah 4:2; 11:1; Jeremiah 23:5; 33:15; Zechariah 3:8; 6:12. Mark does not identify Jesus as a *nazīr,* but Matthew's reference to Jesus being called a Nazarene seems to be doing so (Matt. 2:23).

Fearless Proclamation Because the Angel Gave a Commission Concerning the Resurrection (16:7)

The angel told the women to go and tell the disciples and Peter about the resurrection. All the disciples needed to hear this, but as Mark was writing as the friend and publisher of Peter's version of the Gospel story, he placed a special emphasis on Peter. The express word to Peter would have been as refreshing as a dip in the cool waters of the Atlantic Ocean on an unusually hot day in Greystones, Ireland. Peter would have been relieved to hear that his unfaithfulness to Jesus had not ended in death, but in resurrection to life.

In the commissioning, we hear three important things that sound like the hope of the Great Commission given to each of us. First, *Jesus was going before them* just like He is with us until the end of the world. Jesus' rising from the dead shows that the plan of redemption rests on His sovereign control. He will be ahead of the disciples in Galilee, from which He will prepare them to go into the world. He will be the one with us as we obediently make disciples of all nations, telling them of a risen Savior.

Second, *they will see Him*, just as we will see Him one day. The promise to them is realized *immediately* while it will be realized *eschatologically* to all. Believers stand on the disciples' testimony as eyewitnesses of the resurrection of Christ. Having seen Him alive, and having handled His body, they had all the assurance they and we need to carry out our commission to teach the nations to observe to do all He commanded us.

Third, *Jesus' words will be fulfilled*. He told the disciples in the Upper Room, 'After I am raised up, I will go before you to Galilee' (Mark 14:28). He did that very thing. The hope that Jesus' followers have is that His words will be true, that the risen Savior, who has gone before us to the Father's glory, will return to raise His own from the dead and to take all His people to be with Him in His kingdom forever.

Fearless Proclamation as the Fitting Conclusion (16:8)

In the conclusion of these verses, where one thinks the women would leave their spices for anointing the dead and run out of the tomb shouting, 'He's alive! He's alive!,' they did the opposite. Seized by fear and trembling (like many believers), rather than being seized by hope and joy over a risen Jesus, they left the place where they had come to anoint the dead and did not tell anyone anything, initially! They were as silent about the risen Jesus as many of us are toward more than six billion people today who are heading to a Christless eternity.

The Verification of the Resurrection (16:9-20)

As indicated above, verses 9-20 are disputed as concerns their authenticity. However, whether disputed or not, it is evident the writer pens these verses to verify the resurrection with post-resurrection events. One notes the repetition of 'he appeared' (vv. 9, 12, 14). Also, after appearing, twice there is proclamation by the witnesses to His resurrection and doubt on the parts of the recipients of the proclamation (vv. 10-11, 13). Further there is emphasis on believing the fact of Jesus' resurrection ('believe' in vv. 11, 13, 14, 16 [2x], 17).

The writer indicates that the first post-resurrection appearance is to Mary. He describes her as one from whom Jesus expelled seven demons – an idea gathered from Luke 8:2 rather than previous verses in Mark's account. While she is faithful to proclaim that Jesus is alive to the disciples, the writer indicates she encounters the disciples as they grieve the death of Jesus. The account is written to indicate that they would not believe the report of Jesus being alive, not that they did not trust her words as a woman giving witness.

The next appearance of Jesus to 'two' as they came into the country sounds similar to the Lukan account of the encounter on the Road to Emmaus.[14] These two also are faithful to proclaim that Jesus has risen from the dead. However, they are met with disbelief by the disciples.

The third post-resurrection appearance adds the element of a commissioning. Jesus encounters the eleven as they dine casually. 'Eleven' indicates that Judas is not present, utilizing language found in Matthew, Luke and Acts.[15] The idea of Jesus

---

14. Luke 24:13-35.

15. Matthew, Luke, and Acts reference the 'eleven' in their post-resurrection accounts (Matthew 28:16; Luke 24:9, 33; Acts 1:26; 2:14). However, Matthew is the only one who records the death of Judas (Matthew 27:5). Yet the reference to the

rebuking is not new to the Markan reader.[16] But rebuking the disciples for 'hardness of heart' harkens back to the rebuke of the Jewish leadership in 10:5.

The commissioning is reminiscent of the commissioning in Matthew 28. The eleven are sent into 'all the world ... the whole creation' (in contrast to Matthew's 'all nations'). The scope of the gospel proclamation goes beyond all political and geographic boundaries. In this commissioning, however, the recipients have an explicit responsibility, whereas in Matthew the instructions are to the eyewitnesses only.

As a requirement for salvation, 'believe and is baptized' seems to contradict the simple faith in the gospel one sees throughout the Gospel of Mark. The latter tradition of baptizing those who believe finds ground for such practice in the Matthean version of the Great Commission, and in the practice of the church in Acts. The wording here seems to reflect the practice recorded in Acts.[17]

The addition of 'not condemned' sounds similar to the words of John 3:18. But the promise of accompanying signs to the eyewitnesses is unique to this post-resurrection account. In Acts, signs accompany the apostles' proclamation of the good news. But the promise of such signs is absent from the endings of Matthew, Luke, and John.

The signs themselves involve unique elements. The disciples previously have cast out demons, and one finds this occurring in Acts 16:18. Speaking in tongues is a new concept to the story recorded in Mark, but Acts gives witness to the phenomenon in Acts 2:4; 10:46, and 19:6. The picking up of serpents with one's hands occurs in the life of Paul in Acts 28:35, but is recorded nowhere else in the New Testament.

The drinking of deadly poison without harm has no corresponding episode in Acts. Among the accompanying signs to the proclamation of the gospel, it stands alone without subsequent verification in Acts. One wonders of the writer's and/or audience's experience with drinking poison; it may be

---

death of Judas in Acts 1:16-20 indicates Luke was aware of an account of Judas' death. In Mark 1:1-16:8, there is no indication for the reader that Judas suffered fatal consequences for his betrayal.

16. Mark 1:25; 4:39; 8:33; 9:25.

17. See Acts 2:38, 41; 8:12, 13, 36, 38; 9:18; 10:47, 48; 16:15, 33; 18:8; 19:5.

that the report of a related miracle lies behind these words. But the laying on of hands to heal the sick has verification in Acts 5:15-16; 8:7; 9:12, 17.

The writer's account of the ascension concludes with Jesus returning in triumph to the Father's side – something Luke does not mention in his account of the ascension in Luke or Acts. The statement of Jesus' sitting at the right hand of God brings the theology of Psalm 110:1 into the ending of Mark's Gospel account.

The writer has knowledge of events that go beyond the Matthean and Lukan Gospel endings. The preaching everywhere with confirming signs only occurs after Pentecost, so the writer speaks from this post-Pentecost perspective. The other Gospel accounts only go as far as the ascension.

Reflective Questions

1. What does Mark 16:1-8 give as the reasons why believers should be fearless in their proclamation of Jesus as the resurrected Savior?

2. How does Mark's conclusion without a post-resurrection appearance bring a fitting end to his full presentation of Jesus as a servant?

Subject Index

Scripture Index